2/15

Just Work?

Wildcat: Workers' Movements and Global Capitalism

Series Editors:
Peter Alexander (University of Johannesburg)
Immanuel Ness (City University of New York)
Tim Pringle (SOAS, University of London)
Malehoko Tshoaedi (University of Pretoria)

Workers' movements are a common and recurring feature in contemporary capitalism. The same militancy that inspired the mass labour movements of the twentieth century continues to define worker struggles that proliferate throughout the world today.

For more than a century labour unions have mobilised to represent the political-economic interests of workers by uncovering the abuses of capitalism, establishing wage standards, improving oppressive working conditions, and bargaining with employers and the state. Since the 1970s, organised labour has declined in size and influence as the global power and influence of capital has expanded dramatically. The world over, existing unions are in a condition of fracture and turbulence in response to neoliberalism, financialisation, and the reappearance of rapacious forms of imperialism. New and modernised unions are adapting to conditions and creating class-conscious workers' movement rooted in militancy and solidarity. Ironically, while the power of organised labour contracts, working-class militancy and resistance persists and is growing in the Global South.

Wildcat publishes ambitious and innovative works on the history and political economy of workers' movements and is a forum for debate on pivotal movements and labour struggles. The series applies a broad definition of the labour movement to include workers in and out of unions, and seeks works that examine proletarianisation and class formation; mass production; gender, affective and reproductive labour; imperialism and workers; syndicalism and independent unions, and labour and Leftist social and political movements.

Also available:

Southern Insurgency:
The Coming of the Global Working Class
Immanuel Ness

Just Work?

Migrant Workers' Struggles Today

Edited by
Aziz Choudry and Mondli Hlatshwayo

PlutoPress
www.plutobooks.com

First published 2016 by Pluto Press
345 Archway Road, London N6 5AA

www.plutobooks.com

British Library Cataloguing in Publication Data
A catalogue record for this book is available from the British Library

ISBN   978 0 7453 3584 1   Hardback
ISBN   978 0 7453 3583 4   Paperback
ISBN   978 1 7837 1339 4   PDF eBook
ISBN   978 1 7837 1341 7   Kindle eBook
ISBN   978 1 7837 1340 0   EPUB eBook

This book is printed on paper suitable for recycling and made from fully managed
and sustained forest sources. Logging, pulping and manufacturing processes are
expected to conform to the environmental standards of the country of origin.

Typeset by Stanford DTP Services, Northampton, England
Text design by Melanie Patrick

Simultaneously printed in the European Union and United States of America

Contents

PART III: ASIA AND THE PACIFIC

PART IV: NORTH AMERICA

Acknowledgements

At one level, the idea for *Just Work?: Migrant Workers' Struggles Today* arose from conversations between the two of us, beginning in Johannesburg in 2012 and continuing in our face-to-face and virtual discussions since then. But at another level, as co-editors of this collection, our various engagements in worker and migrant justice struggles grounds and informs our scholarship and the rationale for our collaboration in putting this book together. Choudry currently works as an associate professor in the Department of Integrated Studies in Education at McGill University, is a board member of the Immigrant Workers Centre in Montreal, and has a longer history of working with labour and other movements and organisations, particularly in the Asia-Pacific and North America. Hlatshwayo is a senior lecturer at the Centre for Education Rights and Transformation at the University of Johannesburg, and is involved in organising against xenophobia in South Africa. He has also written extensively on trade unions and immigrant workers in a South African context. This book has very much been a collective effort.

First, we are deeply grateful to all of the chapter contributors for their work – many of whom took precious time away from organising and other responsibilities to work with us. We also acknowledge other colleagues who expressed strong interest in this book project, but who were unable to participate due to their commitments.

Second, we sincerely thank David Shulman at Pluto Press for his enthusiasm and support throughout the process of producing this collection. We have greatly appreciated the encouragement of Manny Ness, as editor of Pluto's new Wildcat series in which this book appears, as well as the professionalism of others at Pluto who have assisted in its production. Désirée Rochat's efficient help in getting the manuscript ready for publication was invaluable.

Finally, we acknowledge the sacrifices and struggles of migrant workers and organisers across the world, both within existing trade union structures and in other forms of organisations and movements – and regardless of their state-ascribed 'legal status'. Visible or not, recognised or not, these daily struggles are not only significant in their own right, but are also key sites of knowledge production – contributing vital ideas for action to resist global capitalism and fight for just working conditions and immigration policies in the twenty-first century.

Aziz Choudry and Mondli Hlatshwayo

All royalties from this book will go to The Immigrant Workers Centre, Montreal (www.iwc-cti.org).

Chapter 12 is adapted from Choudry, A. and Henaway, M. (2014). 'Temporary Agency Worker Organizing in an Era of Contingent Employment'. *Global Labour Journal*, 5(1), 1–22.

List of Abbreviations

ACOMORON	Amalgamated Commercial Motorcycle Riders Organisation of Nigeria
AMCB	Asia Migrants Coordinating Body
ANACOWA	All Nigeria Automobile Commercial Owners and Workers' Association
APMM	Asia Pacific Mission for Migrants
BWI	Building and Wood Workers International
CAIC	Campaign Against Immigration Controls
CBPR	Community-based participatory research
CCMA	Commission for Conciliation, Mediation and Arbitration
CLCF	Committee for Localities with a Concentrated Foreigner Population
CLR	Construction Labour Research
CNT	Commission des normes du travail
COLACOR	Latin American Coalition Against the Cuts
CORAS	Colombian Refugee Association
CoRMSA	Consortium for Refugees and Migrants in South Africa
COSATU	Congress of South African Trade Unions
CSD	Centrale des syndicats démocratiques
CSN	Confédération des syndicats nationaux
CSQ	Centrale des syndicats du Québec
CSST	Commission de la santé et de la sécurité du travail
CWAO	Casual Workers Advice Office
ECOWAS	Economic Community of West African States
EPMU	Engineers, Printers and Manufacturers Union
EQC	Earthquake Commission
EU	European Union
FCC	Filipino Community Centre
FDNS	Front Des Non Syndicats

FDW	Foreign domestic workers
FEONA	Far East Overseas Nepalese Association
FIWON	Federation of Informal Workers' Organisations of Nigeria
FMWU	Filipino Migrant Workers' Union
GAMMI	Indonesian Migrant Muslim Alliance
GCC	Gulf Cooperation Council
GDP	Gross domestic product
GFMD	Global Forum on Migration and Development
GLATUC	Greater London Association of Trade Union Councils
GLMM	Gulf Labour Markets and Migration
GU	General Union
HKCTU	Hong Kong Confederation of Trade Unions
HRW	Human Rights Watch
ILO	International Labour Organization
ILRIG	International Labour Research and Information Group
IMF	International Monetary Fund
IMWU	Indonesian Migrant Workers' Union
INR	Initiative No Racism!
IOM	International Organization for Migration
IPPR	Institute for Public Policy Research
IRMO	Indo-American Rights for Migrants Organisation
IRMW	Initiative for the Rights of Migrant Workers
ITUC	International Trade Union Confederation
IWC	Immigrant Workers Centre
IWGB	Independent Workers of Great Britain
IWW	Industrial Workers of the World
JMIU	All-Japan Metal and Information Machinery Workers' Union
LAWAS	Latin American Workers Association
LCAP	London Coalition Against Poverty
LCP	Live-in Caregiver Program
LHR	Lawyers for Human Rights
LRS	Labour Research Service
MAW	Minimum allowable wage

MERU	Bolivia and Colombia Solidarity Campaigns and Ecuadorian Movement in the UK
MFMW	Mission for Migrant Workers
MHLW	Ministry of Health, Labour and Welfare
MIC	Ministry of Internal Affairs and Communications
MWC	Migrant Workers Committee
NAFTA	North American Free Trade Agreement
NDU	National Distribution Union
NEEDS	National Economic Empowerment and Development Strategy
NGO	Non-governmental organisations
NPL	National Physical Laboratory
NPO	Non-profit organisations
NYU	New York University
NZCTU	New Zealand Council of Trade Unions
OECD	Organisation for Economic Co-operation and Development
ONWU	Overseas Nepali Workers' Union
OSF	Ogoni Solidarity Forum
OTUWA	Organisation of Trade Unions of West Africa
PAR	Participatory action research
PICUM	Platform for International Cooperation on Undocumented Migrants
PILAR	United Indonesians Against Overcharging
PLO	Palestine Liberation Organisation
PWA	Progressive Worker Alliance
SAITF	South African Informal Traders Forum
SFCR	State Forests of the Czech Republic
SOAS	School of Oriental and African Studies
SOMCAN	SoMa Collective Action Network
TAWA	Temporary Agency Workers Association
TFWP	Temporary Foreign Worker Programme
TUC	Trades Union Congress
UAE	United Arab Emirates
UCL	University College London
UK	United Kingdom
UNEMIG	Union Network of Migrants

UNIFEM	United Nations Development Fund for Women
USS	Swiss Federation of Trade Unions
WACMIC	West African Capital Markets Integration Council
WHO	World Health Organization

1

Just Work? Migrant Workers, Capitalist Globalisation and Resistance

Aziz Choudry and Mondli Hlatshwayo

The living and working conditions of migrant workers and the political economy of migration have been examined in many studies. While this body of work helps us to understand the challenges and conditions that migrant workers face, including the dynamics of class, gender, race and immigration status, and the roles that various sections of the global migrant workforce play in labour processes, this international collection of essays illuminates a less-discussed topic: migrant workers' struggles and labour organising experiences. This book centres migrant workers' agency, forms of worker organisation, the politics of solidarity with migrant workers, campaigns to improve their working conditions and the role of trade unions, without neglecting and downplaying constraints and challenges facing migrant workers today. Together, the chapters of this book reflect critically on the possibilities and limitations of organising migrant workers across a number of sectors in five continents in an era of capitalist crisis, the neoliberalisation of immigration regimes (Akers Chacón and Davis, 2006; Arat-Koc, 1999) and 'austerity'. In *Just Work?*, academics and labour organisers collaborate to deepen our understanding of these phenomena, and critically examine recent labour organising efforts and the prospects for improving the economic and social conditions of migrant and immigrant workers in a number of contexts. This global volume contributes to the critical literatures on migration, precarious employment, transformation of paid work and the political actions of migrant workers. It is grounded in critical interdisciplinary scholarship, and activist and organising experiences, exploring contexts which are less well traversed by previous work on migrant and immigrant workers. It also purposefully combines the genres of academic scholarship with chapters written by labour organisers and migrant justice activists – although sometimes these approaches overlap. We believe that it is important and necessary to bring reflexive scholar-activist perspectives on labour migration more squarely into view. Migrant and immigrant workers around the world continue to organise in the face of exploitation and oppression, and often find themselves on the frontlines of struggles against precarity, austerity and other forms of capitalist exploitation which impact all working people. Indeed, their struggles continue to highlight ways in which capital exploits workers through immigration status and the social relations of race, gender and class across the world. Moreover, the struggles, organising and resistance of migrant workers are an indication of an era where migrant and immigrant workers are a vital part of a social and political force in a global power struggle.

Yet in many of the dominant popular representations of migration today, the histories, systems and structures which underpin the terms and conditions of who moves between nation states and how and why they move are often as nameless as most of the migrants themselves. The global free market economy has not led to the building of a 'global village' or a borderless world, despite what many of its advocates have promised. While many barriers to the mobility of capital have been dismantled through policies of liberalisation and deregulation, the majority of the world's people do not experience such freedom to move across borders. Simplistic, populist explanations which dehumanise migrants, criminalise their movements and obscure the reasons why people migrate continue to abound. Indeed, this chapter was written at a time of renewed xenophobic violence in South Africa which left several dead, while forcing thousands from their homes. Meanwhile an estimated 800 people from Africa and the Middle East had just drowned in the sinking of a single overloaded boat – one of many vessels carrying people trying to cross the Mediterranean to Europe, desperate for a future. It is also one of many deadly migration routes which is claiming lives every day. In an April 2015 public address, former Canadian Prime Minister Kim Campbell told a University of Alberta audience that gender equality, which she claimed to be a 'Canadian value' was under threat in a 'society of immigration' (*National Post*, 2015). The start of the 2016 US presidential campaign gave a prominent platform for sometimes virulently racist anti-immigrant posturing by several nominees. On the other side of the Atlantic, the 2015 British election campaign saw most major political parties, once again, trying to talk 'tougher' than each other about curbing and controlling immigration.

From the murders and displacements in South Africa to the drownings in the Mediterranean, migrant deaths are not random 'incidents', but rather they are manifestations of the intentional violence of border policies and anti-migrant racism. Far from bringing people together, flattening the world, or ironing out inequities, capitalist globalisation is deepening gaps between rich and poor within and across nation states through preying on ethnic, racial and religious divisions within the working class. Growing xenophobia is also leading to immigrant-blaming, culture talk, and the securitisation and militarisation of borders fuelled by heightened state-sanctioned politics of fear and loathing against 'migrants' and 'foreigners'. Yet it is important to reiterate that the policing of borders and tighter restrictions on immigration have never been meant to completely stop migration. Rather, various forms of migration and labour management policies seek to control and discipline pools of labour for capitalist exploitation. Many Marxist scholars contend that the so-called developed economies tend to be largely supported by the labour of migrant workers. For example, Cornelius and Rosenblum (2005: 101) suggest that '[f]rom a Marxist perspective, owners of capital also benefit from maintaining a category of job character-ized by a flexible labor supply, allowing lay-offs to minimize losses to capital during economic downturns'. In other words, capital benefits from the use of relatively cheap migrant labour because it is able to further lower the value of its labour power which increases capital's surplus value.

The imperialist exploitation and undermining of many societies in the Global South under earlier eras of colonialism, and historical

institutional arrangements concerning labour, are key to understanding labour and migration in today's era of global capitalism
(Kundnani, 2007; Rodriguez, 2010a). Colonialism and capitalist
economic development have created the structural conditions of
dispossession, poverty and inequality which drive many people to
migrate in search of work. While internal migration within countries
is a major phenomenon across most of the world, and the challenges
faced by internal migrants must not be ignored, this book focuses on
international migration. Capitalist restructuring is the major driving
force behind patterns of migration, as well as a key influence on
immigration and labour policy. When businesses need a specific form
of labour, they demand access to it through laws and arrangements
organised by the capitalist state.

Worldwide, migrant workers and racialised immigrant workers
have long provided pools of 'cheap' labour to be exploited. Migration
sociologist, Anthony Richmond (1994: 204), describes the rise
of 'a system of global apartheid based on discrimination against
migrants and refugees from poorer developing countries'. A global,
often Western-educated elite exists that is relatively mobile, but the
overwhelming majority is temporary, non-status, exploitable and
often underground.

Today, in many countries, border controls increasingly manage
flows of largely temporary migrant workers – a rotating-door labour
market geared to just-in-time production and service provision.
Through a range of systems of closed work permits and sponsorship
by employers, migrant workers are frequently tied to one job with a
single boss, which makes complaints about abuse or substandard or
dangerous working conditions risky and difficult, if not impossible,
with their legal status dependent on remaining at the same workplace.
Arun Kundnani (2007: 145), reflecting on British immigration
history, writes that instead of the idea of the post-Second World War
reserve army of manual workers:

> The new post-industrial migrant workforce was characterized
> by several distinct streams – reserve regiments of labour – each
> adapted to the specific needs of different sectors of the economy. The
> intricacies of the system would be kept subject to constant review

and adjustment, so that the numbers, character and entitlements of workers entering the economy under different schemes could be changed as necessary. Each of these various routes provided employers with a different package of exploitation.

As this book illustrates, the creation and maintenance of categories of workers with different sets of rights tied to their immigration status is a standard policy feature and capitalist strategy which is fundamental to the functioning of many economies, facilitating the provision of reduced labour costs to employers. Pools of undocumented labour are particularly subject to exploitation by capital in order to reduce labour costs and generate greater surplus value. The book also challenges the construction of undocumented migrants and others without immigration status as 'illegal'. These categories of migrants are the most exploited and victimised – by employers and by state authorities in the form of arrests, violence and deportations. In many cases, these workers do precarious and hazardous work and their rights are violated by employers who take advantage of their status. Based on the principles of human solidarity, is it ethical and just to regard other human beings as 'illegal' or 'alien'? Van Driel (2008) argues that the illegal trafficking in people is a feature of globalisation. Corruption, bribery and longer waiting periods for those who have applied for documentation show that 'illegality' is also promoted by states (Van Driel, 2008). For example, in the South African context, Lehulere (2008: 38) argues that the criminalisation of migrant workers runs deep and is also part of the Congress of South African Trade Unions' (COSATU) discourse. COSATU criticised employers for 'employing foreign immigrants, especially the illegal ones', and called on 'employers to stop taking advantage of the desperate situation of foreign nationals'.

In a context of xenophobic attacks and state crackdowns on migrants in South Africa, Europe, North America and other parts of the world, some social movements, activist groups and progressive NGOs have responded to the language of 'illegal migrants' by asserting that 'no one is illegal'. 'By holding on to a perspective that "no one is illegal", the social movements provide a way out of the crisis that is truly internationalist, and that is morally defensible in the eyes of the world' (Lehulere, 2008: 36).

A GLOBAL PHENOMENON

Labour migration is not only a South–North phenomenon. Much labour migration – and a substantial amount of remittance flow – occurs across and among Southern countries. For example, the global literature has tended to ignore migration and the phenomenon of international migrant work in Africa – Southern Africa in particular is emerging as an epicentre of African migration (Segatti, 2011). According to Segatti, the percentage of international migrants in Southern Africa is almost double that in any of the other subregions of Africa. Johannesburg for instance, because of its economic activities, attracts international and domestic migrant workers in particular (Hlatshwayo, 2012; see Chapter 2). In this context of migration in Southern Africa, women migrant workers from Zimbabwe tend to work in precarious conditions in places like Johannesburg. For example, these women are involved in sex work, domestic work and hospitality work (Hlatshwayo, 2010; see Chapter 2).

Turning to Asia and the Pacific, according to the International Organization for Migration (IOM) (2013), 8.6 million Bangladeshis were working as migrants in other countries by 2013. An estimated 10 per cent of the population of the Philippines works abroad. Moreover, according to the IOM, temporary work schemes in both Australia and Aotearoa/New Zealand increase the number of temporary migrant workers, particularly in the latter, which remains the leading destination for migrants from the Pacific Islands, and where in recent years there have been new initiatives from within and outside of the union movement to organise migrant workers and protect their rights.

Within Europe, since the latest global economic crisis, migration from countries such as Greece and Spain to other European countries is accelerating (Dumont, 2013). According to Dumont, migration within the European Union rose by 15 per cent, following a decline of almost 40 per cent during the crisis: 'The trend of people leaving countries hardest hit by the crisis is accelerating, up by 45% from

2009 to 2011' (2013: 1). Across the Atlantic, Stoney et al. (2013) note that the South American immigrant population in the US has grown 30 times since 1960. Migration from Mexico into the US has increased since the North American Free Trade Agreement (NAFTA) negatively impacted Mexican peasant subsistence farmers (Delgado Wise, 2004; Uchitelle, 2007). As Delgado Wise (2004: 592) states in relation to NAFTA:

> behind the integration process and current migratory dynamic that exists between Mexico and the United States there lies a greater subordination of Mexico to the strategic, economic and geopolitical interests of its northern neighbour, wherein Mexican workers – including those who work inside the country as well as those who emigrate and are employed beyond its borders – are compelled to play a tactical role in the United States' process of industrial restructuring.

By 2008, the number of workers entering Canada under temporary foreign worker programmes outnumbered those arriving through the traditional immigration system to become permanent residents for the first time. These programmes are predicated on maintaining qualitatively different sets of rights and status for citizens, permanent residents and temporary workers respectively. Built around labour flexibilisation and labour flexibility, critics, including trade union and immigration justice groups (for example, Choudry et al., 2009; Choudry and Thomas, 2012) have charged that these programmes have few real safeguards, and lead to much actual and potential abuse of workers. During 2013 and 2014, there was sustained media attention and criticism of the Temporary Foreign Workers Programme (TFWP), followed by official announcements of reforms and promises of further changes to the scheme. Yet while some of this debate reflected concerns about the actual and potential exploitation of foreign workers, most demands hinged on the preservation of Canadian jobs. Very few acknowledged the broader historical and contemporary feature of Canada's capitalist economy – its systemic reliance upon exploitation through race, immigration status and shifting forms of 'unfree labour' (for exceptions, see Ramsaroop and

Smith, 2014). Public pressure led the federal government (with its eye on the 2015 federal election), to ban the restaurant industry from using the TFWP (for example, Harper, 2014). Opposition parties and labour unions called for the moratorium to be extended to the entire programme. But the moratorium placed on the use of migrant workers in this sector constitutes a knee-jerk reaction, which fails to address the deeply racialised foundations of Canada's temporary labour migration regime, and the role of capitalist restructuring and broader transformations of work in contributing to the pronounced use of temporary foreign workers across many sectors. Indeed, in mid-2015, thousands of low-skilled temporary foreign workers would be forced to leave Canada, and stay outside for four years before being able to apply for another work permit due to the reforms of the TFWP.

In large part, migrant labour is produced through factors that include structural adjustment imposed in the Global South by the World Bank/International Monetary Fund and other financial institutions, and often supported through bilateral official aid, 'development' projects and restructuring of economies along neoliberal lines through trade and investment liberalisation and aid arrangements. Akers Chacón and Davis (2006: 90) defines 'neoliberal immigration' as 'displacement accompanied by disenfranchisement and often internal segregation in host countries'. Free market capitalist policies force people from their farms, jobs, families and communities and into exploitation and precarity as migrant workers in other countries. Deindustrialisation and the downsizing and privatisation of essential services – accompanied by increasing user fees – are other 'push factors' forcing growing numbers to seek work abroad. The material conditions in workers' countries of origin, as well as the structures of labour markets in the migrant-receiving countries, shape the place of migrant workers. In the current economic crisis, as profits are privatised, costs and losses socialised and externalised, and new 'austerity' measures imposed domestically and internationally by governments, the burden of the devastating impacts of the financiali- sation phase of global capitalism is squarely placed on to working peoples' shoulders. Indeed, as the latest economic crisis mutated to span crises in the housing and financial sectors, to a sovereign debt crisis, we have seen how migrant workers have often been affected at both ends – in their countries of work and countries of origin.

REMITTANCES AND 'MIGRATION AS DEVELOPMENT'

In an era where remittances have become the new 'development mantra' (Kapur, 2004) in many official circles, these money transfers sent back by migrant workers far exceed official development assistance flows. One estimate suggests that worldwide remittance receipts (including those sent to high-income countries) totalled US$583 billion in 2014. Remittance flows are anticipated to reach over US$636 billion worldwide by 2017 (Ratha et al., 2015). Robyn Rodriguez (2010b: 55) contends that the migration-as-development approach promoted by the World Bank, the IOM and the Global Forum on Migration and Development through temporary labour migration programmes allows 'employers to exploit foreign workers, absolve developing states from introducing truly redistributive developmental policies and relieve[s] states from extending the full benefits of citizenship to immigrants'. Remittances have been a way of downloading state responsibility to individual workers, as well as providing a social safety valve for masses of unemployed or underemployed workers in many countries. In both migrant worker sending and receiving countries, a more general trend of state withdrawal from responsibility for provision of social services impacts local and migrant workers alike. A recent illustration of the international policy focus on this issue is the May 2015 conference of the Global Migration Group, an inter-agency group comprising heads of various UN agencies, the World Bank, the IOM, the International Labour Organization (ILO) and the World Health Organization held in New York under the title 'Harnessing Migration, Remittances and Diaspora Contributions for Financing Sustainable Development' (Global Migration Group, 2015). This conference took place against the background of the intergovernmental negotiations at the United Nations General Assembly for the 3rd International Conference on Financing for Development in July 2015, and the United Nations Summit for adoption of the post-2015 development agenda in September 2015.

FORMS OF ORGANISATIONS

Besides the real difficulties and challenges which confront immigrant workers and migrants on a daily basis (Wills et al., 2010; Lutz, 2012; Magalhaes et al., 2010), there are also many positive stories of collective organising, resistance and partial victories. A central topic of this book concerns strategies for organising migrant workers. We argue that migrant workers can be a source of new forms of labour organising as well as a potential force to rethink and reshape traditional union politics. Migrant and immigrant workers and their organisations are beginning to define organisational forms of workers and unionism. Julie Hearn and Monica Bergos (2010: 13) hold that '[o]rganized migrant workers pose two of the greatest threats to employers and the hierarchical and divisive way in which the segmented labour market has been constructed and accepted. Their low wages and working conditions "offer the greatest potential for worker dissatisfaction and protest"'. Yet there are other structural issues that impact migrant labour and influence the possibilities and challenges for migrant worker organising today. Since the 1970s, the global decline in trade union power and the ascendance of neoliberal economic policies has led to the erosion and declining relevance of traditional unions and their power. Many trade unions have failed to mobilise mass rank-and-file militancy to resist the deterioration in workplace conditions and the systematic erosion of workers' power. Further, alongside the bureaucratisation and containment of militancy within the traditional organs of organised labour, in some contexts, some unions have also been hostile or indifferent to migrant workers, and/or failed to support them as they struggle for fair wages and conditions, respect and immigration justice (see, for example, Chapter 2). While there are examples of trade unions that have been proactive in organising and supporting migrant and immigrant workers (see, for example, Chapters 7 and 10), other forms of organising have proven essential to advancing migrant workers' rights, often outside of, and sometimes in tension with, established unions. These include new forms of worker self-organising, which are often grounded in historical antecedents that have been less documented (see Ness, 2014; Suzuki, 2012).

There are three broad forms of organisations which seek to organise migrant workers, and these will be explored and contextualised in the following chapters. The first of these forms of organising migrants is based on the workers' centres which have developed in places such as North America (see Fine, 2006), or forms of community unions which include migrant workers as in Japan (see, for example, Chapter 9 on Japan and Chapter 10 on a hybrid community organising/union model in Aotearoa/New Zealand). Although some are connected with trade unions, workers' centres tend to be community-based and community-led organisations that provide support to low-wage migrant and immigrant workers. Workers' centres often try to fuse elements of community by organising with labour militancy, sometimes in multiracial contexts, or in other cases are rooted in particular communities around national origin or shared language. However, some workers' centres are circumscribed by established trade unions and do not succeed outside of providing services to migrant workers and immigrants. In addition, at times other advocacy/solidarity activism and alliances play significant roles in fighting for migrant workers' rights and immigration justice. Thus, some chapters in the book will examine the role and practice of workers' centres and community unions in organising migrant workers, as well as their successes and challenges.

The second organisational form involves trade unions. Some of the chapters in the book, such as those on Nigeria (Chapter 4) and South Africa (Chapter 2) investigate relationships between trade union federations/national union centres and migrant workers. For example, what tensions and possibilities exist in organising migrant workers from West African countries in Nigeria? The book will also examine reasons for some trade unions' relative success in organising migrant workers, as in Aotearoa/New Zealand, Switzerland and Japan. And what role do migrant workers play in shaping the direction of these unions? What examples of innovation and dynamism exist at the outer edges of existing union tactics and strategies in relation to supporting and organising migrant workers?

Third, there are many non-governmental and/or community organisations which have grown to advocate for the rights of migrant workers. These encompass a range of organisational forms, repertoires of action and political positions, and often lobby for policy change, conduct awareness and education campaigns, and work in coalitions with other groups and organisations (for example, Chapter 3 on the Gulf countries and Chapter 5 on the Czech Republic). While for the most part they do not work to organise migrant workers, they are increasingly active at both national and international levels in their advocacy work.

OUTLINE OF CHAPTERS

Although there are a number of common themes which run across many of the chapters, the book is organised into four parts: (1) Africa and the Middle East; (2) Europe; (3) Asia and the Pacific; and (4) North America. In Part I, and drawing on migrant workers' experiences, in Chapter 2 Mondli Hlatshwayo examines the organisational relationship between immigrant workers and the COSATU, as well as other progressive NGOs and social movements in South Africa. The chapter argues that there are tensions between COSATU's principle of class solidarity and the actual practice of defending the rights of immigrant workers. Yet other, smaller, social movements and NGOs have adopted different approaches that seek to defend the rights of immigrant workers.

Within the six states of the Gulf Cooperation Council (Saudi Arabia, Kuwait, Bahrain, Qatar, the United Arab Emirates and Oman), temporary migrant workers constitute at least half of the total labour force. All of these workers are denied citizenship and basic political rights. Most are concentrated in low-wage, dangerous work such as construction, domestic work and retail. Thus, in Chapter 3, Adam Hanieh focuses on migrant struggles and resistance in the Gulf Arab States, as well as solidarity activists, concentrating particularly on experiences of construction workers in Dubai, Abu Dhabi and Qatar, which have all had considerable resonance in international solidarity campaigns. Hanieh assesses the efficacy of these campaigns, the limitations of more traditional NGO and international legal perspectives around the conditions of migrant workers in the Gulf, as well as the actions of trade union and other worker organisations in labour-sending countries.

In Chapter 4, Baba Ayelabola concludes Part I by discussing problems and prospects for organising undocumented migrant workers in Nigeria, which is both a sending and receiving country. His chapter is a contribution towards addressing the regrettable dearth in the literature regarding the conditions of migrant workers in Nigeria, the majority of whom come from countries in the West Africa subregion. This chapter attempts to put in perspective the possibilities and limitations for their (self-)organising as part of the working class, in defence of their rights and interests, as well as the roles of Nigerian trade unions in relation to migrant workers' rights. It sums up by considering possibilities for (undocumented) migrant workers to win their human rights – as expressly stated in the International Convention on the Protection of the Rights of All Migrant Workers and Members of Their Families – through struggle, and the critical role of organising, involving trade unions and (radical) civil society organisations, in binding the immigrant workers together as part of the working class movement in the country.

In Part II, there are contributions from the Czech Republic, the UK and Switzerland. In Chapter 5, Marek Čaněk focuses on the case of the exploitation of hundreds of migrant workers from Vietnam, Romania, Slovakia and other countries who planted trees and did other work in forestry in 2009 and 2010 in the Czech Republic. During the economic crisis the Czech state co-created a vulnerable ethnicised and criminalised migrant workforce, which fits the demand for cheap labour in forestry. A migrant rights campaign, the first of its kind in the Czech Republic, was organised around the case supported by a variety of organisations (NGOs, trade unions, etc.), informal groups and individuals. It targeted particular subcontractors, sought unpaid wages for the workers and challenged worsening working conditions in state forestry. The chapter maps out the complex character of the campaign, interactions and tensions within the network.

In Chapter 6, Jake Lagnado charts the life of the Latin American Workers Association (LAWAS) in London between 2004 and 2010 on the basis of the author's personal experience. At the start of this period LAWAS entered into a partnership with the British union Unite (previously T&G) at the same time as the latter's Justice for Cleaners (J4C) campaign was in full swing in London, drawing in

Latin American activists and others. In 2010 the relationship broke down, triggered by LAWAS's support for a series of unofficial protests by a group of J4C members, and different approaches to migrant rights campaigning. The chapter covers some of the tensions between different kinds of community and union organising, including mainstream unions' organising approach, independent unionism, the NGO model and the politics of the left and international solidarity.

In Chapter 7, Vasco Pedrina discusses organising migrant workers in Switzerland. His chapter discusses the Swiss inter-industrial union Unia – through the organisations from which it originates – which has had a lot of experience in organising and integrating migrant workers within its structures, from as early as the 1960s. As one of the first unions in Europe to do so, the chapter discusses the evolution, obstacles and successes of Unia's systematic policy of organising and integrating migrant workers in unions. It also considers the impact of the integration of migrants on the orientation of trade union policies, and organising migrant workers at the international level in the light of the Swiss experience.

Part III begins with Chapter 8, which is collectively authored by the Asia Pacific Mission for Migrants (APMM), deals with a study on migrant union organising experiences in Hong Kong conducted in 2012, and is the first of three contributions from the Asia-Pacific region. It is the result of focus-group discussions among the three migrant unions representing foreign domestic workers in Hong Kong: the Filipino Migrant Workers' Union (FMWU), the Indonesian Migrant Workers' Union (IMWU) and the Overseas Nepali Workers' Union (ONWU). Problems that they have resolved along the way as well as current challenges are discussed. The chapter concludes that migrant unionism has the advantage of representing migrant workers in Hong Kong's Labour Tribunal, and can become a channel of workers' solidarity if properly oriented. As a strategy 'from below', different from the trade union-initiated 'top-down' approach, the Hong Kong model in migrant union organising is offered as an effective model in areas where local labour unions are weak or stagnant, but where the right to organise is guaranteed by national laws and policies.

Hiroshi Ueki explores the possibilities and limitations of organising immigrant workers in Japan in Chapter 9. This chapter discusses the case of the local union of the All-Japan Metal and Information Machinery Workers' Union (JMIU), which has organised South American workers of Japanese descent in Shizuoka. It contends that the successful organising of immigrant workers by the union is based on two factors. The first is that the local union has characteristics of a community union which any worker can join as an individual, irrespective of employment status or nationality. Second, it has much experience in organising enterprise-level locals, based on JMIU's plan. The chapter also discusses the limitations of local union activities in relation to the lives of migrant workers.

Migrant workers have long occupied an important role in the development of capitalism in Aotearoa/New Zealand. In Chapter 10, Edward Miller and Dennis Maga argue that migrant workers are now indispensable to the reconstruction projects that followed the Christchurch earthquakes of 2010 and 2011, and this has brought with it a significant rise in migrant worker exploitation. The chapter discusses the development of community-based migrant worker organising through the Union Network of Migrants (UNEMIG, a division of FIRST Union) and its approach to organising migrants.

Part IV comprises chapters which cover US and Canadian migrant worker organising experiences. In Chapter 11, Valerie Francisco discusses building Filipino migrant worker leadership in the Bay Area of California through community-based research. It looks at how research and leadership development focused on caregivers and migrants works in the domestic care sector to identify the key issues and potential organising strategies for this migrant worker population. Developing a core of migrant worker organisers through the CARE Project became the basis for establishing an approach to migrant worker organising that could begin with research and common goals. This chapter argues that participatory research can be an avenue to spark much consciousness and solidarity between migrant workers. It also explores the limits of community-based research in sustaining migrant worker organising.

Finally, in Chapter 12, Aziz Choudry and Mostafa Henaway write about labour organising among racialised immigrants and migrants working for temporary labour recruitment agencies in Montreal. They discuss building worker agency, leadership and independent organisations of agency workers, and explore broader campaigns against temp agency industry practices, often characterised by low wages, poor working conditions and labour law violations. Their chapter contextualises these conditions and workers' struggles within broader historical and contemporary trends in national and global labour, the transformation of work, immigration and economic policymaking at a time of capitalist crisis and austerity.

We hope that *Just Work?* not only makes a contribution to the critical literatures on migration, precarious employment, transformation of paid work and the political actions of migrant workers, but that it is of relevance to organisers. Relatively few books in these areas are grounded in activism and address the dynamics and tensions of organising. In addition, the contexts and struggles presented in our book have not been well-documented, if at all, and far less brought together in a collection which introduces them into a critical conversation on migrant workers, globalisation and resistance. Yet we hope that these approaches and the cases shared here will contribute to both scholarly and activist thought and action for justice for migrant workers.

REFERENCES

Akers Chacón, J. and Davis, M. (2006). *No One is Illegal: Fighting Racism and State Violence on the US–Mexico Border*. Chicago: Haymarket Books.

Arat-Koc, S. (1999). 'Neoliberalism, State Restructuring and Immigration: Changes in Canadian Policies in the 1990s'. *Journal of Canadian Studies*, 34(2), 31–56.

Choudry, A., Hanley, J., Jordan, S., Shragge, E. and Stiegman, M. (2009). *Fight Back: Workplace Justice for Immigrants*. Halifax: Fernwood.

—— and Thomas, M. (2012). 'Organizing Migrant and Immigrant Workers in Canada'. In Ross, S. and Savage, L. (Eds), *Rethinking the Politics of Labour in Canada* (pp. 171–83). Halifax and Winnipeg: Fernwood.

Cornelius, W. A. and Rosenblum, M. R. (2005). 'Immigration and Politics'. *Annual Review of Political Science*, 8, 99–119.

Delgado Wise, R. (2004). 'Critical Dimensions of Mexico–US Migration under the Aegis of Neoliberalism and NAFTA'. *Canadian Journal of Development Studies*, 25(4), 591–605.

Dumont, J.-C. (2013). 'Migration Picking Up but Rising Unemployment Hurting Immigrants. OECD, June 13. www.oecd.org/els/mig/migrationpickingupbutrisingunemploymenthurtingimmigrants.htm (accessed August 2015).

Fine, J. (2006). *Worker Centers: Organizing Communities at the Edge of the Dream.* Ithaca, NY: Cornell University Press.

Global Migration Group (2015). 'Harnessing Migration, Remittances and Diaspora Contributions for Financing Sustainable Development'. Conference agenda, May. www.globalmigrationgroup.org/sites/default/files/Agenda_May_26-27_v8.pdf (accessed August 2015).

Harper, T. (2014). 'Jason Kenney Suspends Food Services Sector from Foreign Worker Program'. *The Toronto Star*, April 24. www.thestar.com/news/canada/2014/04/24/a_flood_of_foreign_workers_drives_up_western_unemployment_tim_harper.html (accessed August 2015).

Hearn, J. and Bergos, M. (2010). 'Learning from the Cleaners? Trade Union Activism among Low Paid Latin American Migrant Workers at the University of London'. Identity, Citizenship and Migration Centre, Working Paper No. 7, University of Nottingham. WP 10-07.

Hlatshwayo, M. (2010). *COSATU's Responses to Xenophobia.* Johannesburg: Strategy and Tactics.

—— (2012). 'COSATU's Attitudes and Policies towards External Migrants'. In Buhlungu, S. and Tshoaedi, M. (Eds), *COSATU's Contested Legacy: South African Trade Unions in the Second Decade of Democracy* (pp. 228–58). Cape Town: Human Science Research Council Press.

International Organization for Migration (Dhaka). (2013). *Facts and Figures.* http://www.iom.org.bd/page/facts-and-figures/ (accessed August 2015).

Kapur, D. (2004). 'Remittances: The New Development Mantra?' G-24 Discussion Paper, No. 29. www.cities-localgovernments.org/committees/fccd/Upload/library/gdsmdpbg2420045_en_en.pdf (accessed August 2015).

Kundnani, A. (2007). *The End of Tolerance: Racism in 21st Century Britain.* London and Ann Arbor, MI: Pluto.

Lehulere, O. (2008). 'The Xenophobia Outbreak in South Africa: Strategic Political and Organisational Questions facing the New Social Movements'. *KHANYA, A Journal for Activists*, 19(July), 32–44.

Lutz, H. (Ed.). (2012). *Migration and Domestic Work: A European Perspective on a Global Theme.* Aldershot: Ashgate.

Magalhaes, L., Carrasco, C. and Gastaldo, D. (2010). Undocumented Migrants in Canada: 'A Scope Literature review on Health, Access to Services, and Working Conditions'. *Journal of Immigrant and Minority Health*, 12(1), 132–51.

National Post. (2015). 'Canadian Gender Equality Under Threat from "Society of Immigration": Former PM Kim Campbell'. *National Post*, 16 April. http://news.nationalpost.com/news/canada/canadian-gender-equality-under-threat-from-society-of-immigration-former-pm-kim-campbell (accessed August 2015).

Ness, I. (2014). *New Forms of Worker Organization and Migration in a World of Inequality.* Oakland, CA: PM Press.

Ramsaroop, C. and Smith, A. A. (2014). The Inherent Racism of the Temporary Foreign Worker Program. *The Toronto Star*, 21 May. http://thestar.com/opinion/

commentary/2014/05/21/the_inherent_racism_of_the_temporary_foreign_worker_program.html (accessed 2 May 2015).

Ratha, D., De, S., Dervisevic, E., Plaza, S., Schuettler, K., Shaw, W., Wyss, H., Yi, S. and Yousefi, S. R. (2015). *Migration and Development Brief 24*. Migration and Remittances Team, Development Prospects Group, World Bank, 13 April. http://siteresources.worldbank.org/INTPROSPECTS/Resources/334934-1288990760745/MigrationandDevelopmentBrief24.pdf (accessed August 2015).

Richmond, A. H. (1994). *Global Apartheid: Refugees, Racism and the New World Order*. Don Mills, ON: Oxford University Press.

Rodriguez, R. M. (2010a). *Migrants for Export: How the Philippine State Brokers Labor to the World*. Minneapolis: University of Minnesota Press.

—— (2010b). 'On the Question of Expertise: A Critical Reflection on "Civil Society" Processes'. In A. Choudry and D. Kapoor (Eds), *Learning from the Ground Up: Global Perspectives on Social Movements and Knowledge Production* (pp. 53–68). New York: Palgrave Macmillan.

Segatti, A. (2011). 'Migration to South Africa: Regional Challenges versus National Instruments and Interests'. In A. Segatti and L. B. Landau (Eds), *Contemporary Migration to South Africa: A Regional Development Issue* (pp. 9–30). Washington, DC: World Bank.

Stoney, S., Batalova, J. and Russell, J. (2013). *US in Focus: South American Immigrants in the United States*. Migration Policy Institute, May. www.migrationinformation.org/USfocus/display.cfm?id=949#1 (accessed August 2015).

Suzuki, A. (Ed.). (2012). *Cross-National Comparisons of Social Movement Unionism: Diversities of Labour Movement Revitalization in Japan, Korea and the United States*. Bern: Peter Lang.

Uchitelle, L. (2007). 'NAFTA Should Have Stopped Illegal Immigration, Right?' *New York Times*, 18 February. www.nytimes.com/2007/02/18/weekinreview/18uchitelle.html (accessed August 2015).

Van Driel, M. (2008). 'Understanding Xenophobia in Democratic South Africa'. *KHANYA, A Journal for Activists*, 19, 5–21.

Wills, J., Datta, K., Evans, Y., Herbert, J., May, J. and McIlwaine, C. (2010). *Global Cities at Work: New Migrant Divisions of Labour*. London: Pluto.

Part I

Africa and the Middle East

2

Xenophobia, Resilience, and Resistance of Immigrant Workers in South Africa: Collective and Individual Responses

Mondli Hlatshwayo

The literature on xenophobia in South Africa has extensively examined the nature and forms of xenophobia perpetrated by ordinary South Africans, the state and its various arms such as the police, and the media (for example, Everatt, 2011; Landau, 2011; Sigsworth et al., 2008). This scholarship largely discusses the xenophobic attacks on immigrants in working class and poor residential areas inside cities and towns (Amisi, 2009; Bruce, 2002; Everatt, 2011; Landau, 2011; Sinwell, 2011). It plays a critical role in analysing xenophobia as a post-apartheid South African phenomenon and in understanding how it affects immigrants. But with very few exceptions (Amisi, 2009; Polzer and Segatti, 2011), it does not view immigrant communities as social agents capable of shaping their own conditions. In addition, immigrant communities do not tend to be seen as permanent features of the present and future South African society and economy.

Another relatively small strand of literature examines the relationship between trade unions and immigrant workers, especially in a context of the massive xenophobic attacks on immigrants in May 2008 (Di Paola, 2013; Hlatshwayo, 2011). This contributes towards understanding union attitudes to immigrants in South Africa, but it does not locate immigrants and migrant workers as a central point of the inquiry. Rather, immigrant workers and immigrants are discussed through the prism of trade unions, especially in regard to union attitudes to immigrants.

However, it is the conditions of immigrant workers and their various expressions of social agency that form this chapter's starting point and unit of analysis. First I argue that immigrant workers are a permanent feature of the post-apartheid South African economy. This largely arises from the relative strength of the South African economy on the African continent. Drawing on interviews with around 30 immigrant workers, I then examine the working conditions of immigrants in the context of the rise of generalised precarious working conditions or what is regarded as the 'race to the bottom', which entails the lowering of labour standards and wages. I then discuss the resilience of immigrant workers. This is graphically captured in the risky journeys they undertake from their countries of origin to major cities like Johannesburg due to the hunger for work and the struggle for survival in a context of economic meltdown in countries like Zimbabwe. While a generalised 'race to the bottom' affects all workers including South Africans, immigrant workers face even bigger risks and obstacles such as deportation and victimisation by employers. It is easier for employers to victimise immigrant workers because many of them are not documented. Undocumented immigrants are considered to be 'illegal' and are most likely to be detained and deported by the state authorities. Their stories are not listened to since they are presumed to be guilty because they are considered to have entered the country 'illegally'.

The rest of the chapter examines individual and collective responses of immigrant workers in the generalised precarious industrial relations of South Africa. Immigrant workers as social agents interact among themselves, work with some South Africans, are assisted by NGOs, and form their own organisations in order to navigate the difficult and unfriendly terrain in South Africa.

THE PRESENCE OF IMMIGRANTS IN SOUTH AFRICA

Lehulere (2008: 37) states that immigration into South Africa is a permanent aspect of the South African economy and relates to the sociopolitical context in Africa and especially Southern Africa. He argues that:

Immigration into South Africa will not be stopped by some action that will or can be undertaken by the South African state. On the contrary, it is the actions of the South African state that ensure that immigration into South Africa will continue with or without the Zimbabwean crisis. As an agent of South African capital, the South African state is responsible for policies that undermine African economies, it is responsible for policies that extract wealth from Africa into South Africa, and it is responsible for policies that are concentrating the capital of the continent – both human and financial – into South Africa.

He then emphasises that the migration of people tends to follow capital – people go to places where there are chances of earning an income. At the moment, the direction of migration reflects South Africa's economic strength on the African continent. Should this change in the future, migration patterns will also change (Lehulere, 2008).

While there are no exact figures for immigrants in South Africa, there is a general agreement that the number of immigrants seeking economic opportunities and immigrants in general has increased drastically, and the immigrant question is a post-apartheid phenomenon. In 2013, the South African Government News Agency (SAGNA) reported that the country's population was expected to have grown from just below 51.8 million in 2011 to close to 53 million. The agency announced that the population's natural rate of increase fell from 1.05 per cent per year in 2002 to 0.99 per cent in 2013. Thanks to a net inflow of migrants, the population increased faster per year in 2013 than over ten years ago. The population grew by 1.34 per cent between 2012 and 2013. The increase between 2002 and 2003 was by 1.3 per cent (SAGNA, 2013: 1).

In 2013, SAGNA (2013: 1) further reported that '[a]n estimated 998,000 African migrants are expected to enter the country between 2011 and 2015'. Lehulere (2008) and Gordon (2005) argue that African 'immigrants' and immigrant workers are not just visitors who are going to return to their countries of origin after a couple of years, but they must be understood and conceptualised as part of the South African working people and the poor.

THE CONDITIONS OF IMMIGRANT WORKERS

Having established that the presence of immigrant workers in South Africa is not just a temporary aberration which will disappear, we can now discuss their working conditions. Ighsaan Schroeder, coordinator of the Casual Workers Advice Office (CWAO), which advises atypical workers on their rights and is involved in campaigning for the rights of vulnerable workers in South Africa, reflected on the conditions of immigrant workers and workers in general:

> The levels of exploitation of workers has intensified so much ... I am not saying that this holds for everybody but a lot of the time most workers belong to a category of vulnerable workers. The level of exploitation and degradation and depression of workers, denial of their rights has become so generalised. You know, that the immigrant workers are just like all the other workers. (I. Schroeder, interview, 6 September 2011)

However, Schroeder also stated that the question of documentation and immigrant workers' status as non-citizens makes them extremely vulnerable, and they are always faced with deportation as soon as they start demanding their rights (I. Schroeder, interview, 6 September 2011). Tafira (2013: 14) writes about the extremely precarious position of immigrant workers, noting that '[i]mmigrant workers thereby come to constitute a "lower stratum" of the working class which becomes fragmented'. The level of unionisation among vulnerable workers and immigrant workers occupying precarious positions is very low or close to non-existent (Hlatshwayo, 2013). For example, this chapter is largely based on 30 in-depth interviews with immigrant workers living in Johannesburg, none of whom belonged to a union. Testimonies of these immigrant workers show that they are extremely vulnerable, and earn very low wages.

Jay Ginger,[1] an immigrant worker from Zimbabwe who lives at the Central Methodist Church in Johannesburg, had this to say about his precarious position in South Africa: 'We are not part of unions. We have no rights. We earn starvation wages. We are victimised by the police and some South Africans. We can be deported back to Zimbabwe any time' (J. Ginger, interview, 6 October 2014).

IMMIGRANT WORKERS' RESILIENCE AND THE JOURNEY TO SOUTH AFRICA

Maduna (2008) narrates the dangers and difficulties that immigrant workers face on their way to South African cities like Johannesburg. This journey is an individual and collective struggle, as it requires resilience and solidarity. She reflects:

> The process of migration though is fraught with dangers and difficulties, exposing migrants to considerable risks (that is, physical and/or gender-based violence, economic exploitation, detention, etc), health problems and ongoing hardship. Nevertheless, migration remains a livelihood option to many. Migrants continue to travel alone or together with friends and family, often paying *Magumaguma* [thieves], *Malayitsha* [smugglers], or government authorities for their entry to South Africa. The survey reveals that many respondents travel off the main roads and through the bush to avoid detection by authorities and very often encounter thieves in the isolated areas near the Limpopo River. Nearly a third of all respondents had experienced some form of violence during their journey. (Maduna, 2008: 3)

Tenga Thengwayo, a bricklayer from Mozambique working in Johannesburg said: 'In 1998, I came to South Africa. I just crossed the border illegally. I did not use my passport and visa. I took a taxi. I went through Lebombo Mountains. We went through the farms. ... I then went to Jozi [Johannesburg]' (T. Thengwayo, interview, 6 September 2014). Oshman Mohazi, a tailor originally from Tamale in Ghana, now a South African citizen, spoke about his very long journey to South Africa:

Travelling is not like being at home. When you go outside you learn. I used to take stuff from the farms and sell in the city. I did so almost for 3 to 4 years. I organised money so that I can come to South Africa. I knew nothing about travelling. I went to the agent and I applied for my visa. I collected the money, and said I am going to Swaziland. When I went to Swaziland I had only had US$100. I did not have a visa. We walked by foot and reached South Africa at 4 am. I then took a taxi to Johannesburg. (O. Mohazi, interview, 7 September 2014)

Ginger from Shamva District in Zimbabwe said: 'I came with *Malayitsha* [smugglers]. I gave them a thousand Rands [US$100]. You speak to security guards. This is safer than going through the water. I know the *Magumaguma* [thieves] can kill you. Those guys are dangerous. I came here to the Methodist Church [in Johannesburg]' (J. Ginger, interview, 6 September 2014).

The situation is worse for women immigrants. According to Musetha, 'Three out of 10 Zimbabwean women are gang-raped while trying to illegally cross the border into South Africa through undesignated entry points along the Limpopo River' (2012: 1). Pamela Khumalo, a woman migrant worker working in South Africa's early childhood development sector said, 'We have to persevere. Resilience keeps us going. We have to survive against all odds and that has to do with the fact that there are no job and economic opportunities in Zimbabwe. We survive violence on the way to South Africa, because we are looking for work' (P. Khumalo, interview, 10 October 2014).

INDIVIDUAL RESPONSES

Given the poor organisation of immigrant workers, their responses to challenges in the workplace tend to be highly individualised. Jay Ginger came to Johannesburg and lived with his uncle in 2014. He recalled, 'I worked for my uncle and the pay was bad. I do not have a work permit. I get treated like a slave.' One of his individual responses was to move to other, better jobs. He said: 'I left that job, and found other better jobs like painting and washing cars. There are no unions to look after us' (J. Ginger, interview, 3 October 2014).

Women immigrant workers face even more serious obstacles and gender-based discrimination. Sizani Gumede, an immigrant worker from Zimbabwe, said:

I bought groceries. I was paying R70 [US$7] per week for rent. We would go and work in Mayfair doing piece jobs and we were getting R50 [US$5] or R70 [US$7] per day. I then got contract work in Crown Mines and they did not see that we are pregnant. They then chase me away as they realised that I was pregnant. ... I got fired. I realised that if I was not pregnant I would be working. We just have to be strong and resilient, because the situation is worse in Zimbabwe. There are no piece jobs. (S. Gumede, interview, 6 October 2014)

When asked about how she deals with workplace challenges, Pamela stated that 'you just ignore [these problems] so that you can stay well. That is how we are taught. Religion and God play an important role in our lives' (P. Khumalo, interview, 10 October 2014).

Sizani Gumede had to rely on her individual initiative, religion, belief and networks to survive. She stated that she relies on belief in the existence of God. She believes that God is the one looking after her. She said that she should pray to go and actively look for a job. Her husband was not with her in Johannesburg, and she was pregnant. She had to survive against all these odds. Then she was hired by a Nigerian migrant to distribute flyers advertising his business. Subsequent to that she was hired by a South African street vendor, and had to sell fat cakes in the streets of Johannesburg. This new job required her to wake up at 2 o'clock in the morning and she would normally complete the sales at 9 am. She also stated that South Africans are not all the same. Like her employer, other South Africans care about migrants from other African countries (S. Gumede, interview, 6 October 2014).

Asked about whether there are organisations that helped her to defend her rights as a pregnant woman and workers, she responded: 'There was no organisation that assisted me. I cannot talk about trade unions as I have never interacted with them. I was helped by relatives, friends and some South Africans' (S. Gumede, interview, 6 October 2014).

Pamela Khumalo also complained about lack of support from South African trade unions and how immigrant workers are left to their own devices. She argued:

Trade unions do not speak for us as foreigners. ... No one cares about how much you are getting. Whether you are paid peanuts or not is not an issue for them because they say this [working in a private pre-school] is private thing. I went to CCMA[2] [Commission for Arbitration Mediation and Conciliation] but it does not help at all. My previous employer would brag about the fact that I could not do anything. I just had to leave my money. (P. Khumalo, interview, 10 October 2014)

TRADE UNIONS, NGOS AND COLLECTIVE RESPONSES

There is a strong yearning for South African-based trade unions to provide solidarity to immigrant workers. Blessing Katari, a street vendor in Johannesburg who is from the Chimanimani District in Zimbabwe, argued: 'If I were to be formally employed, I would belong to the union' (B. Katari, interview, 6 August 2014). Phumzile Khuboni, an immigrant domestic worker from Zimbabwe, also stated that: 'Maybe I want to be part of a union. Maybe they can be helpful' (P. Khuboni, interview, 6 August 2014).

Elsewhere I have stated that trade unions under the banner of the Congress of South African Trade Unions (COSATU) have not been able to organise immigrant workers, related to the fact that there was no appreciation that immigrant workers are a permanent feature of the South African economy and that these COSATU unions are largely interested in established skilled and semi-skilled workers who are South Africans (Hlatshwayo, 2011, 2012, 2013). COSATU is the biggest trade union federation in South Africa with possibilities of reaching out to all workers, but it has adopted a narrow nationalist chauvinist approach which prioritises organising South African workers located in relatively permanent positions, or what I regard as 'low-hanging fruits', to the exclusion of vulnerable workers and immigrant workers. COSATU has also complained about immigrant workers taking over the jobs of South African workers, and stated that immigrant workers are prepared to accept low wages, thereby 'undercutting' South African workers. Instead of viewing immigrant workers as part of labour in a struggle against capital, COSATU has tended to see immigrants as a problem that must be fixed through tighter border controls (Hlatshwayo, 2013).

Jinah (2012: 33) reflects on the role of international NGOs in relation to immigrant workers and states that: 'Generally international organisations, which have the authority to intervene at government level, believe that poor working and living conditions of farm workers stems from their state of being undocumented and economically, politically, and socially marginalised'. She then states that the orientation of these organisations is to use legal means in order to normalise the status of immigrant workers. Local NGOs operating in the South African border near Zimbabwe contend that international NGOs are not in touch with immigrant workers on the ground, and are 'bureaucratic and uncaring' (Jinah, 2012: 33). The local NGOs provide immigrant workers, especially farm workers, with support by ensuring that they access HIV and AIDS treatment, better working conditions and wages. Some of these NGOs conduct workshops on the rights of immigrant workers and help them to access their rights via the Department of Labour (Jinah, 2012: 33). While to some extent immigrant workers take part in these NGO-led campaigns, they also want to be part of some direct organisational response to their conditions.

According to Jinah (2012), international NGOs do not seem to share knowledge with local NGOs so that problems of farm workers can be addressed collectively. She proposes that there should be joint work between international and local NGOs, the Department of Labour and the Department of Home Affairs, and that immigrant workers have to work together in order to improve the living and working conditions of workers. However, in the Western Cape province, there has been some collaboration to build an organisational response to xenophobia and around the challenges facing immigrant workers. COSATU's Western Cape provincial office supports NGOs such as the International Labour Research and Information Group (ILRIG), the Labour Research Service (LRS) and the Ogoni Solidarity Forum (OSF), an organisation of immigrants (Jara and Peberdy, 2009).

Gaetan Imbula-Bofale of the OSF elaborates on the Western Cape initiative, reflecting on a discussion which took place in 2008 between leaders and officials of LRS, ILRIG, Western Cape COSATU and the OSF. They spoke about developing strategies and tactics for opposing xenophobia and building organisational responses which would contribute towards the unity of migrant workers from other African countries and South African workers in the Western Cape. According to Imbula-Bofale, it was these discussions which led to the formation of the Migrant Workers Committee (MWC), a group of migrants and refugees which acted as an organising platform for migrant workers and refugees in 2010 (Imbula-Bofale, 2010).

Imbula-Bofale sees the MWC as a space for dialogue and solidarity between South African and immigrant workers. The MWC created space for dialogue and debate among migrants, trade unionists, NGO activists and organisations of migrants. Some of the discussions had practical implications for migrant workers. Some people were referred to government institutions dealing with labour matters so that their problems could be solved. There were also discussions about building a platform of pan-African workers in the South African context. In other words, South African workers had to see themselves not just as South African workers, but as pan-African workers or workers belonging to the African continent (Imbula-Bofale, 2010: 1).

Barry Wuganaale of the OSF, who is also part of the MWC, spoke about the relationship between immigrant workers and COSATU in the Western Cape, indicating that immigrant workers and immigrants in general and their organisations have received concrete solidarity and support from COSATU in the Western Cape. This makes immigrant organisations feel welcomed (cited in Hlatshwayo, 2013: 286).

Imbula-Bofale (2010) noted that an important aspect of the work involves immigrant women workers. For example, he observes that the MWC has sought to build links with Building Women Activism, an ILRIG women-only space, and the South African Domestic Cleaning and Allied Workers Union, to empower and help organise migrant women. However, the Western Cape initiatives led by COSATU in the Western Cape, immigrant organisations and NGOs have not been sustained. Organisations have tended to focus on their specific issues, and that has led to a lack of interest in building broad immigrant worker formation.

In Durban there have also been attempts to unite and organise street traders regardless of their nationality. Pat Horn, a leader of StreetNet International, an international alliance of unions and other membership-based organisations of street traders, with local structures in South Africa, and a veteran of South Africa's labour movement, reflected on these efforts:

> All our affiliates are from different countries. The question of favouring citizens of another country is not even on the agenda. We have 36 affiliates in 32 countries. International solidarity is our starting point because we are an international organisation. That framework helps to tackle xenophobia because when you talk of international solidarity you cannot entertain any xenophobic interest. Twenty of our affiliates are in Africa, and in Zimbabwe and Namibia our affiliates are an alliance of informal economy organisations which are part of cross-border trade organisations. (Cited in Hlatshwayo, 2010: 34)

Horn argued that xenophobia is an issue that StreetNet had to confront. One creative strategy employed to do so included exchange visits where South African members of StreetNet would visit other African countries. She stated that this has yielded positive results because it reinforces the notion of international solidarity among street traders of different nationalities operating in Southern Africa. She noted that street vendors in Zambia and Namibia have formed cross-border organisations that can negotiate at the level of the South African Customs Union (Hlatshwayo, 2010).

According to Horn, StreetNet's mobilisation of street vendors regardless of nationalities led to those without South African identity documents being granted trade permits in the streets of Durban in 2005 (Hlatshwayo, 2010). The efforts of local and immigrant traders ensured that immigrant vendors are granted some relief in the form of trade permits. In 2014, immigrant and South African traders both faced evictions from Johannesburg's city centre. According to the Consortium for Refugees and Migrants in South Africa (CoRMSA), an NGO that services migrants in South Africa:

> One of the highlights of campaigns in the year 2014 was legal victory regarding the eviction of informal traders in the Johannesburg city centre. With the support of legal teams, the South African Informal Traders Forum (SAITF) and the displaced traders approached the Constitutional Court with the objective of seeking relief. On the 4th of April 2014, the Constitutional Court handed down a judgement explaining its reasons for ordering the City of Johannesburg to allow informal traders to return to their stalls in the inner city of Johannesburg. (CoRMSA, 2014: 4)

The SAITF, a forum representing immigrant and local traders, was able to work with lawyers and NGOs and used the law to advance and defend the rights of traders regardless of their nationality. Oshman Mohazi, a street trader, had this to say about the eviction and unity among street traders: 'We were united as African brothers and sisters. We are all working and the city was violating our right to work and trade' (O. Mohazi, interview, 7 September 2014).

USING LEGAL SPACES AND ADVICE WORK

There have also been positive developments with regard to labour law and undocumented migrants. These are some of the small but important steps which begin to stretch the borders of citizenship. According to Hweshe (2010: 1), in 2010, for the first time, South Africa's Labour Appeal Court said sex workers could take their bosses to the CCMA for unfair dismissal. One immigrant sex worker, Kylie, worked for Brigitte's brothel for more than a decade, seeing more than ten clients 'on a good day'. But in 2006, when she complained of 14-hour working days, no days off and refused to give oral sex to clients, she was fired. The Sex Worker Education and Advocacy Taskforce, with the help of lawyers, took up her case, but it was rejected by the CCMA who said sex work was illegal. The CCMA said undocumented or 'illegal' immigrant workers could not claim labour rights. The labour court said the same in 2008. But in May 2010, the labour appeals court ruled in favour of Kylie. This court victory means that undocumented migrant workers have a right to use courts and other legal processes to challenge unfair labour laws as well as a limited notion of citizenship and rights.

Immigrant workers earning low wages also benefit from free legal support provided by the NGO, Lawyers for Human Rights (LHR). Given the need to provide legal support for immigrants and immigrant workers, the LHR established a Refugee and Migrant Rights Programme. The programme team consists of eight lawyers, a social worker, two paralegals and two administrators who operate from the programme's legal advice offices in Johannesburg, Pretoria, Durban and Port Elizabeth (LHR, 2014: 1).

CWAO, introduced earlier in the chapter, 'provides free advice and support to workers, privileging casual, contract, labour broker and other precarious workers. The organisation was formed out of the recognition that the traditional labour movement appears incapable or unwilling to organise the new kinds of workers created by neo-liberalism' (CWAO, 2014: 1).

CWAO coordinator Ighsaan Schroeder stated that the advice office advises immigrant workers on their rights, seeks to build unity among all vulnerable workers in South Africa, and provides free support to workers. He spoke about the kind of support provided to immigrant workers, which includes representing them at the CCMA free of charge. He said:

> If it's a dismissal, we then tend to do the referral of the dispute to the CCMA, so we complete the form, we'll fax it to the employer, and we will then tell the employee where the CCMA is. If you can't fax the employer, we will pay for the registered postage. But all of that comes after we've had a lengthy interview with the worker to inform them of his or her rights. We will even sit with the worker and argue the case with them, prepare the case, write it up in point form for them. (I. Schroeder, interview, 6 September 2014)

The advice office was also involved in the collective struggle of immigrant and other atypical workers in 2013. Schroeder recalled that a company called Savemore in Kwa-Thema, an area in the east of Johannesburg, had hired over a hundred workers, including permanent staff, through labour brokers (companies which hire workers and deploy them to various workplaces) and casual workers. Of these, around 30 immigrant workers received no payslips, paid sick leave or annual leave. They were underpaid. They received R500 a week as a wage (I. Schroeder, interview, 6 September 2014).

The workers were involved in a campaign to fight for their rights. Schroeder explained: 'Those were now South African workers, Zimbabwean, Mozambican workers. And the workers from the onset were keen to keep the unity and that looked good on the South African workers, you know, there wasn't a hint of xenophobia and they all live in the Kwa-Thema community'. (I. Schroeder, interview, 6 September 2014).

The unity was disturbed by the mere mention of the Department of Labour. Schroeder recalled: 'The minute the issue of the Department of Labour was raised, the Zimbabwean and Mozambican workers seemed to disappear into the background.' Being identified as an undocumented worker by the Department of Labour would have led to their arrest and deportation.

However, Schroeder notes that there is unevenness among workers. He argued:

It's interesting, what strikes you about the Zimbabwean workers, they seem a lot more confident to come forward and we have tried to understand why. It seems there might be a whole range of different reasons for that, the one is just like a straight pragmatic question of language, these workers speak English, they can speak to other workers and get to know about their rights, they can come to the office and speak to you and say what the problem is, it might be the consequence of a slightly better education in Zimbabwe, than here, so there is a slightly greater level of confidence that comes with that. (I. Schroeder, interview, 6 September 2014)

MWA-SA ORGANISES IMMIGRANT WORKERS

Other organisational initiatives of immigrant workers included the formation of the Migrant Workers Association South Africa

(MWA-SA) in 2011. Established by immigrant workers based in South Africa, the organisation seeks to be a platform for immigrant workers who have no organised voice. The objective of the organisation is 'to mobilise, educate and represent migrant workers in order to protect their rights. It also aims to negotiate for better working conditions for all migrant workers and ensure they are not exploited in the labour market and they receive their benefits if terminated' (Nyathi, 2014: 1). Butholezwe Nyathi, National Coordinator of the MWA-SA, explained:

> Fellow migrant workers; it is upon us to organise ourselves and collectively address the common challenges we face in the different host countries we find ourselves in. As migrants, there are socio-economic and labour related challenges that we can put our heads together to alleviate and eradicate. Join us in this struggle as an activist, donor or partner for the PROMOTION and PROTECTION of migrant worker rights. (2014: 1)

Ezra Maplanka, a MWA-SA spokesperson, said that there are two membership categories. First, full membership, which first started in January 2014, was held by about 780 people who paid an annual subscription at the time of writing. Second, associate membership includes others who want to be part of the organisation (E. Maplanka, interview, 28 October 2014).

The MWA-SA uses social media to inform and mobilise immigrant workers. The organisation uses Facebook and Twitter to inform members and interested individuals about their rights and information on documentation. At the time of writing this chapter, 2,500 people 'liked' the Facebook page and there were 600 Twitter subscribers (E. Maplanka, interview, 28 October 2014). According to Maplanka, the organisation uses social media and face-to-face contact to inform and educate ordinary immigrant workers about the Zimbabwe Special Dispensation Permit (ZSDP), a process through which Zimbabwean immigrants can formalise their stay in South Africa. Maplanka further said, 'we assist them just for free' (E. Maplanka, interview, 28 October 2014).

However Dumile Ndlovu, a Zimbabwean immigrant working in South Africa, disputed this and stated that the organisation wanted her to pay a service fee of R150 for assistance with regard to her visa. She was told that the money would go towards administrative costs. She further stated that she wanted to know why the organisation would charge for this service because she believed the programme was already funded, upon which she was told it is not (D. Ndlovu, personal communication, 1 November 2014).

There is general agreement among those interviewed that immigrant workers in South Africa need to have some organisational expression. A hybrid form of organising seems to be emerging. Trade unions are called upon to organise immigrant workers, because immigrants are now a permanent feature of the South African economy. Immigrants are also looking at organising themselves. Nyathi stated that 80 per cent of catering industry workers are immigrant workers. There are also farm workers working in the South African border areas near Mozambique and Zimbabwe. MW-SA has been in discussions with COSATU-affiliated unions organising in the catering and agricultural sectors about organising immigrant workers.

Ezra Maplanka, an MWA-SA spokesperson, states:

> On our relationship with COSATU, we sit on the committee task team which is called Vulnerable Workers Task Team. That team ... caters for vulnerable workers who are earning less than R3500 [US$350]. They target farm workers, cleaners and migrant workers as well. So as an organisation we represent migrant workers on that platform. Farm workers, domestic workers, cleaners, street hawkers and traders and then migrant workers they fall in that category. MWA-SA as an organisation, it represents migrant workers on that committee. And we spoke about the strategy ... we are open to any nationality. (E. Maplanka, interview, 28 October 2014)

MWA-SA is working with other organisations to help Zimbabweans whose SA permits are about to expire. Most permits obtained freely under the Zimbabwean Documentation Project are nearing expiry. However, the limit of the organisation is that it only helps its membership. Maplanka appealed to all those who would like to be represented by the organisation to join it so that they can be assisted (E. Maplanka, interview, 28 October 2014). He further stated that the application forms had no option for renewal as in all other permits. The Dispensation of Zimbabweans Project[3] permits fell below even the ones that were given to Mozambicans in the year 2000, which gave them five years and an option to either go back home or apply for permanent residence. He elaborated that it is well known that most Zimbabweans are not in South Africa by choice, but because of the bad political and economic situation in Zimbabwe. He further indicated that his organisation has complied with the South African state's Department of Home Affairs' (DHA) process which requires documentation of immigrants and immigrant workers in particular, but the DHA has indicated that some work permits will not be renewed (E. Maplanka, interview, 28 October 2014).

CONCLUSION

This chapter provides some examples of both collective and individual responses to discrimination and precarious forms of existence in South Africa. Immigrant workers are not just victims of xenophobia and the 'race to the bottom', but are resilient agents seeking to improve their working and living conditions in a South Africa char-acterised by generalised precariousness, affecting all sections of the poor and working class. That is to say that the working class and the poor in general are faced with the deepening crisis of unemployment, poverty and lack of adequate access to basic services such as water and electricity. However, immigrant workers have a bigger burden of precariousness because in addition they have to deal with the fact that they are not South African citizens.

As individuals, immigrant workers face hardships as they leave their homes on their way to South Africa, and women tend to be most vulnerable as they face sexual attacks en route. Individual resilience, as shown in the interviews cited in this chapter, is char-acterised by determination, faith and hope which become tools of navigation from places of origin to cities and workplaces. Elsewhere I have argued that COSATU, the biggest trade union federation in

Just Work?

South Africa, has not been able to conceptualise immigrant workers as a permanent feature of South Africa's post-apartheid economy. Therefore immigrant workers have to be organised so that they can contribute towards strengthening the labour movement and the building of workers' unity within South African borders. Some NGOs, together with immigrant workers, form part of collective and individual responses to difficulties they face. Immigrant workers have also started to form their own organisations, such as MWA-SA which seeks to mobilise immigrants so that they can advance their rights. However, the general approach to organising immigrant workers in South Africa is still in a transition phase, as there seems to be no realisation that immigrant workers are part and parcel of the South African economy and society.

NOTES

1. All interviewees are identified by a pseudonym.
2. The Commission for Arbitration Mediation and Conciliation is a state body established by South African labour law. Its role is to mediate and/or arbitrate disagreements between workers and employers.
3. In 2009, the South African government announced a new policy called the Dispensation of Zimbabweans Project. The aim of this policy, according to the government, was to 'normalise' the stay of Zimbabweans in South Africa.

REFERENCES

Amisi, B. (2009). *Migrant Voices*. Research Report. www.gcro.ac.za/sites/default/files/News_items/Xeno_reports_July2010/synthesis/8_Migrant_voices.pdf (accessed August 2015).

Bruce, D. (2002). 'Police Brutality in South Africa'. Mwanajiti, N., Mhlanga, P., Sifuniso, M., Nachali-Kambikambi, Y., Muuba, M. and Mwananyanda, M. (Eds), *Police Brutality in Southern Africa: A Human Rights Perspective*. Lusaka: Inter-African Network for Human Rights and Development (Afronet). Research Report. http://s3.amazonaws.com/academia.edu.documents/31111189/policebrutality_1_.pdf?AWSAccessKeyId=AKIAJ56TQJRTWSMTNPEAandExpires=1434460149an dSignature=XSA9ArISoY88D9cS7uRWm9kZCT4%3Dandresponse-content-disposition=inline (accessed August 2015).

CoRMSA. (2014). *Protecting and Promoting the Rights of Asylum Seekers, Refugees and Migrants in 2014*. CoRMSA Annual Report 2013. www.CoRMSA.org.za (accessed August 2015).

Di Paola, M. (2013). 'A Labour Perspective on Xenophobia in South Africa: A Case Study of the Metals and Engineering Industry in Ekurhuleni'. Unpublished master's thesis, University of the Witwatersrand, Johannesburg.

Everatt, D. (2011). 'Xenophobia, State and Society in South Africa 2008–2010'. *Politikon: South African Journal of Political Studies*, 38(1), 7–36.

Gordon, S. 2005. 'The Trade Union Response to Alien Workers within Post-Apartheid South Africa: An Analysis of the Nature of the Response of the South African Trade Union Movement to the Issue of Illegal Migrant Workers, Using The National Security & Unqualified Workers Union as a Case Study'. Unpublished master's thesis, University of KwaZulu-Natal, Durban.

Hlatshwayo, M. (2011). 'Is there Room for International Solidarity within South African Borders? COSATU's Responses to the Xenophobic Attacks of May 2008'. *Politikon: South African Journal of Political Studies*, 38(1), 169–89.

—— (2012). 'COSATU's Attitudes and Policies towards External Migrants'. In Buhlungu, S. and Tshoaedi, M. (Eds), *COSATU'S Contested Legacy: South African Trade Unions in the Second Decade of Democracy* (pp. 228–58). Cape Town: Human Science Research Council.

—— (2013). 'Immigrant Workers and COSATU: Solidarity versus National Chauvinism?'. *Alternation: Special Edition*, 7, 267–93.

Hweshe, F. (2010). 'Sex Worker Wins Appeal'. *Sowetan Live*, 3 June. www.sowetanlive. co.za/sowetan/archive/2010/06/03/sex-worker-wins-appeal?filter=all_comments (accessed August 2015).

Imbula-Bofale, G. (2010). 'The Migrant Voice'. *The Migrant Voice: An Authentic African Voice for Migrants and Refugees*, Newsletter, 1 May 2010.

Jara, M. K. and Peberdy, S. (2009). 'Progressive Humanitarian and Social Mobilisation in a Neo-Apartheid Cape Town: A Report on Civil Society and the May 2008 Xenophobic violence'. Research Report, *The Atlantic Philanthropies*. www.atlanticphilanthropies.org/sites/all/modules/filemanager/files/2_Cape_town_c.pdf (accessed August 2015).

Jinah, Z. (2012). '"We Have to Go into the Bush": Understanding the Responses of NGOs and Government in Addressing Conditions Faced by Cross Border Migrant Workers in Musina'. Research Report, African Centre for Migration and Society, University of the Witwatersrand.

Landau, L. (Ed.). (2011). *Exorcising the Demons Within: Xenophobia, Violence and State in Contemporary South Africa, Johannesburg*. Johannesburg: Wits University Press.

Lehulere, O. (2008). 'The Xenophobia Outbreak in South Africa: Strategic, Political and Organisational Questions Facing the New Social Movements'. *Khanya Journal*, 19, 32–45.

LHR. (2014). *Refugee and Migrant Rights Programme*. www.lhr.org.za/programme/refugee-and-migrant-rights-programme-rmrp/information (accessed 11 December 2014).

Maduna, L. (2008). *Migrants' Needs and Vulnerabilities in the Limpopo Province, Republic of South Africa, Phase One. November–December 2008.* Johannesburg: International Organization for Migration.

Musetha, N. (2012). 'Border Jumpers Raped and Intimidated'. *Limpopo Mirror*, November 19. www.limpopomirror.co.za/articles/news/15902/2012–11–19/border-jumpers-raped-and-intimidated (accessed August 2015).

Nyathi, B. (2014). 'MWA-SA: Migration – A Human Right!'. Migrant Workers Association. www.migrantworkersassociation.org (accessed August 2015).

Polzer, N. and Segatti, A. (2011). 'From Defending Migrant Rights to New Political Subjectivities: Gauteng Migrants' Organisations after May 2008'. In L. Landau (Ed.), *Exorcising the Demons Within: Xenophobia, Violence and Statecraft in Contemporary South Africa* (pp. 173–99). Johannesburg: Witwatersrand University Press.

SAGNA (South African Government News Agency). 2013. 'Inflow of Migrants Pushes Population to 53 Million – Stats SA'. http://sanews.gov.za/south-africa/inflow-migrants-pushes-population-53-million-%E2%80%93-stats-sa (accessed August 2015).

Sigsworth, R., Ngwane, C. and Pino, A. (2008). *The Gendered Nature of Xenophobia in South Africa.* Johannesburg: Centre for the Study of Violence and Reconciliation. www.csvr.org.za/images/gnoxsa_report.pdf (accessed August 2015).

Singh, A. and Zammit, A. (2004). 'Labour Standards and the "Race to the Bottom": Rethinking Globalization and Workers' Rights from Developmental and Solidaristic Perspectives'. *Oxford Review of Economic Policy*, 20(1), 85–104.

Sinwell, L. (2011). 'Obtaining "Peace", Searching for Justice: Evaluating Civil Society and Local Government Responses to Xenophobia in Alexandra'. *Politikon: South African Journal of Political Studies*, 38(1), 131–48.

Tafira, K. (2013). 'Steve Biko Returns: The Persistence of Black Consciousness in Azania (South Africa)'. Unpublished doctoral dissertation, University of Witwatersrand, Johannesburg.

3

States of Exclusion: Migrant Work in the Gulf Arab States

Adam Hanieh

Over the last few years, Western media, international NGOs, trade unions and a growing number of solidarity campaigns have begun to voice major concern around the conditions of migrant workers in the six Arab states of the Gulf Cooperation Council (GCC: Saudi Arabia, Kuwait, Qatar, Bahrain, United Arab Emirates (UAE) and Oman). Migrant workers make up at least half of the labour force in all GCC states – the highest proportion of migrant workers of any country or region in the world. Taken as a whole, the GCC is the destination of more migrants than any other region in the Global South. These workers are typically brought to the Gulf on a work visa that binds them to a sponsor (the so-called *kafala* system), and find themselves systematically excluded from any political and civil rights, subject to dangerous and low-paid working conditions, and liable to deportation at the employer's whim. This exclusionary labour market system rests upon a strict demarcation of citizenship-based rights, frequently justified through a heavily racialised discourse that emphasises the ever-present 'threat' that migrants pose to the region.

Much of the increasing international attention towards the Gulf's migrant workers has been spurred by reports of the deaths of hundreds of migrants in Qatar in the wake of the country's successful 2022 World Cup bid. In March 2014, the International Trade Union Confederation (ITUC) reported that around 1,200 migrants had died since the bid was won in 2010, a rate of more than one worker each day (ITUC, 2014). This estimate was based upon data from just two countries, Nepal and India, so the real figure is undoubtedly much higher. By the time the first World Cup match kicks off in 2022, it is conservatively predicted that as many as 4,000 people will have died (ITUC, 2014). Qatar, however, is not alone in facing increasing scrutiny over its treatment of migrant workers. Scores of recent investigative reports and fact-finding missions have revealed similar cases of abuse and mistreatment in construction sites, factories, private homes and migrant detention camps across all Gulf states (see *Guardian*, 2014; *Times Of India*, 2012; Human Rights Watch (HRW), 2014).

These stories have begun to turn the spotlight on the decades-long pattern of institutionalised exploitation of workers in the Gulf. Yet much of the discussion of this issue has tended to remain fairly superficial – focused on documenting human rights abuses faced by migrants and lobbying Gulf governments to change their policies and legislation around migration.[1] While these efforts can play a useful role in raising awareness, this chapter contends that the Gulf's treatment of migrant workers needs to be seen as much more than simply a problem of government policies, unscrupulous employers or legislative weakness. Rather, this system is functionally entwined with the sharply hierarchical nature of political and economic power in the Gulf; it is an essential component of how elites continue to reproduce their dominant positions in Gulf societies. For this reason, Gulf rulers – or the domestic and international businesses that also profit from migrant labour exploitation – will not willingly dismantle this system. Substantive improvement in migrant labour conditions will not occur without challenging the dominance of these political and economic interests.

With this perspective in mind, the chapter aims to map the migrant labour structure in the Gulf and the various challenges to it from both inside and outside the Gulf. It begins by outlining the early foundations of Gulf migration and its recent evolution through three distinct phases following the discovery of oil in the region. It then turns to examine the various institutional mechanisms that govern and control contemporary migration to the Gulf. The third section focuses upon the myriad ways this structure is being contested today. In this regard, the chapter foregrounds the self-organisation and mobilisation of Gulf migrant workers themselves – too often viewed as passive or depoliticised – as well as some recent examples of global solidarity initiatives that are not simply focused on lobbying Gulf governments, but target the complicity of international businesses and other institutions.

THE FOUNDATIONS OF MIGRANT LABOUR IN THE GULF

Migration has long been a prominent feature of Gulf societies. Throughout the nineteenth and early twentieth centuries, the Gulf formed an important link within Britain's colonial network – intimately related to control of neighbouring India, the centrepiece of the British Empire (AlShehabi, 2014). In this period, Britain coordinated the movement of people to the Gulf to serve in its colonial administration and to staff Gulf militaries and security forces (Abdulhameed, 2014). These migrants were brought mainly from the UK or the Indian subcontinent, and were consciously discouraged from forming any integrative links with local Gulf communities.

With the discovery of oil in the Gulf in the early twentieth century – followed by the beginnings of commercial exploitation in the post-Second World War period – these migration patterns were to shift decisively. The region as a whole was transformed from a relatively underdeveloped area largely based on pearling and entrepôt trade into a central node of an emerging oil-based global capitalism (Hanieh, 2011). There were three clear phases to this transformation as it related to migration. During the first phase (1950–73), increasing numbers of migrant workers found employment in the oil and public sector workforces; citizen labour, however, continued to constitute a majority of the overall labour force. In this period, most migrant workers – particularly in Saudi Arabia, the centre of the region's oil production – were drawn from Arab countries.[2]

This first phase coincided with the growth of wider political movements in the Middle East, including emerging nationalist, anti-colonial and left wing struggles. The Gulf was no exception to this trend, with important examples of labour strikes in the region's oil sector occurring in Saudi Arabia, Bahrain, Kuwait and Qatar during this time (Hanieh, 2011). These strikes frequently took aim at the conditions of work in British and US oil camps, whose racially segregated structures have been compared by scholars to the Jim Crow laws prevailing in the American South (Vitalis, 2007). Oil workers also sought greater control over oil revenues and protested the complicity of Gulf rulers with Western domination of the Middle East, taking inspiration from struggles in Egypt, Palestine and elsewhere.

The second distinct phase of migration to the Gulf began in the early 1970s as Gulf states gained formal independence from their former colonial rulers and consequently a greater degree of control over the vast oil revenues associated with the export of hydrocarbons. This so-called Second Oil Boom saw the emergence of new inflows of temporary migrant labour which became central to the distinctive pattern of class formation in the newly independent states. Most importantly, a systematic institutional cleavage was established between citizens and the growing mass of migrant workers. Citizens were granted a range of benefits including free education, healthcare, subsidised housing, employment in the public sector, and access to land and other financial support (such as generous marriage dowries) (Hanieh, 2011). These benefits were provided on the proviso that they demonstrated loyalty to the state and the ruling family, and the potential revocation of citizenship became a powerful means of disciplining the population (a threat that continues through to the contemporary period). A complex system of 'vertically segmented' groups based on religious affiliation, regional origin, tribal identity and so forth mediated the relationship between citizen and state (Khalaf, 2014). In the context of centrally determined access to wealth, group rivalry became an ever-present feature of political and social culture, acting to encourage the internalisation of norms that stressed loyalty and allegiance to the ruling family and state structures (Khalaf, 1985; Lackner, 1978). Simultaneously, migrant workers came to be defined by their exclusion from this system. There was no institutional route to citizenship or permanent residency available to migrant workers or their children, regardless of the length of time they were present in the country. An elaborate system of governance mediated the relationship between migrant–citizen–state (see below)

– consciously designed to maximise the exploitation of labour and minimise the possibility of political protest.

During this post-independence phase, the majority of migrant workers continued to be drawn from Arab countries – primarily Egypt, Yemen, Palestine, Jordan, Lebanon and Syria. These workers were involved in construction and low-wage activities, as well as teaching, engineering, medicine and other professional work.[3] The numerous wars and other crises occurring through the region at the time helped to reinforce these migratory flows to the Gulf. In the case of Palestine, for example, the Israeli occupation of the West Bank and Gaza Strip led to nearly 40 per cent of the available Palestinian labour force migrating for work through the mid-1970s, much of which ended up in the Gulf (Zahlan and Zahlan, 1977). Other Arab governments – such as Egypt, Jordan and Lebanon – viewed migration to the Gulf as a useful mechanism for dealing with their own internal social and economic challenges. As a consequence of these migration flows, the level of remittances from the Gulf to the rest of the Arab world tripled between 1973 and 1980 (Shaw, 1983).

The third phase of migration to the Gulf began in the 1980s and continues through to the current day. Fearful of the potential threat posed by Arab political movements in the Gulf, and mindful of the increasing desire of Arab migrants to bring their families or settle permanently in the Gulf, ruling families began to shift away from a largely Arab-based migrant workforce, towards one centred on the Indian subcontinent and East Asia (AlShehabi, 2014). Gulf rulers believed that these non-Arab workers would form a pliable, lower-paid workforce, which – for cultural and linguistic reasons – could be more easily separated from the citizen population. The logic behind this shift was not entirely without precedent; in the late 1970s, for example, South Korean conglomerates had marketed themselves to the Saudi and Bahraini governments as providers of a 'semi-militarized labor force' of former soldiers who would be housed in labour camps away from other workers or citizens, and supposedly immune to any political or labour protest (Disney, 1977: 24). The 1980s and 1990s, however, were to mark a decisive generalisation of this policy of 'containerisation of labour' across the wider Gulf.

The first Gulf War of the early 1990s proved to be a major turning point in this regard. With the US-led attack on Iraq in 1990–1, Gulf states used the support shown to Iraq's Saddam Hussein by the Palestine Liberation Organisation and the Yemeni government to justify mass deportations of Palestinian and other Arab workers. It is estimated that up to two million Arabs were deported from the Gulf at the time of the invasion (Fergany, 2001). In their place, millions of South and East Asian migrants were brought to the Gulf over the 1990s and 2000s. From 1975 to 2000, the Arab proportion of migrant workers in the Gulf had fallen from 72 per cent to around 25–9 per cent, replaced with labour from Asian countries (over the same period, the total number of migrant workers in the Gulf states increased from 1.1 million to 8.5 million workers) (Kapiszewski, 2004). By 2005, the proportion of Arab workers in Gulf migrant labour forces had fallen to 40 per cent in Qatar, 31 per cent in Saudi Arabia and Kuwait, 12.42 per cent in Bahrain, 8.7 per cent in the UAE and 5.6 per cent in Oman (ILO, 2009). These new Asian workers found employment in construction, service and other important economic sectors in the Gulf, helping to underpin the region's massive urban development boom of the 2000s. In turn, many neighbouring countries became critically dependent upon the Gulf as a labour destination and source of remittances.

MECHANISMS OF CONTROL

The composition of Gulf societies has shifted dramatically as a result of these four decades of labour migration. According to the most recent statistics from the region, the percentage of non-nationals has reached a remarkable 48 per cent of the Gulf's 49 million-strong total population (GLMM, 2014a). The proportion of non-nationals within Gulf labour forces is even higher, ranging from between 56 to 82 per cent of the employed population in Saudi Arabia, Oman, Bahrain and Kuwait, to around 93–4 per cent in Qatar and the UAE (GLMM, 2014b). Across the entire Gulf, 70 per cent of the total employed population is made up of non-nationals (GLMM, 2014b). The vast majority of this migrant labour force – around 88 per cent of all foreign workers – is found in the Gulf's private sector (GLMM, 2014c).[4]

As these figures suggest, the critical element to the governance of migration in the Gulf is the distinction between citizen and non-citizen, and the array of differential rights that are connected to these two categories. Entrance to a Gulf country for the purpose of work takes place through the *kafala* system, a complex sponsorship arrangement in which a Gulf citizen or company is delegated (from the state) the right to control the entry and employment of a migrant. In this manner, the employer owns the work permit, and the state 'subcontracts' the surveillance and control of migrant labour to individual citizens and businesses (Longva, 1997). Not only does the *kafala* system provide lucrative profit-making opportunities for citizens (through the sale of permits), but it also positions Gulf citizenry as an extended arm of the state's disciplining of labour (Dito, 2014). Migration, in other words, must be seen as involving more than just the relationship between the migrant and the Gulf state; it is also an important feature of how Gulf citizens themselves are integrated into their societies.

Numerous authors have pointed out the similarity between the *kafala* system and bonded labour – workers are tied to particular employers, denied mobility between jobs, frequently have their passports withheld, and are often trapped with significant levels of debt associated with purchasing their work permit (see Dito, 2014, for detailed discussion of these mechanisms). Overlaying these features are extremely restrictive laws that ban migrant workers from forming unions, going on strike or engaging in any kind of political activism.[5] Through these characteristic elements of 'unfree' labour, employers wield an enormous degree of power over a migrant's living and working conditions. This is reflected in very low wages, long hours and hazardous, substandard conditions of work – particularly in economically significant sectors such as construction.[6] There are no minimum wages in the private sector (where most migrants are found), and huge wage differentials exist between citizen and non-citizen labour – even more pronounced if non-wage costs are included (such as access to education, health and housing).[7] Studies have even documented differences in pay for the same work depending upon the national origin of workers (notably in domestic work).

The control over migrant labour is further enhanced through restrictions on movement within the country. The policy of containerisation is now standard across the region, with low-paid migrant workers located in specially designed labour camps and their movement to and from work organised through employer-provided transportation (HRW, 2014). Often mobility restrictions are a natural outcome of economic barriers, with worker accommodation consciously located far away from citizen or tourist areas. Sometimes, however, these restrictions are legally enforced. In 2011, for example, Qatari authorities issued a law banning male migrant workers from living in established residential areas (Kovessy, 2014). Female domestic workers are particularly affected by restrictions on movement as they typically live with their employer and may be prevented from leaving the house unaccompanied. Indeed, one researcher examining domestic workers in the UAE found that close to one-half of all the workers she interviewed had never left the houses of their employers alone over the two years that they had been in the country (Gambard, 2009).

These features of migrant labour governance in the Gulf are underpinned by a powerful and sustained discourse that fashions migration and migrants as variously imagined threats – 'security', 'demographic', 'cultural' and 'sexual' dangers are the typical tropes wielded by government spokespeople and in the region's media. Thus, at a October 2004 regional meeting of GCC labour ministers, the Bahraini representative, Majeed Al-Alawi, was to describe migrant workers as a 'strategic threat to the region's future' (Qatar Peninsula, 2004) and the Kuwaiti delegate called on GCC states to 'control the demographic structure in order to preserve the Gulf's social and political identity' (*Island*, 2004). Similarly, GCC Secretary-General Abdul Rahman Al Attiya has depicted the large number of migrant workers as a 'national security issue' (Toumi, 2005). In Qatar, the aforementioned restriction on migrant workers' residential location was justified by their alleged 'lack of respect ... for local values and traditions and menaces to the Qatari way of life' (Kovessy, 2014). Likewise, in a recent perceptive analysis Michelle Buckley (2014: 142) has noted that male construction workers – frequently described as 'bachelors' regardless of their marital status – are often portrayed as a potential sexual threat and thus made subject to 'ethnonationally-focused forms of surveillance targeting specific groups of men'.[8]

Governed through these institutional and discursive means, the role of migrant labour is foundational to the reproduction of power in the Gulf and the ongoing dominance of the Gulf monarchies. Any attempt at worker mobilisation or political protest can be (legally) met with termination of employment and immediate deportation, producing a state of permanent precarity for the vast majority of the Gulf's working classes. The cheap labour of these workers has directly fed the accumulation of massive conglomerates that span both the Gulf's state and private sectors (a large number of these conglomerates are centred upon the construction sector where migrant labour is most exploited and controlled). The towering real estate projects that dot the skylines of all Gulf cities are highly visible embodiments of this labour exploitation, pointing to the importance of looking beyond simply 'petrodollars' to explain the Gulf's glittering urban landscapes.[9]

Moreover, at significant moments, this structure of migrant labour has been utilised by the Gulf states to overcome the potential effects of crisis. One example of this was the impact of the 2008–9 global financial crisis, which initially appeared to present a major threat to a development model based upon debt-driven real estate bubbles and global capital inflows. Nonetheless, following the collapse of construction activities in the wake of the global downturn (notably in Dubai), Gulf states were able to partially displace the impact of the crisis by slowing the hiring of workers, cutting back their workforces, and deporting migrants back to their home countries. Coupled with accumulated petrodollar surpluses, this spatial displacement of the crisis enabled the Gulf to overcome its worst effects (Hanieh, 2011).

Factors such as these posit migrant labour at the core of the Gulf's class structure. Yet this reliance on a temporary migrant workforce is not without significant contradictions for Gulf societies. Prominent among these is a rising level of youth unemployment among citizens, the effects of which are particularly accentuated in a region where over 50 per cent of the population is under the age of 25 (Malecki and

Ewers, 2007). These very high unemployment levels, coupled with the continued provision of social benefits to citizens, place considerable pressure on Gulf budgets and many analysts argue that this is unsustainable in the medium to long term. As a means of addressing this, all Gulf states have put in place so-called 'Gulf-isation' programmes, which seek to set business quotas for the employment of nationals and ostensibly reduce the reliance on migrant labour. These policies, however, have largely failed – citizens are unwilling to accept the low wages and working conditions of migrants, and the private sector continues to depend almost exclusively on a foreign labour force. Once again, there is no legislative solution to this dilemma – it is difficult to conceive of any reversal of the status quo given the ongoing systemic need for a cheap and precarious workforce in the Gulf. Moreover, any significant level of proletarianisation of Gulf citizenry would raise precisely the kinds of problems that the reliance on migrant labour acts to undercut – the potential of domestic labour movements that may challenge existing ruling regimes.

MIGRANT STRUGGLES AND INTERNATIONAL SOLIDARITY

Despite the very significant barriers described above, it is essential to emphasise that migrant workers in the Gulf continue to mobilise, protest and engage in a variety of different strategies of resistance. Indeed, there were numerous important examples of such struggles during 2013 and 2014, including:[10] a five-day strike in June 2014 by thousands of Indian, Sri Lankan, Bangladeshi and Burmese workers at the MRS Fashions Factory in Bahrain – a company that produces clothing for Macy's, J. C. Penney, Wal-Mart, GAP, H&M, Abercrombie and Fitch, Sears, Target and other major retailers;[11] a strike by Indian women cleaners at a Saudi hospital in March 2014; a two-day strike by South Asian porters at the King Abdulaziz International Airport, Saudi Arabia, also in March 2014; an August 2013 strike by Nepalese workers in Sitra, Bahrain, following a death by suicide of a 22-year-old worker; a demonstration in October 2013 by over 1,300 Ethiopian nurses in Kuwait, challenging non-payment of salaries and racial discrimination in wage levels; a strike by 10,000 South Asian workers in Oman in March 2013, in protest of poor safety conditions and the death of an Indian worker on the job, and a successful 6,000-strong strike by cleaners in Saudi Arabia (Migrant Rights, 2014). Although strike leaders were imprisoned and deported in most of these cases, they indicate that migrant workers in the Gulf are prepared to challenge the entrenched institutional barriers to on-the-job protest. Moreover, in many of these actions, workers were able to win some concrete victories.

Perhaps the most strategically significant Gulf country with regard to the potential impact of labour militancy is the UAE. Due to the enormous economic weight of the country's construction and real estate sector, closely linked to other sectors such as banking and finance (Buckley and Hanieh, 2014), the UAE's development model is particularly dependent upon the availability of large numbers of poorly paid construction workers who are denied any effective labour rights. Despite the country's reputation for widespread persecution of labour activists – including the documented use of arrest, torture or deportation against hundreds of people in 2013 – strikes are relatively frequent and have involved thousands of workers in labour actions over the last few years (Kannan, 2014).[12] Of these recent strikes, two in particular are noteworthy:

1. In October 2013, 3,000 workers involved in building the New York University (NYU) campus in Abu Dhabi embarked on a two-day strike. According to one participant interviewed by the UK newspaper, *The Independent*, workers received around US$198 a month (equivalent to, at most, US$0.75 an hour) and were seeking to increase this to US$265 a month (South and Bland, 2014). Workers also complained of having their passports confiscated on arrival, and having to pay back recruitment fees equivalent to one year's wages (Kaminer and O'Driscoll, 2014). UAE authorities responded to the strike with extreme repression – a staggering 10 per cent of the workforce (300 workers) were arrested, beaten and deported. The workers' employer, BK Gulf – a joint venture involving the British firm, Balfour Beatty – allegedly reported the formation of the strike committee to the UAE security forces and filmed striking workers (South and Bland, 2014). In a statement to the media following the strike, Balfour Beatty observed

– correctly, although undoubtedly without the unintended irony – that they 'complie[d] with all UAE laws regarding the employment, welfare and accommodation of employees' (South and Bland, 2014). Strikes by workers involved in building NYU Abu Dhabi are particularly significant because of the ongoing transnational solidarity that has developed around them. This has included high-profile campaigns by the Coalition of Fair Labor at NYU, and other US-based groups, who have highlighted the university's complicity in the abuse of migrant workers. Their efforts have resulted in front-page coverage in the *New York Times* and *Guardian* newspapers, and forced public responses by NYU administrators (Holmes and Lipsitz, 2014).

2. In May 2013, a four-day strike was launched by thousands of construction workers employed by the UAE-based Arabtec. Arabtec is a large construction company with close ties to the Emirati ruling family, and was part of the consortium that built Dubai's Burj Khalifa, the world's tallest building. The striking workers were seeking an increase in their wages, which range from US$160 to US$190 a month (McGinley, 2013). The most important feature of this strike was the fact that it was spread across a range of different Arabtec worksites in the UAE, and thus broke from the usual pattern of small, workplace-based actions in the Gulf. In the wake of the strike, news reports claimed that 1,000 workers had been deported (the company stated that these workers had left on 'their own accord'). Nonetheless, despite facing repression and large-scale deportation, the workers reportedly managed to win a 20 per cent increase in wages for 36,000 Arabtec workers across the country (*Construction Week Online*, 2013).[13]

In addition to shattering the image of Gulf migrant labour forces as passive and unwilling to engage in labour protest, these two strikes indicate the potential to build international solidarity campaigns around labour issues in the Gulf. The UAE is particularly vulnerable to such campaigns, due to government policy aimed at attracting high-profile international partners for sponsorship, branding, finance, consultancy and engineering work on the country's construction projects. Such international links have presented important opportunities to target foreign corporations and institutions around poor working conditions or repression against strike action in the UAE. In addition to the NYU Abu Dhabi campaign noted above, another salient example of solidarity is the campaign launched by prominent artists to support workers on Abu Dhabi's Saadiyat Island (Island of Happiness), a massive development project projected to cost US$27 billion that involves the construction of museums, hotels, resorts, golf courses and housing for more than 125,000 residents. The artists have established a campaign group, Gulf Labor, which has targeted international institutions partnering with the UAE government on the Saadiyat project, including the Guggenheim Abu Dhabi, Louvre Abu Dhabi and the Sheikh Zayed National Museum (built in collaboration with the British Museum). Through creative actions aimed at these museums in the West, as well as the production of artwork highlighting the campaign itself, the Gulf Labor campaign has forced these international institutions to respond publically to the repeated claims around working conditions and abuse of migrant workers.[14]

Any discussion of international organising around migrants in the Gulf also needs to consider the potential transnational links between movements in sending countries and workers abroad. This is undoubtedly a relatively weak area in regards to the Gulf, although the recent strikes – and associated deportations of leading activists – clearly raise the possibility for sharing experiences and lessons between different waves of migrant workers. As yet, however, there do not appear to be any longer-term institutional forms aimed at developing these links. The one partial exception to this is the work of the Filipino worker organisation, Migrante. Migrante has established an office in the UAE, which provides legal advice, shelter, counselling and other services for victims of employer abuse, particularly that faced by domestic workers. Migrante also consciously emphasises the importance of campaigning around social conditions in the Philippines itself, understanding the ways in which the root causes of migration need to be addressed as part of any long-term solution to the problems facing migrant workers outside of the country (Ellao, 2013). In this sense, Migrante's work echoes the recent argument expressed by US activist David Bacon (2013), that migrants not only need to seek greater rights in their country of work, but they also have 'the right to stay home'.

In contrast to standard narratives that abstract from relations of domination and exploitation, this chapter has stressed the necessity of placing migrant labour at the core of understanding political and economic processes in the Gulf states. The position of Gulf rulers crucially depends upon the presence of a precarious class of migrant workers drawn from nearby countries. This class has supplied the essential labour responsible for the spectacular reworking of Gulf urban environments over recent decades; its exploitation has thus directly enriched a narrow layer of Gulf conglomerates – both state and privately owned alike. Politically, the citizen/non-citizen divide that underpins this reliance on migrant labour is constitutive of ruling class power in the Gulf – helping to bind national allegiance to the region's leading families and state structures. At times of economic turmoil, the ever-temporary nature of migrant work has been utilised as a means of effecting a spatial displacement of crisis – shifting the burden of globally induced problems on to labour-sending countries. For all of these reasons, migrants in the Gulf constitute one of the most important parts of the Arab world's population.

Moreover, this particular form of class structure has significant global implications. Precisely because of the Gulf's centrality to global capitalism – not least, in the ways that the Gulf's integration into the architecture of US power has enabled the latter to develop and extend its hegemonic position globally since the Second World War – the structure of class in the Gulf is not just of concern to local rulers. The contrast between the GCC and neighbouring Iraq and Iran – both of which have a long history of militant, indigenous working classes – is instructive here. The history of global capitalism would likely have taken a profoundly different path if the world's key oil-producing states had not rested upon this type of class structure.

This perspective implies that the treatment of migrant workers in the Gulf is not merely the outcome of poor policymaking, a lack of awareness around international norms, unregulated labour recruitment agencies or legislative oversight. Rather, the exploitation of migrant workers is structurally foundational to how Gulf rulers maintain and extend their power over society, and is deeply enmeshed in wider regional and global hierarchies. While the political strategy of many NGOs and other international bodies aimed at encouraging Gulf governments to alter legislation around the conditions of migrant work can be useful and important, it holds little hope of success without a more fundamental challenge to the structures of power within the Gulf. A narrow focus on government legislation does nothing to address the real structural causes that underpin the Gulf's exclusionary labour markets. Indeed, in several cases, Gulf governments have utilised cosmetic changes to legislation – or commissioned 'audits' by well-remunerated international consultants – to claim that substantive progress is being made. Any significant improvement in the conditions of workers in the Gulf – such as the right to organise, the extension of political and civil rights or the ability to gain permanent status – is fully bound up with challenging the position of the ruling regimes in the Gulf itself.

International solidarity can make a potentially important contribution to the eventual success of such movements, and the campaigns discussed in this chapter represent novel and promising examples of this. Precisely because so much of the Gulf's urban development model is premised upon the institutionalised exploitation of migrant workers – and yet simultaneously oriented towards attracting foreign capital and international partnerships – it is possible for those living outside the region to act directly against companies complicit in the abuse of migrant workers in the Gulf. While these campaigns are still relatively new and untested, the seemingly never-ending intensification of the Gulf's relationship with global capital means that they represent a strategically vital area for future solidarity with the region.

Finally, although this particular structure of migrant labour is in many ways unique to the Gulf states, similar patterns of exploitation can increasingly be found in many countries around the world. Numerous states have begun to implement policies such as sharply differentiating the social and political rights of citizens and non-citizens (e.g. the right to strike or organise collectively); spatially segregating migrant workers from the rest of the population; the use of short-term, limited contracts for temporary migrant labour; and the generalisation of *kafala*-like systems targeting potential workers in the Global South. In this respect, the Gulf constitutes a global laboratory for labour exploitation today – a region that can teach us much about migrant workers and their place in contemporary capitalism.

NOTES

1. These demands typically include ending the practice of charging fees for worker recruitment, permitting job mobility, banning the confiscation of passports and improving workplace inspections.
2. One important sector of these Arab migrants were Palestinian refugees. Saudi Arabia, for example, established labour recruitment offices in refugee camps that brought Palestinians to work in the oil industries and related sectors.
3. In 1975, 75 per cent of Yemeni migrant workers, 50 per cent of Egyptian workers and 40 per cent of Jordanian workers were involved in construction. Professional activities were dominated by Palestinian and Egyptian migrants (Shaw, 1983).
4. This figure does not include the UAE, for which figures are unavailable but are likely of a similar magnitude.
5. In Bahrain and Kuwait, migrant workers are permitted to join established unions (but not to form their own). In practice, however, there is a great deal of reluctance from these unions to recruit or ally with migrant workers. None of the GCC states (except for Kuwait) have ratified the two key International Labour Organization (ILO) conventions governing the right to freely form and join worker organisations, organise and collectively bargain (Conventions No. 87 and 98).
6. Wages in the Gulf do not reflect the cost of living in the Gulf states themselves, but are more appropriately compared to those in the home country of the worker.
7. The exception to this trend is found in sectors such as high-level management, banking and finance, where a different type of migrant worker can be found (usually from Western countries).
8. Buckley has further described how labour-sending countries employ particular tropes of masculinity to market their nationals as hard working, loyal and adaptable to the harsh climate of the region.
9. Indeed, even the International Monetary Fund (IMF) has recently noted this point in relation to Qatar, commenting that while the poor conditions of work had made 'global headlines', any change in the availability or cost of this labour 'would hinder growth, since the success of Qatar's current development model

depends importantly on the ability to rapidly hire expatriate workers' (IMF, 2014).

10. This list is drawn from the superb documentation of migrant conditions in the Gulf, available at the website of the campaign group, Migrant Rights (www. migrant-rights.org).

11. Prior to the strike, workers were paid around US$0.77 per hour and forced to work 60 hours a week with no overtime. Workers also complained of having their passports confiscated, and being beaten by management if they complained about their conditions. Despite the deportation of eleven strike leaders, the workers won some partial victories, including a small wage increase and forcing management to backtrack on new production targets (www.globallabourrights. org/alerts/improvements-follow-strike-at-walmart-jcpenney-sweatshop-in-bahrain, accessed 5 December 2014).

12. According to the UAE newspaper, *The National*, 78 strikes took place across the country in 2012 and 2013 (Kannan, 2014).

13. It should be noted that according to reports by Arabtec workers to a *Gulf Labor* investigation in March 2014, this pay rise has not materialised (http:// gulflabor.org/wp-content/uploads/2014/04/gl_REPORT_APR30.pdf, accessed 5 December 2014).

14. See the organisation's website (http://gulflabor.org).

REFERENCES

Abdulhameed, K. T. (2014). 'Bahrain's Migrant Security Apparatus'. In Khalaf, A., AlShehabi, O. and Hanieh, A. (Eds), *Transit States: Labour, Migration and Citizenship in the Gulf* (pp. 153–69). London: Pluto Press.

AlShehabi, O. (2014). 'Histories of Migration to the Gulf'. In Khalaf, A., AlShehabi, O. and Hanieh, A. (Eds), *Transit States: Labour, Migration and Citizenship in the Gulf* (pp. 3–38). London: Pluto Press.

Bacon, D. (2013). *The Right to Stay Home: How US Policy Drives Mexican Migration*. Boston, MA: Beacon Press.

Buckley, M. (2014). 'Construction Work, "Bachelor" Builders and the Intersectional Politics of Urbanisation in Dubai'. In Khalaf, A., AlShehabi, O. and Hanieh, A. (Eds), *Transit States: Labour, Migration and Citizenship in the Gulf* (pp. 132–52). London: Pluto Press.

—— and Hanieh A. (2014). 'Diversification by Urbanisation: Tracing the Property–Finance Nexus in Dubai and the Gulf'. *International Journal of Urban and Regional Research*, 38(1), 155–75.

Construction Week Online (2013). 'UAE's Arabtec Raises 36,000 Labourer Wages by 20%'. 30 September. www.constructionweekonline.com/article-24487-uaes-arabtec-raises-36000-labourer-wages-by-20/#.Ux8WgPTV_YQ (accessed August 2015).

Disney, N. (1977). 'South Korean Workers in the Middle East'. *Middle East Report*, 61, 22–4.

Dito, M. (2014). 'Kafala: Foundations of Migrant Exclusion in GCC Labour Markets'. In Khalaf, A., AlShehabi, O. and Hanieh, A. (Eds), *Transit States: Labour, Migration and Citizenship in the Gulf* (pp. 79–100). London: Pluto Press.

Ellao, J. (2013). 'Filipino Migrants' Rights Advocates Join High-Level Talks on Migration'. *Bulatlat*. http://bulatlat.com/main/2013/10/07/filipino-migrants-rights-advocates-join-high-level-talks-on-migration/ (accessed August 2015).

Fergany, N. (2001). *Aspects of Labor Migration and Unemployment in the Arab Region*. Cairo: Almishkat Center for Research.

Gambard, M. (2009). 'Advocating for Sri Lankan Migrant Workers: Obstacles and Challenges'. *Critical Asian Studies*, 41(1), 61–88.

GLMM (Gulf Labour Markets and Migration). (2014a). 'GCC Total Population and Percentage of Nationals and Non-Nationals in GCC Countries Latest National Statistics 2010–2014'. http://gulfmigration.eu/gcc-total-population-and-percentage-of-nationals-and-non-nationals-in-gcc-countries-latest-national-statistics-2010–2014/ (accessed August 2015).

—— (2014b). 'Percentage of Nationals and Non-Nationals in Employed Population in GCC Countries'. http://gulfmigration.eu/percentage-of-nationals-and-non-nationals-in-employed-population-in-gcc-countries-national-statistics-latest-year-or-period-available/ (accessed August 2015).

—— (2014c). 'Percentage of Non-Nationals in Government Sector and in Private and Other Sectors'. http://gulfmigration.eu/percentage-of-non-nationals-in-govpercentage-of-non-nationals-in-government-sector-and-in-private-and-other-sectors-in-gcc-countries-national-statistics-latest-year-or-period-available (accessed August 2015).

Guardian, The. (2014). 'Saudi Arabia Says It Has Deported More than 250,000 Foreign Migrant Workers'. *The Guardian*, 22 January. www.theguardian.com/world/2014/jan/22/saudi-arabia-deported-foreign-migrant-workers (accessed August 2015).

Hanieh, A. (2011). *Capitalism and Class in the Gulf Arab States*. New York: Palgrave Macmillan.

Holmes, H. and Lipsitz, A. (2014). 'Reports of Worker Abuse Continue at NYU's Newly Completed Abu Dhabi Campus'. *The Nation*, 20 May. www.thenation.com/blog/179933/reports-worker-abuse-continue-nyus-newly-completed-abu-dhabi-campus# (accessed August 2015).

HRW (Human Rights Watch). (2014). *'I Already Bought You': Abuse and Exploitation of Female Migrant Domestic Workers in the United Arab Emirates*. 23 October. www.hrw.org/node/129798 (accessed August 2015).

ILO (International Labour Organization). (2009). *International Labour Migration and Employment in the Arab Region: Origins, Consequences and the Way Forward*. Thematic Paper, Arab Employment Forum. Geneva: ILO.

IMF (International Monetary Fund). (2014). *Qatar: 2014 Article IV Consultation Concluding Statement of the IMF Mission.* February. www.imf.org/external/np/ms/2014/030714.htm (accessed August 2015).

Island, The. (2004). 'Gulf States to Cut Dependence on Expatriate Workers'. www.island.lk/2004/10/14/news19.html (accessed August 2015).

ITUC (International Trade Union Confederation). (2014). *The Case Against Qatar.* www.ituc-csi.org/IMG/pdf/the_case_against_qatar_en_web170314.pdf (accessed August 2015).

Kaminer, A. and O'Driscoll, S. (2014). 'Workers at N.Y.U.'s Abu Dhabi Site Faced Harsh Conditions'. *New York Times,* 18 May. www.nytimes.com/2014/05/19/nyregion/workers-at-nyus-abu-dhabi-site-face-harsh-conditions.html?_r=0 (accessed August 2015).

Kannan, P. (2014). 'Number of Labour Strikes in Dubai Falls Almost 25%'. *The National,* 17 April. www.thenational.ae/uae/government/number-of-labour-strikes-in-dubai-falls-almost-25 (accessed August 2015).

Kapiszewski, A. (2004). 'Arab Labour Migration to the GCC State'. In *Arab Migration in a Globalized World,* 2003 edition (pp. 115–33). Geneva: International Organization for Migration and League of Arab States.

Khalaf, A. (1985). *Labor Movements in Bahrain.* MERIP Report, 132, 24–9.

—— (2014). 'The Politics of Migration'. In Khalaf, A., AlShehabi, O. and Hanieh, A. (Eds), *Transit States: Labour, Migration and Citizenship in the Gulf* (pp. 39–56). London: Pluto Press.

Kovessy, P. (2014). 'Crackdown on Partitioned Homes Continues with Amended Qatar Law'. *Doha News* 9 June. http://dohanews.co/crackdown-partitioned-homes-continues-new-law/ (accessed August 2015).

Lackner, H. (1978). *A House Built on Sand: A Political Economy of Saudi Arabia.* Reading: Ithaca Press.

Longva, A. N. (1997). *Walls Built on Sand: Migration, Exclusion and Society in Kuwait.* Boulder, CO: Westview Press.

Malecki, E. and Ewers, M. (2007). 'Labor Migration to World Cities: With a Research Agenda for the Arab Gulf'. *Progress in Human Geography,* 31(4), 467–84.

McGinley, S. (2013). 'UAE's Arabtec Raises 36,000 Labourer Wages by 20%'. *Arabian Business,* 30 September. www.arabianbusiness.com/uae-s-arabtec-raises-36–000-labourer-wages-by-20--520756.html (accessed August 2015).

Migrant Rights. (2014). *Labor Strikes in the GCC, Deportations and Victories in 2014.* www.migrant-rights.org/research/labor-strikes-in-the-gcc-deportations-and-victories-in-2014/ (accessed August 2015).

Qatar Peninsula. (2004). 'Gulf Ministers Okay Steps to Cut Reliance on Foreign Labour'. 13 October.

Shaw, R. P. (1983). *Mobilizing Human Resources in the Arab World.* London: Kegan Paul.

South, T. and Bland, A. (2014). 'Dubai Workers for British Firm Beaten by Police over Strike'. *The Independent,* 25 May. www.independent.co.uk/news/world/

middle-east/dubai-workers-for-british-firm-beaten-by-police-over-strike-9432149.html (accessed August 2015).

Times of India, The. (2012). 'An Indian Ends Life Every Sixth Day in Oman'. *The Times of India*, 30 April. http://timesofindia.indiatimes.com/nri/middle-east-news/An-Indian-ends-life-every-sixth-day-in-Oman/articleshow/12934364.cms (accessed August 2015).

Toumi, H. (2005). 'Call for Prudent Labour Import Policy'. *Gulf News*, 24 November. http://gulfnews.com/news/gulf/bahrain/call-for-prudent-labour-import-policy-1.445829 (accessed August 2015).

Vitalis, R. (2007). *America's Kingdom: Mythmaking on the Saudi Oil Frontier*. Stanford, CA: Stanford University Press.

Zahlan, A. and Zahlan, R. (1977). 'The Palestinian Future: Education and Manpower'. *Journal of Palestine Studies*, 6(4), 103–12.

4

Undocumented Migrant Workers in Nigeria: Labouring in the Shadows of Regional Integration

Baba Ayelabola

Nigeria is the demographic and socio-economic powerhouse of West Africa. Out of roughly 340 million people in 16 states, nearly 180 million live in Nigeria (National Bureau of Statistics, 2014), which overtook South Africa as the continent's largest economy in 2014.

The impressive economic growth rate of recent years has not been of much benefit for the vast majority of the population. With the official unemployment rate at 23 per cent (while youth unemployment is at 53 per cent) and with an average life expectancy of only 53 years, the tendency for emigration, particularly of the country's youth, has been high. But despite the abysmal state of life in Nigeria, it still serves as a destination for many migrants from neighbouring countries, especially those who share similar ethnic identities (in bordering countries) or history (British colonialism for countries like Ghana).

'In general, there is a dearth of data and information on international migration in Nigeria' (Afolayan, 2008: 22). But the country occupies a significant position in international migration as a sending, transit and receiving country. Net immigration has been relatively stable at 0.2 per 1,000 people in 2000, 0.3 in 2005 (Afolayan, 2008: 15) and 0.22 in 2013 (National Bureau of Statistics, 2014). Around 90 per cent of immigrant workers in Nigeria come from countries in the West African subregion. Data from the Economic Community of West African States (ECOWAS) on residence permits and the National Population Commission indicate that the proportion of total documented migrants from the subregion increased from 63 per cent in 2001 to 97 per cent by 2005 (ECOWAS, 2006). Undocumented immigrants often have only the most precarious of jobs with the lowest wages. They work in the shadows of the informal economy, or as casual labour in the formal sector, representing labour migration from below (Adetula, 2009).

This chapter considers issues of concern to these workers, within the context of regional integration, as part of globalisation from above that has failed to ensure the protection of migrant workers *as subjects* of West Africa's development. As a call to action, it concludes with an interrogation of the prospects for the organising of migrants, to enable them to regain their dignity. The chapter shows that the formal adherence to conventions, such as the International Convention on the Protection of the Rights of All Migrant Workers and Members of Their Families, amounts to nought without struggle, involving the trade unions and (radical) civil society organisations, binding immigrant workers to the wider general working class movement.

HISTORICAL OVERVIEW OF MIGRATION AND MIGRANTS

Yaro (2008: 2) notes: 'West Africa has a long history of population mobility, both regionally and internationally'. Migration trends and patterns in West Africa in general, and in Nigeria in particular, could be broadly categorised into precolonial, colonial and postcolonial periods.

Migrants in precolonial Nigeria came in relatively high numbers 'largely in search of security, new land safe for settlement and fertile for farming' (Adepoju, 2005: 1). While migration in the Sahel region involved the movement of peoples along the trans-Saharan trade routes, the tendency was for peoples to move southwards to the more fertile coastal regions. The transatlantic slave trade from the fifteenth century led in the opposite direction – to increased migration towards the hills and mountains of what is now the middle belt of Nigeria.

A POLITICAL ECONOMY OF MIGRATION AND MIGRANT WORK

Generally, there have been two approaches to migration theory. One is the livelihood approach, which analyses the micro-level causes and consequences of migrants, rooted in neoclassical traditions of rational markets (Harris and Todaro, 1970; Stark and Bloom, 1985).

The other approach is political economy, which prioritises the structural, institutional and power relations at the macro level of the (international) economy. It situates migration within the dynamics of historical contexts that grasp the critical place of countries within the international division of labour. The advanced economies, global and subimperialist powers regionally, are thus considered more likely to be receiving countries than sending countries.

This chapter utilises a political economy approach. This enables us to grasp the complexity of Nigeria as a migrant-receiving country within the subregion which is equally a sending country internationally. This dynamic reflects both its subimperialist dominance in West Africa and at the same time its neocolonial status globally.

Migration in the Colonial Period

Migration during the earlier period of colonialism had some continuity with the past and was mainly for improved subsistence and the facilitation of long-distance trade. Generally though, colonialism changed migration patterns. As Adepoju (2005: 1) puts it:

> [The] Colonial regime altered the motivation and composition of migration by introducing and enforcing various blends of political and economic structures, imposing tax regimes and establishing territorial boundaries. A series of economic and recruitment policies – compulsory recruitment, contract and forced labour legislation and agreements – were employed to stimulate regional labour migration from Mali, Togo and Upper Volta to road networks, plantations and mines in Gold Coast and Ivory Coast.

Quotas of able-bodied men were set for chiefs to deploy to the plantations and mines and 'taxation and brute force were the main instruments used during this period to stimulate migration' (Adepoju, 2005: 4). The division of West Africa, largely between France and Britain, played a key role in establishing linkages between sending and receiving countries. Thus, for example, Burkina Faso, Mali and Guinea Conakry were major sending countries to the coffee fields in Côte d'Ivoire. Nigeria, Liberia and Sierra Leone were major sources of labour for the cocoa plantations in Ghana. However, free migration also continued, particularly to major urban centres like Lagos and Kano.

Migration in the Immediate Aftermath of Independence

The 1960s saw independence and the introduction of 'indigenisation' programmes and the provision of social services. While espousing pan-Africanism in some form or other, as expressed in the formation of the Organisation of African Unity, many countries introduced greater regulation. 'The elaborate visa and passport regulations, customs and controls, and the need for "foreign" workers to obtain work permits ushered in a period of restrictions on intra-regional free movement of persons across West Africa' (Adepoju, 2005: 3). The Immigration Act of 1963 codified the regulation of migration. However, immigration was not considered to be a significant issue, as the Nigerian economy was not then as attractive as those of Ghana and Côte d'Ivoire. The collapse of the prices of primary commodities in the 1960s and the spike in oil prices in the late 1970s resulted in changes in the pattern of migration. Nigeria became a major destination for migrants from across West Africa.

ISSUES AND CHALLENGES BESETTING MIGRANTS

The era of neoliberal globalisation commenced barely a decade and a half after flag independence had been won. The dynamics of this reorganisation of capitalism over the last three decades largely shaped the trends and characteristics of migration. This period also saw transformations in the body politic of Nigeria and the rise of militant Islamism. Economic downturns were not unrelated to the broader globalist neoliberal restructuring, but were equally impacted upon by the legendary corruption and fractured hegemony of the local ruling class. It was mainly undocumented migrants who were scapegoated with two mass expulsions of 'illegal aliens' in the 1980s (Adepoju, 1994; Afolayan 1988; Brydon, 1985; Gravil, 1985) and a smaller number in the early twenty-first century. This was despite Nigeria's promotion of subregional integration, particularly on the platform of ECOWAS with commitment to free migration. This support for regional integration is to further the subimperialist expansion of Nigeria's economy through the business ventures of its indigenous capitalists and entrepreneurs.

Regional Integration and Migrant Workers

Neoliberal globalisation's mantra of 'free trade' includes the expansion of multilateral initiatives promoting regional economic cooperation and development. This saw the establishment of several regional economic blocs, including ECOWAS in 1975, that inadvertently promoted free movements of people within subregions.

During the Nigerian oil boom, increased employment prospects encouraged the migration of workers from neighbouring and other nearby countries. De Haas (2006: 3) noted that '[r]ising incomes of the urban middle class and rapid industrialisation attracted substantial numbers of West African labour migrants'. The largest numbers of these were from Ghana. In 1970, of the 360,000 migrants from the subregion, almost 130,000 were Ghanaians. By 1975, this had increased to about 584,000 migrants from the subregion, with more than 310,000 being from Ghana (Arthur, 1991: 74). Ghanaian migrants included a significant proportion of professionals. They were particularly renowned for being excellent secondary (and post-secondary) school teachers.

Partly as a result of the language divide, larger proportions of migrant workers from the francophone countries were semi-skilled and unskilled, working in the construction sector and industry. James (1987) notes that the bulk of Chadian migrants, for example, worked in the informal economy as cobblers, car washers, domestic servants or security guards. This situation remains largely the same today. In 1980, the protocol of the Treaty on Free Movement of Persons was ratified by ECOWAS states. This formally provided citizens of member states with right of entry and the right to stay in any other member state for up to 90 days without a visa. But in actuality, it was part of a broader process where 'distinctions ... made between legal and illegal aliens, based on proof of nationality, passport, visa, residence and work permits which were hitherto irrelevant to the migrants' became entrenched (Adepoju, 2005: 4).

In Nigeria, the government and captains of industry were circumspect with regard to possible high immigration from sister member states, and called for close monitoring of the protocol and the containment of mass influx of migrant workers, in the interest of national security (Onwuka, 1982). However, Nigeria had no clear and consistent policy on labour and migration until 2014.

The spate of fratricidal wars within the region, including Liberia in the 1980s, Sierra Leone in the 1990s and Côte d'Ivoire at the turn of the century, brought about increased migration. But this was never a major problem for the Nigerian government as the numbers and proportions were not significant. Refugees accounted for less than 1 per cent of immigration even at the peak of such forced influx during those wars (Afolayan 2009: 65). With the gradual return of peace in Liberia and Sierra Leone there has been a sharp decline in the number of refugees from these countries.

Governments of the region did not put poor people at the heart of the regional integration process. The ECOWAS Treaty was revised in 1993, representing what Aryeetey (2001: 1) rightly described as a move away from the 'overly bureaucratic inter-governmental agency of the past' towards a 'people-centred organisation'. Essentially, the revision introduced a *social dimension* to the regional integration goal and vision of ECOWAS (Roberts, 2004: 9–11). Social policy integration was now considered, at least formally, as being at least as important as economic integration. A commitment to the harmonisation of employment and labour laws was introduced. However, both steps are primarily meant to 'enhance the flexibility and availability of labour in the sub-region', with the aim of 'enlarging opportunities for workers being arguably secondary' (Roberts, 2004: 19).

The ECOWAS Social and Cultural Commission equally adopted the General Convention on Social Security. This Convention, formulated with technical support from the International Labour Office (ILO), requires equal rights for migrant workers from ECOWAS member states who are resident in sister member states. The spirit of these reforms are consistent with the earlier enactment of the African Charter on Human and People's Rights and the general 'pro-democratic' upsurge in the wake of the collapse of the East European regimes.

In 1984, ECOWAS established the Organisation of Trade Unions of West Africa (OTUWA). This was meant to foster improved relations between the national trade union centres, in defence of workers' rights. OTUWA has, however, remained the weakest of the subregional trade union federations on the continent. Having said that, there have been renewed efforts towards reviving the federation with the establishment of a technical committee for this purpose in 2013. A draft constitution was formulated and October 2015 was envisaged for a conference that could herald OTUWA's rebirth. Unfortunately though, while the draft constitution and reports of the technical committee's meetings copiously refer to the defence of trade union and human rights of workers, there is no single reference to the topical subject of migration.

Similarly, the establishment of bilateral ties between the two strongest national trade union centres, the Ghana Trade Union Congress and the Nigeria Labour Congress (NLC) in 2002 has not had much impact in forging transborder union activism. On the subject of migrant workers there was absolutely no resolution. They did not feature as any item of discussion for the few meetings held before this bilateral got sucked into the 'trilateral' meetings of the two federations and the Congress of South African Trade Unions (COSATU).[1]

Global union federations with migrant programmes in the subregion, such as Public Services International, have robust migration projects. But the focus of these (which bring together unions in the same sector within the subregion) has been more on ensuring informed *emigration* out of the subregion to the Global North.

The universalisation of some rights for workers, as for other democratic and human rights, is ideologically crucial for capitalism's legitimisation. It is in this light that the formulation of such fundamental principles as the ILO conventions can be understood. Nigeria, like most other ECOWAS member states, is a signatory to the ILO (and UN) conventions on migrant workers' rights. The ILO has also collaborated with ECOWAS to provide technical support to situate labour migration within the context of regional integration and socio-economic development. The ECOWAS 'passport' which came into effect in 2000 was a huge step forwards, as it is easier to obtain than normal passports. However, it still limits the stay of an immigrant to 90 days at a time. Yet the phenomenon of undocumented migration continues. On the one hand, there are those who enter a country with an ECOWAS passport or their country's international passport and stay well beyond the 90-day limit. On the other hand, many more migrants appear not to bother obtaining either of these travel documents. Considering the shared ethnic identities between several Nigerian nationalities and those of many migrants in neighbouring countries, transborder migration is hardly taken as international migration within the region, by them. The Nigerian state is much more concerned with fostering capital integration within ECOWAS than it is with labour mobility and 'human' integration. While the timelines for the phased expansion of the scope of the freedom of movement of people in the subregion keep being extended, those for the integration of capital markets have to a great extent been on track. As revealed at the fifth meeting of the West African Capital Markets Integration Council, in March 2015, capital markets in the region should be fully integrated by the first quarter of 2016.

Economic Restructuring, Sociopolitical Crises and Xenophobic Tendencies

The collapse of oil prices in the early 1980s ushered in what is generally described in Nigeria as the period of 'austerity measures'. This was heralded by the 1981 Economic Stabilisation Act. Hardship became the order of the day for poor working people. The NLC had to fight for the institution of a national minimum wage. It demanded a ₦250 (US$152.50) monthly minimum wage, but won only ₦150 (US$91.50) after a two-day general strike. It also developed a Workers Charter of Demands, but this did not refer to migrant workers. With these protests, and others by students and peasants, the popularity of the federal government plunged. However, the most violent events were the religious Maitatsine riots of 1980–4, which marked a turn to militant political Islamism. By 1978, religion also became an important elite strategy for political mobilisation, starting with the Constituent Assembly debate over the inclusion of *sharia* in the 1979 constitution (Falola, 1998: 2–3). To a great extent this has remained the case.

It was within this context that the first expulsion of undocumented migrants was announced by Ali Baba, the Minister of Internal Affairs, on 17 January 1983. All 'unskilled foreigners residing and working illegally' in the country were ordered to leave by 31 January 1983. 'For the skilled aliens they were allowed to stay until 28 February 1983' (Aremu, 2013: 340–1). Meanwhile, the federal government directed all 'legal aliens' to report to the state-level headquarters of the immigration service by 14 February, for authentication of their residency status and fresh registration. Accurate statistics of the number of migrants affected by this order varies, 'but up to two million people are thought to have been eventually obliged to leave, of whom about half were Ghanaians' (Van Hear, 1992: 8). The four major reasons given by the federal government for this enforced exodus were: enthronement of the sanctity of the Nigerian immigration laws; the economic downturn, with its adverse effects on the country's revenue on the one hand and the rate of employment on the other; the active participation of (undocumented) migrants (particularly from Niger, Chad and Cameroon) in religious riots; and the association of foreigners (particularly Ghanaians) with crimes like armed robbery and prostitution in the urban centres, and Lagos in particular. But as Aremu (2013: 341) also notes: 'apart from these official reasons cited by government, a reasonable implied rationale for the 1983 expulsion order was probably the growing frustration among Nigerian policy-makers over the failure of ECOWAS to adequately serve Nigeria's national interest and leadership ambitions in the West African sub-region'.

There was an international outcry against the expulsion, including from: the United States government (Brown, 1989: 254–5; Aluko, 1985: 423); the European Economic Commission (*Sunday Concord,*

1983); and Pope John Paul II (ibid). The leaders of five francophone ECOWAS member states also jointly issued a communiqué condemning the expulsion of their citizens, as being 'contrary to the spirit of African hospitality and various international agreements' (Afolayan 1988: 18–19). But the expulsion order was not reversed. 'Employees of federal, state and parastatals as well as citizens of Cameroon and Chad who had come to Nigeria before 1963, were however excluded from the expulsion order "irrespective of what they do"' (Aremu, 2013: 341).

ECOWAS governments were properly informed of the expulsion before the order was enacted (Adepoju, 1984). Further, according to Fafowora (1983), who was then the Nigerian Ambassador to the United Nations, they all showed an understanding of the problems the Nigerian government faced, with a large number of unskilled and undocumented migrants. They also agreed that the expulsions did not contravene the ECOWAS protocol on the free movement of people and goods within the subregion. This demonstrates that the fate of poor working people is not of central concern for the ruling class across the subregion and that the ECOWAS protocol on the free movement of people and goods does not regard labour migration as central to regional integration.

The expulsion of 'illegal aliens' in 1983 was part of the election campaign leading up to the general elections that took place seven months after the deportations started. This was why *The Economist* (in its 5 February 1988 edition, as cited by Aremu, 2013: 345) opined that the expulsion was 'Nigeria's president's xenophobic way of courting votes in next summer's elections at a time when his country's economy is in well deserved tatters'.

Some scholars have attempted to justify the expulsion order after the fact. Aremu (2013: 350) argues that 'all said and done, the 1983 expulsion of illegal aliens by the Nigerian government was not an illegality at all'. He justifies this statement by citing earlier deportations (including Nigerians) by other West African states. Choosing to forget that most of these were before the establishment of ECOWAS, he avers that 'if other countries have expelled aliens from their territories without much cry, all the foul cries against the Nigerian action in 1983 may best be regarded as mere hypocrisy by the international community against Nigeria'. Similarly, Anyanwu et al. (1997: 531) posit that 'mobility of labour' in ECOWAS brought about 'socio-economic and political problems of alien-influx', which Nigeria had 'been experiencing before the expulsion of illegal immigrants', creating 'unemployment for Nigerian nationals'. They also claimed that undocumented migrants 'participated in religious riots and other social vices like armed robbery and prostitution'. However, Aremu (2013: 349) was forced to admit that there was a need 'to look inwards henceforth for solutions to our economic woes rather than blaming foreigners'.

A review of the literature fails to identify xenophobia from below in 1983 and subsequently. Primordial sentiments that caught on as a divisive ideology within the mass of working and other poor people were more hinged on ethno-regional identities. On the contrary, what we find is the dangerous promotion of xenophobia by the state as a gambit to retain power. There is no record of resistance on the part of immigrants being deported during the expulsion. Equally, the NLC never condemned the deportations outright. According to Sylvester Ejiofoh, a leading light of the trade union movement for several decades, unionists recalled the expulsions of Nigerians by the Ghanaian state earlier (S. Ejiofoh, interview, 1 June 2015). This had affected several trade unionists. The movement had to provide accommodation and stipends for a while. Thus, it was seen as a payback of sorts for Ghana.

The National Party of Nigeria government was victorious at the heavily rigged polls in August 1983. It is not clear if the anti-immigrant sentiments it stirred helped in securing this. But only four months later, on 31 December 1983, the military struck, bringing General Muhammadu Buhari to power. The regime pursued an agenda of discipline and nationalism, instituting a 'war against indiscipline'. It was forced to continue with austerity measures, but this only deepened the economic crisis. Eventually, on 3 May 1985, out of desperation, it also expelled 700,000 undocumented migrants, giving them barely a week to leave. These were mainly supposed to be migrants who had evaded the net in 1983, or who had returned illegally. 'The government claimed that immigrants were taking jobs to the disadvantage of Nigerians, and blamed them for heavy involvement in crime' (Van Hear, 1992: 9). Eventually about a quarter of a million undocumented workers were deported.

Barely three months after the mass expulsions, there was another coup. The succeeding junta led by General Ibrahim Babangida introduced a structural adjustment programme in 1986, which led to an unprecedented expansion of the informal economy where undocumented workers were able to scrape a living. Subsequent economic policies and programmes consolidated this trend. These included: the National Economic Empowerment and Development Strategy, which was a national version of the New Economic Partnership for Africa; the short-lived 'seven-point agenda'; and the 'transformation agenda' of Dr Goodluck Jonathan.

Xenophobic tendencies have been stirred again in recent years. Undocumented migrants have again been charged with contributing to sociopolitical crisis, particularly in the form of religious insurgency. This has been led by Boko Haram waging war in the north-eastern region. This new turn to the scapegoating of foreigners started in 2012. It led to deportations of undocumented migrants, particularly those from Niger.

Probably the first inkling of this turn came from Samuel Igoche, the Comptroller of Immigration in the south-western Ekiti state, in March 2012. Makinde (2012) reported his request to 'the state government to assist the command with operations vehicles to enable it to perform its duties effectively in the state'. These duties were more explicitly defined as 'working in collaboration with other security agencies to curb influx of illegal immigrants into the country'. To successfully carry out such an onerous task, he explained: 'Our men make sure they interrogate strange faces and those suspected to have the capability of constituting danger to the society.' Barely a week and a half later, the Minister of the Interior said that the federal government had uncovered '1,497 routes into Nigeria' as reported by Ogbu (2012) in *This Day*: 'In a bid to check the influx of illegal immigrants into the country', the government was to 'erect border plazas at the 84 legal border posts', in order 'to secure the lives and properties of its citizens' in the words of the minister, as if illegal migrants as a rule necessarily threaten the lives and properties of Nigerian citizens.

By 2013, the federal government moved to mass deportation, albeit not on the scale witnessed in 1983 and 1985. Between February and August, over 22,000 'illegal immigrants' were deported, according to the Minister of the Interior (Odunsi, 2013). A number of undocumented migrants, particularly those from Niger, who constituted the largest number of undocumented migrants in the country (at least in the north) chose to return home rather than face the indignities and oppressive actions that go with the arrest and deportation of (suspected) illegal immigrants (Akinkuoto, 2013).

A reported case is that of Mohammed Lawal, a father of one child, who used to be a cyclical undocumented migrant who would work in the north of Nigeria for six months and then go back home to Niger to farm for the other half of the year. In an interview with *The Guardian* (2012), he said: 'If you have no papers, police throw you in jail.' He further added that: 'They fine you 1,000 naira and keep you locked up for a few days. The police do sweeps where people wait for work and check to see whether you are Nigerian.'

Despite this stereotyping and demeaning treatment of undocumented migrants, there is an understanding that migrant workers contribute significantly to economic development. For example, Daniel Cole – an entrepreneur and Managing Director of Humsford Realties, speaking to Meshack Idehen of the *National Mirror* (2013) – said that 'he had to depend on the special set of construction skills that immigrant workers from Mali, Ghana, Benin and Senegal had before he was able to complete a major building project he was involved with in Lagos'. Indicating some of those 'unique skills' as 'including building with natural materials like cane, bamboo and other tree crops', he summed up by saying that 'the presence of those immigrant workers made all the difference in regards to the successful completion of his work'.

National electoral politics might again beam a searchlight laden with prejudice on undocumented migrants. The spokesperson for President Goodluck Jonathan, during his failed re-election bid in 2015, alleged that underage voters accounted for the huge number of votes polled by the opposition General Muhammadu Buhari in several northern states. He went on to claim that the bulk of these were illegal migrants from neighbouring Niger, Chad and Cameroon.

The land borders had been closed for several days before the elections in an attempt to stop such activities.

While this could be considered a case of sour grapes, matters were not helped by the fact that the immigration service had earlier, in December 2014, reported that 20 voter cards had been seized from undocumented migrants from Niger. These were some of the 430 'illegal immigrants' it had apprehended in Jigawa state (in the north-western zone), between January and July (*Premium Times*, 2014).

National Politico-Legal Framework for Migration and the Civil Society Movement

In a recent document, the Nigerian government's National Commission for Refugees, Migrants and Internally Displaced Persons (NCFRMI, 2015: 7) stated: 'Migration did not gain prominence in national discourse until 2002' and when it did, it was because 'the Federal Government was confronted with the reality of Nigerian youths transiting through the Sahara desert to sojourn abroad in search of greener pastures'. Legislation on migration however dates back to the 1963 Immigration Act, consolidated and amended as the Immigration Act, 1990.[2]

Neither in 1963 nor the early 2000s was much concern shown for *immigrant workers*, particularly for those from sister African countries. The Immigration Act appears to give greater consideration to migrants from Commonwealth countries (and Eire) than it does to citizens of ECOWAS member states. This is despite the fact that the immediate neighbouring countries, forming a substantial proportion of immigrants, are francophone and not part of the Commonwealth. It is also noteworthy that, while the Labour Act upholds the rights of employees irrespective of their nationalities, it has been established as case law that 'no foreigner can accept employment with (the) Federal Government of Nigeria or state government without the consent in writing of the Director of Immigration' in the first place (Aturu, 2005: 21).

The evolution of a national migration agenda towards the formulation of a migration governance framework could be divided into two phases in the twenty-first century. The first decade witnessed efforts at formulating a coherent approach to the question of migration, with labour migration at its centre. In 2004, Nigeria's government embarked on proactive measures to regulate regular migration, as well as to manage irregular migration, by establishing an International Labour Migration Desk within the Federal Ministry of Labour and Productivity (2010). The Ministry sought and received technical support from the ILO that same year and also collaborated with the International Organisation for Migration towards formulating the first draft of a national Labour Migration Policy.

The process for formulating a generalised National Migration Policy only started two years later, in 2006. The Labour Migration Policy was eventually adopted in 2014, while the National Migration Policy came into effect on 15 May 2015. The National Commission for Refugees, Migrants and Internally Displaced Persons is vested with the responsibility of providing overall coordination for migration and related development issues. It does this at four levels: a Ministerial Sector Peer Review Committee; a Technical Working Group; five thematic Sectoral Groups, which include the Labour Migration Working Group; and the various state and non-state agents, being 'organisations whose activities are related and have an impact on migration' (NCFRMI, 2015: 16). There is a dire lack of involvement of migrant workers' organisations at any of these four levels. Migrant workers and their organisations have equally not been included in the 'national migration dialogue' thus far.

It appears that the condition of migrant workers in general, and undocumented migrant workers in particular, is not of paramount concern for the government. Indeed, 'protection of migrant workers and promotion of their welfare and that of families left behind' is one of the three key objectives of the Labour Migration Policy, but there are no identifiable activities to achieve these objectives. In 2014, Nigeria's president presented the priorities of the state concerning migration. The 'five key priority issues' he listed were: 'Protection of Nigerian Migrants within the context of its foreign Policy'; 'Diaspora Contributions to National Development'; 'Internal Migration and the Threat of Ethnic Tensions'; 'Migration and Citizenship'; and 'Insurgency and the Challenge of Displacement' (NCFRMI, 2015: 13–14). Thus the Nigerian state is more concerned with *internal* migration, particularly within the context of continued social strife, including what is literally a civil war in the north-eastern region of the country and conflicts between 'indigenes' and 'settlers', resulting in perennial friction and conflicts in several parts of the country. Second, the real concern of the government regarding international migration relates to *emigrants* and their remittances. Unfortunately, there is thus little room for ensuring the protection of immigrant workers and their families.

Migrant workers do not have separate union organisations. While regular migrants could belong to unions, irregular migrants 'are not members of any workers unions in the country' (IOM, 2015). Civil society organising on migration is equally very recent and still nascent. In January 2013, civil society organisations and the trade union centres participated in a symposium on 'empowering and protecting migrants in Nigeria' organised by the Platform for International Cooperation on Undocumented Migrants and the development Research and Projects Centre (dRPC) in collaboration with the Institute for Public Policy Research. This was part of the European Union-supported Beyond Irregularity project aimed at stemming irregular migration from sub-Saharan Africa to Europe. It sowed the seeds for the formation of the Centre for Migration and Development Aid (CMDA), which is led by the NLC.

One of the first actions of the coalition was to collaborate with the IOM in drafting an information brochure on the rights of migrants in Nigeria. The brochure stated that 'Whether you hold a residence and work permit or not, you are entitled to the fundamental human rights by virtue of being human' (IOM, 2015: 2), but also opined that the 'irregular status' of some migrants denied them the right to be trade union members. The concern of the Coalition has focused more on emigration (J. Eustace, migration officer of the NLC and Chair of the CMDA, interview, 3 June 2015). Thus far, it has not spurred organising of immigrants or the defence of immigrants' rights, despite drafting the brochure.

The bulk of irregular immigrants continue to eke a living in the informal economy. They are organised, in a broad sense of the word, informally along kinship lines, bonding together as communities of fate, as much as possible. Where they have been organised on union-like lines, this has been as part of and as an outgrowth of informal workers' organisations. The sharpest example of this is within the milieu of commercial motorcycle (popularly called *okada*) riders in Lagos, the commercial capital of Nigeria. The All Nigeria Automobile Commercial Owners and Workers' Association (ANACOWA) which broke out from the Amalgamated Commercial Motorcycle Riders Organisation of Nigeria (ACOMORON) included a large number of Nigeriens. Its founding president was a Nigerien.

ANACOWA was at the forefront of the struggle against the ban on *okadas* plying 497 routes in the city. It had the support of the Joint Action Front, the radical civil society coalition that is a part of the Labour Civil Society Coalition, with the NLC and TUC. When it lost a court case against this gentrification project of the state, the association literally collapsed, according to Gbenga Komolafe, General-Secretary of the Federation of Informal Workers' Organisations of Nigeria (FIWON), with which both ACOMORON and ANACOWA were affiliated (G. Komolafe, interview, 4 June 2015). He added that most Nigerien members of ANACOWA subsequently moved back home or to the northern states. Komolafe further discussed the efforts of FIWON to organise migrant domestic workers alongside local domestic workers. This was resisted by local domestic workers who were of the view that the migrants' acceptance of lower wages was detrimental to their interests. In fact, they wanted FIWON to issue a statement against migrant domestic workers. FIWON resisted this. But it has been constrained in organising migrant domestic workers for several reasons. The Federation's lean resources require that it is stringent with its target priorities. The domestic workers targeted have been those employed by upper-middle-class professionals within estates that can be easily gathered together. Most of the migrant domestic workers who are recruited irregularly through trafficking networks or by madams who go to pick them from their relations in the Republic of Benin and Togo work downtown, employed by local food sellers, market women and so on. Further, considering their irregular migration status and fear of the viciousness with which their madams could respond if they belonged to unions, they choose to distance themselves from the

FIWON efforts. Consequently, no single migrant worker belongs to the domestic workers' initiative established by the Federation.

Tackling migration as a trade union issue got a fillip in June 2015 when the Public Services International affiliates in the country inaugurated the National Working Group on Migration. The Group commenced research on migration in the public services. While the focus of its work is on emigration and situated in the formal sector, this pacesetting agenda is likely to have ripple effects that would benefit the quest for (undocumented) migrants in Nigeria to have a voice and achieve greater respect for their human and workers' rights.

CONCLUSION

There is a long history of migration in Nigeria. Colonialism and subsequently neocolonialism reconfigured the flow and dynamics of this, integrating it into the broader political economy of the accumulation of capital and its different regimes. The bulk of immigrants, particularly since independence in 1960, have been from the West African subregion. This trend was deepened in the 1970s in the wake of the oil boom in Nigeria and the formation of ECOWAS. Migration as a topical issue of discourse became more pervasive only in the twenty-first century. The state and civil society have been more concerned with emigration and internal migration, with emphasis on internally displaced persons regarding the latter. There is a near absence of self-organising, as unions or in other forms of organisation, by immigrants. The trade unions which play a central role in the nascent coalition of civil society organisations in the field of migration are pivotal to bringing about a living struggle in defence of migrants' rights and for stimulating the emergence of migrant workers' organisations as an integral part of the labour movement. Recent developments point towards this possibility, which could harness the repertoire of international, subregional and national policy frameworks in the coming period. This chapter is a contribution borne out of practice in this direction, with the aim of putting people at the centre of migration, which in Nigeria and West Africa as a whole must entail the liberation of integration from below, from the penumbra, in ECOWAS.

NOTES

1. The author was involved in drafting the communiqués of both the 1st and 3rd Trilateral Conferences at Accra and Abuja in 2010 and 2014 respectively. Similarly, the earlier 'bilaterals' (between the NLC and TUC Ghana on the one hand and between the NLC and COSATU on the other) did not discuss this topic.
2. Available online: www.nigeria-law.org/Immigration%20Act.htm (accessed August 2015).

REFERENCES

Adepoju, A. (1984). 'Illegals and Expulsion in Africa: The Nigerian Experience'. *International Migration Review*, 18(3), 426–36.

—— (1994). 'Preliminary Analysis of Emigration Dynamics in Sub-Saharan Africa'. *International Migration*, 32(2), 197–216.

—— (2005). 'Migration in West Africa'. Paper prepared for the Policy Analysis and Research Program of the Global Commission on International Migration, Human Resources Development Centre, Lagos, Nigeria. www.gcim.org/attachements/RS8.pdf (accessed August 2015).

Adetula, V. A. (2009). 'West African Labour Migrants and National Security in Nigeria'. In Ki-Zerbo, L. and Arrous, M. B. (Eds), *African Studies in Geography from Below*, CODESRIA (pp. 269–95). Oxford: African Books Collective.

Afolayan, A. A. (1988). 'Immigration and Expulsion of ECOWAS Aliens in Nigeria'. *International Migration Review*, 22(1), 4–27.

—— (2009). *Migration in Nigeria: A Country Profile*. Geneva: International Organisation for Migration. http://publications.iom.int/bookstore/free/Nigeria_Profile_2009.pdf (accessed August 2015).

——, Ikwuyatum, G. O. and Abejide, O. (2008). 'Country Paper: Dynamics of International Migration in Nigeria (A Review of Literature)'. Paper prepared as part of the African Perspectives on Human Mobility Programme, International Migration Institute, University of Oxford.

Akinkuoto, E. (2013). 'Nigeriens Top Illegal Aliens in Nigeria –Immigration'. *The Punch, 18* April. www.punchng.com/news/nigeriens-top-illegal-aliens-in-nigeria-immigration (accessed August 2015).

Aluko, O. (1985). 'The Expulsion of Illegal Aliens from Nigeria: A Study in Nigeria's Decision-Making'. *African Affairs*, 84(337), 539–60.

Anyanwu, J. C., Oyefusi, A., Ohaikhenan, H. and Dimowo, F. A. (1997). *The Structure of the Nigerian Economy (1960–1997)*. Onitsha: Joanee Educational.

Aremu, J. A. (2013). 'Responses to the 1983 expulsion of Aliens from Nigeria: A Critique'. *African Research Review*, 7(3), 340–52.

Arthur, J. A. (1991). 'International Labour Migration Patterns in West Africa'. *African Studies Review*, 34(3), 65–87.

Aryeetey, E. (2001). 'Regional Integration in West Africa'. Working Paper No. 170. Ottawa: OECD Development Centre.

Aturu, B. (2005). *Nigerian Labour Laws (Principles, Cases, Commentaries and Materials)*. Lagos: Friedrich Ebert Stiftung.

Brown, M. L. (1989). 'Nigeria and the ECOWAS Protocol on Free Movement and Residence'. *The Journal of Modern African Studies*, 27(2), 251–73.

Brydon, L. (1985). 'Ghanaian Responses to the Nigerian Expulsions of 1983'. *African Affairs*, 84(337), 561–85.

De Haas, H. (2006). *International Migration and National Development: Viewpoints and Policy Initiatives in Countries of Origin – The Case of Nigeria*. Oxford: International Migration Institute, University of Oxford.

ECOWAS (Economic Community of West African States). (2006). *ECOWAS Social and Economic Indicators, 2006*. Abuja: ECOWAS Commission.

Fafowora, O. O. (1983). 'On the Expulsion of Illegal Immigrants from Nigeria'. *Population and Development Review*, 9(2), 391–2.

Falola, T. (1998). *Violence in Nigeria: The Crisis of Religious Politics and Secular Ideologies*. New York: University of Rochester Press.

Federal Ministry of Labour and Productivity. (2010). 'Labour Migration Policy for Nigeria'. Revised Draft, 15 December.

Gravil, R. (1985). 'The Nigerian Aliens Expulsion Order of 1983'. *African Affairs*, 84(337), 523–37.

Guardian, The. (2012). 'Niger's Migrant Workers Lose a Lifeline as Unrest Turns Nigeria into No Go Zone'. *The Guardian*, 23 January. www.theguardian.com/global-development/2012/jan/20/niger-migrant-workers-lose-lifeline (accessed August 2015).

Harris, J. R. and Todaro, M. P. (1970). 'Migration, Unemployment and Development: A Two-Sector Analysis'. *The American Economic Review*, 60(1), 126–42.

Idehen, M. (2013). 'Immigrant Workers Contributing to Economic Growth'. *National Mirror*, 17 September. http://nationalmirroronline.net/new/immigrant-workers-contributing-to-economic-growth/ (accessed August 2015).

IOM (2015). *Rights of Migrants Workers*. Abuja: International Organisation for Migration Mission in Nigeria.

James, I. (1987). 'Human Mobility in the Lake Chad Basin'. *Annals of Borno*, 4, 57–67.

Makinde, F. (2012). 'Immigration Seeks Govt Assistance for Effective Security'. *The Punch*, 4 March. www.punchng.com/news/immigration-seeks-govt-assistance-for-effective-security (accessed August 2015).

National Bureau of Statistics. (2014). *Annual Abstract of Statistics*. Abuja: National Bureau of Statistics. www.nigerianstat.gov.ng (accessed August 2015).

NCFRMI (2015). 'National Migration Dialogue, 2014 Maiden Report, 18 February'. Submitted to the 2nd National Migration Dialogue held at the Yar'Adua Centre, Abuja, 24 March 2015.

Odunsi, W. (2013). 'Nigeria Deports 22,000 Illegal Immigrants in Six Months'. *Daily Post*, 26 August. http://dailypost.ng/2013/08/26/nigeria-deports-22000-illegal-immigrants-in-six-months/?wt=2 (accessed August 2015).

Ogbu, A. (2012). 'FG Uncovers 1,497 Routes into Nigeria'. *This Day*, 15 March. www.thisdaylive.com/articles/fg-uncovers-1-497-illegal-migration-routesinto-nigeria/111514/ (accessed August 2015).

Onwuka, R. I. (1982). 'The ECOWAS Protocol on the Free Movement of Persons: A Threat to Nigerian Security?'. *African Affairs*, 81(323), 193–206.

Premium Times (2014). 'Illegal Immigrants from Niger Caught with Nigerian Voter Cards'. *Premium Times*, 20 December. www.premiumtimesng.com/news/top-news/173585-illegal-immigrants-niger-caught-nigerian-voter-cards.html (accessed August 2015).

Roberts, R. (2004). 'The Social Dimension of Regional Integration in ECOWAS'. Working Paper No. 49. Geneva: International Labour Organisation.

Sunday Concord (1983). 'Editorial Comment'. Lagos. 13 February.

Stark, O. and Bloom, D. E. (1985). 'The New Economics of Labour Migration'. *The American Economic Review*, 75, 173–8.

Van Hear, N. (1992). 'Consequences of the Forced Mass Repatriation of Migrant Communities: Recent Cases from West Africa and the Middle East'. Discussion Paper No. 38, November. Geneva: United Nations Research Institute for Social Development.

Yaro, J. A. (2008). 'Migration in West Africa: Patterns, Issues and Challenges'. Legon: Centre for Migration Studies, University of Ghana. http://waifem-cbp.org/v2/dloads/MIGRATION%20IN%20WEST%20AFRICA%20PATTERNS.pdf (accessed August 2015).

Part II

Europe

5

Migrant Rights Activism and the Tree Workers Case in the Czech Republic

Marek Čaněk

The collective representation of precarious workers' rights by trade unions or other labour organisations has been rather limited in Central and Eastern Europe (Czarzasty and Mrozowicki, 2014), including migrant workers in low-skilled and low-paid jobs who have been a growing presence in some of these countries since their inclusion in the capitalist economy since 1989.[1] Unlike other trade unions in this region, in recent years Czech union strategy documents have mentioned migrant workers. However, migrant workers' union membership has been low (Čaněk, 2014). Nor have there been other kinds of organisations (like workers' centres, for example, Fine, 2006) in the Czech Republic that would organise them. Thus the recent tree workers campaign against violations of migrant forestry workers' rights seems exceptional. This campaign involved several hundred migrant workers from Vietnam, Romania, Slovakia and elsewhere who, in 2009, 2010 and beyond, did not get paid, or received only small portions of their wages, and were exposed to unfair working conditions in the Czech Republic.

This chapter begins by examining the recruitment of migrant workers, their working conditions and possibilities for worker agency. Ethnicised groups of migrant workers from European Union (EU) and non-EU states with varying legal status and rights in the labour market were recruited by the temporary labour agency Affumicata and other companies.

The tree workers case's structural causes are then analysed from the point of view of the development of the Czech forestry economy, the globalisation of production, the commodification of labour (Overbeek, 2003), and the conditions of migrant workers since the 2008 global economic crisis. Since possible relocation of production in forestry is limited, the Czech forestry industry has relied on labour migration, mainly from Central, Eastern and south-eastern Europe.

The tree workers campaign is discussed from two main perspectives, namely the promotion of migrant workers' rights and an anti-human trafficking discourse. The author was involved in this campaign as he combined activism with research. In 2010 and 2011, interviews were carried out with mostly migrant workers involved in the tree workers case, and in 2014 selected persons from the campaign were interviewed in order to reflect back on it.

MIGRANT WORKERS IN FORESTRY AND THE ECONOMIC CRISIS IN THE CZECH REPUBLIC: THE TREE WORKERS CASE

In March 2009, several recruitment meetings for unemployed Vietnamese migrant workers were held in Prague for tree plantation and other manual forestry work. These workers had been dismissed mainly from low-skilled temp agency jobs in manufacturing and other industries, or arrived recently in the Czech Republic only to discover that the promised work no longer existed following the beginning of the global economic and financial crisis in autumn 2008. Around 150–200 workers attended each meeting. They were stranded in the country due to high debts for their visas and without knowledge of the Czech language.

What initially seemed to be an opportunity became a case of major labour rights violations involving hundreds of migrant workers from Vietnam and several Central and Eastern European countries, including Slovakia, Romania and Hungary. In the tree workers case, several interrelated companies, Affumicata, Wood Servis Praha, Madera Servicio and others, were subcontracted by Less & Forest (formerly one of the biggest Czech forestry companies) on public bids in forestry and verge maintenance mostly between 2009 and 2011. The workers were owed unpaid wages; some were starving or threatened with violence, especially when they demanded their wages.

RECRUITMENT, WORKING CONDITIONS AND WORKERS' AGENCY

Some of Affumicata's owners and bosses had already had experience with the Vietnamese community from their previous and parallel businesses. This included their involvement in the recruitment of over a thousand workers in Vietnam in 2008, for jobs which never materialised, although the US$1,147 million it received as a deposit was not paid back, and nor were 1,807 passports returned (Křížková and Čaněk, 2011).

Affumicata realised that many of the Vietnamese migrants became unemployed during the economic crisis and would not return to Vietnam before repaying their debts and earning some extra money (*iDNES.cz*, 2009). The former head of Affumicata presented its recruitment efforts as giving a helping hand to the Czech state by offering work to unemployed migrant workers: 'We knew that in 2009 the economic crisis came and there were hundreds to thousands of unemployed Vietnamese ... It was a problem that the Czech Republic was worried about, [they] were committing crimes' (personal communication, 11 November 2010). Affumicata negotiated successfully with Less & Forest for access to the forestry sector. Workers mostly planted trees, working seven days a week, for 9–12 hours per day.

One unemployed Vietnamese migrant described the beginning of the economic crisis and the cultivation work for Affumicata in this way:

Before we drove into the forest, we had to wait for five days in the Sapa Vietnamese market in Prague where we went to a Buddhist shrine to beg for food. There was no heating, hot water, nothing. It was terrible ... Then we drove to the forest tree nursery. There we got 6,200 Czech crowns [US$300] for the first month. For the three hundred hours of work in the next month we never got a penny ... Although it was raining or snowing heavily and we were very cold, we still had to work. (Former Affumicata employee, personal communication, 26 March 2011).

Tree planting and other forestry work for the Vietnamese workers were not considered official employment. They had a 'trainee contract' which did not mention any compensation for work. The company using the 'trainee contract' for Vietnamese workers in 2009 was fined for employing 'illegal' migrants by two labour offices in northern Bohemia.

The labour force employed by Affumicata and other subcontractors was highly segmented by ethnicity, race, citizenship, legal status and gender. These companies tapped certain labour pools in particular areas in different countries. Each year new labour pools were sought: in 2009 they mostly targeted workers from Vietnam and Slovakia; in 2010 those from Romania or Slovakia; and in 2011 recruitment occurred in Romania, Lithuania and Hungary.

New companies were set up to avoid possible legal actions concerning fraud or labour rights violations. Companies such as Affumicata blamed the workers for any problems, while their reputation on social networks suffered as information about the workers' conditions spread due to the tree workers campaign.

The capacity to hire from diverse pools each year was made possible through local partners and recruiters who spoke the language of the country or the area, confirming the centrality of such transnational labour subcontractors or employment agencies to the entire operation (Pijpers, 2010). The seasonal nature of forestry work, the cost of visas and the restricting of legal labour migration to the Czech Republic during the crisis made the EU citizens from Central and Eastern Europe a privileged group of flexible workers. In contrast to Vietnamese workers, Central and Eastern European workers had either regular or precarious work contracts. The workers were usually uninsured, including those where the regular kind of employment contract obliged the employer to provide insurance. Work injuries were frequent; employers either paid in cash for the health treatment, or the employees did not receive proper health checks.

Many workers left after learning that there were issues with the work and its payment, or after becoming suspicious of the company and its bosses. Some workers were concerned for their security, since work coordinators in some workplaces were reported to have guns. Some workers fled, but those who were owed substantial amounts of money often thought that they would never see the money if they left. 'Everyone's concern is to have a job to be able to earn some money for the family. When they tell you "wait, you'll get your money later" ... they keep you at bay' (former forestry worker, personal communication, 26 October 2011). For example, the economic situation in eastern Slovakia was such that some workers were glad to receive small weekly deposits and not be a burden to their families (former forestry worker, personal communication, 26 October 2011).

Workers were discouraged from making official complaints. The company owners spread rumours about their connections to the police and politicians. Many workers thus never complained officially or did not know where to find support: 'How can an average person from eastern Slovakia look for a lawyer in Prague? ... I lost some of my pennies but returned home healthy. I'm glad for this and will not try my luck again' (former forestry worker, personal communication, 15 June 2011). Some workers complained to the police or the State Labour Inspection Office without any success. When one work coordinator called at the Labour Inspection Office, he was told: 'a check is not possible now'. He concluded: 'you have nowhere to turn to. You are owed months of wages, your life expenses are not covered and they just get away with it' (former Affumicata employee, personal communication, 18 May 2010).

Some workers visited the company's office and tried unsuccessfully to get their money paid back. Another strategy was to stop working. Work stoppages by Romanian workers became common as in the Krkonoše National Park in 2010. Two security guards tried to discipline the workers. This did not concern the Slovak workers, one of whom recalls: 'Such practices aren't something normal. Well, these [Romanian workers] are also humans. They also worked there, they're also people, they have their own rights. I didn't feel the same way. I was from Slovakia ... I'm also a foreigner but anyway I understand the language; however, [the Romanian workers] had no clue' (former forestry worker, personal communication, 26 October 2011). While there was some solidarity among workers of different nationalities, they often did not have a common language, and different groups of workers were quite isolated from each other in the forests, which made resistance more difficult.

PRECARISATION AND FLEXIBILISATION OF FORESTRY WORK

Affumicata's role in the public bids won by Less & Forest were criticised by Transparency International Czech Republic, which in 2011 researched into the State Forests of the Czech Republic (SFCR). It reported the cutting down of labour costs by temp agencies with a criminal background such as Affumicata (Transparency International, 2011a, 2011b). A substantial decrease in labour costs for cultivation work reportedly happened in 2009 by about 40 per cent compared to the previous year: 'People started to get agitated but [Less & Forest] didn't care ... they thought that saved the company a lot of money' (former Less & Forest employee, telephone communication, 6 December 2010; see also Čaněk, 2011). I turn now to the flexibilisation of the forestry economy in the Czech Republic and its inclusion in the global labour market.

After 1989, principles of a self-regulating market (Polanyi, 2001) were introduced in the Czech forestry industry. A new model of administration of state forests was established in 1992, based on the outsourcing of planting and woodcutting services. With its public tendering approach in forestry and deregulatory labour market policies, the state has substantially impacted upon various dimensions of precariousness such as the degree of certainty in continuing employment, degree of regulatory effectiveness, control over the labour process and adequacy of the income package (Vosko, 2010: 3).

The transfer of entrepreneurial risk on to the workers was marked by the shifts from employee status to that of self-employment (Slavnic, 2010). The number of employees in standard employment relationships also declined. The state has had an important role in the changes to employment relationships and the restructuring of many wood and forestry companies. For example, in the area of tree cultivation, mostly temporary contracts have been used. 'Traditionally' women carried out this kind of work. Today more men work in tree cultivation than there used to be (SFCR employee, 21 April 2011); this has also been a growing sector in the use of migrant workers.

Uncertainty of state contracts shared by the companies, as well as the emphasis placed on price as the main criterion in winning public bids, and heightened competition have been two of the factors leading employers to reduce labour costs and subcontract labour on a temporary basis.

The flexibilisation in state forestry along with the conditions of public procurement have had several consequences for workers in the 'public tender chain'. This term is used here to explain how the principles of public procurement, introduced with entry into the EU and realised under conditions of state capture and neoliberal principles (i.e. 'cost' being largely the only criterion in winning a public tender), have had negative effects on workers at the bottom of subcontracting chains. At the top of the public tender chain in the tree workers case were the SFCR, the Šumava National Park, the Krkonoše National Park and the Headquarters of Roads and Highways. In the middle was Less & Forest that won the public tenders. At the lowest level were the agencies or subcontractors supplying workers to work on the public contracts.

The intensification of production (Rogaly, 2008) and the relocation of workers according to the needs of Less & Forest from one part of the country to the other have made this kind of work less accessible to 'local' workers. The migrants, who worked for the subcontractors of Less & Forest were in an unequal position in relation to the company in the upper parts of the production or public tender chain (see Pun and Lu, 2010: 150). Uncertainties in the market and in public procurement in forestry have been transmitted on to them.

MIGRATION CONTROL POLICIES IN TIMES OF ECONOMIC CRISIS

Externalisation of costs (Vosko, 2010: 23) by employers and the state assumed a new dynamic during the economic crisis. In this context, the separation of renewal and maintenance costs (Burawoy, 1976) established between the receiving and sending states breaks down. The receiving state now has to bear costs of unproductive labour in times of the crisis and prefers to pass these on to the sending state.

However, there were also differences regarding two broad legal categories of unemployed migrant labour: EU citizens, with a right to free movement, would react to economic developments, while non-EU citizens would be coerced into leaving (Ciupijus, 2011: 545). In the eyes of state bureaucrats and politicians, the concern was with the citizens of Vietnam, Mongolia and other countries, some of whom had accumulated debts ranging from US$7,000 to US$13,000 (Ministry of the Interior, 2009a) for the costs of arranging visas and work in the Czech Republic.

Unemployment among migrant workers was rising since the 2008 economic crisis began. It was expected that thousands of migrant workers would become unemployed. The state's main policy proposals included a 'voluntary return' programme, increased monitoring and regulation of both non-EU migrants present in the Czech Republic, as well as a temporary stoppage of labour migration from selected countries (Ministry of the Interior, 2009a).

For those who would lose their jobs, but would not use the 'voluntary return' option and become illegal, there was a threat: 'foreigners should be aware of the fact that the alternative to the voluntary return is only an enforced return, which includes detention'. Unemployed migrants would thus become criminalised and 'illegal'. Migrants who stayed on might be abused as forced labour, which meant that an image of a vulnerable migrant appeared in the governmental reports (Ministry of the Interior, 2008, 2009a).

Vietnamese migrants found themselves stuck between a bad employer (Anderson, 2010) and the state, which offered the indebted unemployed non-EU migrant workers either a 'voluntary' return or 'voluntary' exploitation. Both the employer and the state presented themselves as being generous to migrants by offering them assistance in the economic crisis. However, as the Czech state predicted, most Vietnamese migrants did not make use of the 'voluntary return'[2] offers, and thus their susceptibility to labour exploitation increased (Ministry of the Interior, 2009a).

Through its migration policies, the state co-created a vulnerable, ethnicised and criminalised migrant workforce during the economic crisis, which corresponded to the demand for cheap labour in forestry. Increasing migration control, illegalisation and reduced access to a pool of migrants from non-EU countries were important factors in the change in some employers' and intermediaries' employment strategies, which started to tap (more) labour pools in several Eastern European countries. In the tree workers case, workers from Romania and Slovakia faced similar experiences of exploitation as those from Vietnam before them, highlighting structural problems in the labour market and public procurement in the forestry sector.

During the crisis, the state's role was made largely invisible (see also Šafránková Pavlíčková, 2009) with respect to the position of migrant workers. This is true for the state's political economy (support for foreign direct investment), its role in the weak regulation of labour market standards (for agency and other workers on the secondary labour market), as well as in the productive role of the law and migration policies (in creating cheap migrant labour by limiting migrant workers' rights).

With this background in mind, I now turn to the campaign itself. The tree workers campaign was an attempt by some organisations and initiatives to reinterpret the role of migrant workers in the economic crisis. The case was used to oppose the Ministry of the Interior's blaming and criminalising of unemployed migrants and to place responsibility for the protection of migrant workers' rights on the state.

THE TREE WORKERS CASE CAMPAIGN

The campaign that is described here took place mainly in 2010 and 2011. The most intensive period in terms of other activities and the involvement of many organisations and individuals lasted until 2012, but the legal case was ongoing at the time of writing, three years later. The campaign's three main aims have been: financial compensation for unpaid wages and damages to workers; the quick investigation of the case by the Czech police; and the stopping of labour exploitation by the companies involved.

The campaign did not meet these initial aims, apart from contributing to the spread of information about the abuses the workers faced in the Czech Republic and internationally, including their countries of recruitment. However, it was important in two main respects in the Czech context. First, it reacted to one of the biggest cases of migrant workers' rights violations in the Czech Republic. Second, this was the first migrant rights campaign to involve such a variety of actions, including legal, media and various kinds of political activist strategies. Crucially, it combined the targeting of concrete abusive employers and tried to explain and address migrant rights violations from a structural perspective.

THE CAMPAIGN AS A NETWORK OF LAWYERS, PROFESSIONAL NGOS AND INFORMAL INITIATIVES

The campaign's complex character was due to its composition as a relatively loose network of various formal and non-formalised organisations and individuals. It was based on a functional division of labour between various tasks among lawyers representing the workers and professional NGOs, and informal migrant and anti-racist initiatives. This kind of wide cooperation was seen as one of the campaign's positive aspects: 'The campaign and the fact that more people were joining in was giving me a lot of strength', said one of the legal representatives of the tree workers (Matouš Jíra, personal communication, 18 July 2014).

The division of tasks within the network also explains quite different understandings of the campaign. This chapter views the campaign in the wider sense, encompassing the whole range of actors and activities in support of the tree workers case. But for certain actors, like some of the main lawyers from the Prague Attorneys' law office, it was mostly about the media, public awareness and activist parts. The distinction between the legal case as represented by the lawyers and some NGOs on the one hand, and the more activist approach on the other hand, was, however, blurred. It was a deliberate strategy partly to distinguish the two parts of the campaign, for the following reasons. The lawyers, at least initially, did not wish to be seen to be critical of the work of the police and state prosecutors with whom they needed to cooperate. Some of the professional NGOs providing social and legal services to migrant workers, especially at the beginning of the campaign, were also hesitant to put their full weight behind the case and make their public support for some of the campaign's activities visible. For example, this manifested itself in the publication of the first press releases on the tree workers case, which were published by informal initiatives and not by the professional NGOs involved. Thus the role of the more informal initiatives (described below) was useful. Some of the professional NGOs saw involvement in this case as potentially conflicting with their main roles as providers of social and legal services to individual clients. Also, the informal initiatives seemed a safer vehicle through which to attack Affumicata, related companies and their representatives, who could have sought compensation for damages to their reputation. This never happened, although the SFCR threatened potential legal action against La Strada Czech Republic (La Strada) in 2012 for promoting a film screening of the documentary *Tree Workers Case* directed by Daniela Agostini.

Although a loose network, there was a core group of individuals and organisations. Among the most powerful in the group were the lawyers, especially those from the Prague Attorneys' law office, whose important role was strengthened with a 2010 grant from the Organisation for Security and Co-operation in Europe. Anti-human trafficking NGO La Strada gradually joined the case and started to coordinate the core group. This organisation also received a grant in October 2011 to support the case from the United Nations Voluntary Trust Fund for Victims of Human Trafficking.

MIGRANT WORKERS, RIGHTS AND HUMAN TRAFFICKING PERSPECTIVES

Czech NGOs assisting migrants, and a few lawyers, learned about the case almost a year after the main recruitment of Vietnamese workers started in March 2009. The scarce information and rumour that some individuals in migration NGOs had about Vietnamese workers engaged in forestry work from 2008 (Daniel, 2010) was confirmed by a former worker who came to be represented by a lawyer in 2009/2010.

There were two main broad perspectives in the campaign. The first was about the need to build new organisational structures, strengthen a discourse in support of migrant workers' rights and eventually lead to the organising of migrant workers, including in the unions. The second perspective concerned the use of anti-human trafficking mechanisms, discourse and grants from international donors fighting trafficking for labour exploitation. These can be seen as complementary perspectives. For example, without the use of at least partial funding for a case 'fighting human trafficking' it would have been almost impossible to mount a legal battle involving scores of workers or to coordinate the campaign on a long-term basis (Matouš Jíra, personal communication, 18 July 2014).

The migrant workers' rights perspective in the campaign was especially promoted by some individuals in the Initiative for the Rights of Migrant Workers (IRMW), founded as an informal organisation in spring 2010. The report from the first meeting of what later became the IRMW stated: 'Various kinds of people (from migration and migrant NGOs, migrants, academics, [Czech] citizens, anarchists, etc.) have come to [this] meeting. The fact that we have met here this way shows that there are a number of big issues [to be dealt with] as well as only a few possibilities to express ourselves in the name of migrant rights' (report from the meeting, 31 March 2010). This initiative was established due to the limited ability of the professional migration NGOs – which have played a crucial role in the social and legal assistance to migrants and refugees since the 1990s – to: gain larger public support for migrant rights; politicise the position of migrants in the Czech economy and society; and face the issues of labour rights violations as well as overcome the social isolation of NGOs in relation to migrants by involving migrants in these political activities (Szczepaniková, 2010). The aim was also to use hitherto rarely used repertoires of action by migration NGOs such as demonstrations and other kinds of activism.

The IRMW and Initiative No Racism! (INR) organised their first public protest in June 2010: a march for migrant rights. Both of these initiatives quickly became involved in the tree workers campaign. Their main roles involved organising public events and protests (for example, the Week for the Rights of Tree Workers in March 2011), outreach to Czech and international media, spreading information in workers' countries of origin, a letter campaign targeting Less & Forest in 2011 and looking for information about the tree workers case. In 2011 the case became one of their main activities in the field of migrant workers' rights. The involvement of the two initiatives in the case almost died out after 2011. Some members felt exhausted from long involvement without much success for the workers. The IRMW struggled to find a meaningful existence. But its activities were partially transferred to the Consortium of Migrants Assisting Organisations in the Czech Republic, an umbrella association of migration and migrant rights NGOs, coordinated by two former IRMW members (see Figure 5.1).

Figure 5.1   March in Support of Tree Workers, 27 March 2011, Prague. Photo by Anna Šolcová.

Was the campaign an opportunity to organise migrant workers and to involve them in the trade unions or alternative types of organisations? Such was the hope of some people in the IRMW (Iniciativa Za práva pracovních migrantů a migrantek, 2010). A tree workers trade union was even formally set up as a civil society organisation, but never used. Selected unions and their representatives became partially involved in the campaign. This included the Trade Union of Workers in Woodworking Industry, Forestry and Management of Water Supplies, but it was reluctant to support the campaign very openly. One reason for this was that the union had been through difficult collective bargaining negotiations with the SFCR, and was afraid that this could harm talks. The head of the Czech Metalworkers' Federation (OS KOVO) supported the tree workers' case at the meeting of the tripartite (the representatives of the unions, employers and the state) in May 2010. International trade unions such as Building and Wood Workers' International were interested in supporting the case but could not do so without the endorsement from its national trade union member. On the other hand, the International Trade Union Confederation (ITUC) launched a project to combat labour trafficking in 2012 in cooperation with La Strada and the Czech Moravian Confederation of Trade Unions, among others.

The tree workers campaign helped bring Czech unions' attention to the case. But it did not lead to any substantial changes in their relation towards migrant workers who rarely happen to be members (Čaněk, 2014). Nor has it led to other kinds of migrant worker organising. Among the reasons for this are the fact that the case involved seasonal workers dispersed in many parts of the country who worked for only short periods of time, making it difficult for them to organise. With this kind of abusive employer the business model could hardly become more 'civilised' even if workers were organised in a union. The nature of the forestry industry made it complicated for the initiatives from an urban area to connect directly to migrant forestry workers. In addition, most of the migrant workers employed by these companies were usually contacted only after they had stopped working for them and left the country.

The anti-human trafficking perspective in the campaign was especially promoted by La Strada. This organisation was aware of the Czech Programme on Support and Protection of Victims of Trafficking in Human Beings (the State Programme), residence permits for victims of human trafficking as well as potential international support. The tree workers were a case of strategic representation (Kutálková et al., 2013). La Strada offered support and started cooperating with lawyers from the Prague Attorneys' office, who 'reflected on the framework of trafficking in human beings. The case fulfilled the definition of human trafficking and there was a great number of people who could have made use of services provided by

the state' (Petra Kutálková, personal communication, 14 July 2014).
I will now briefly describe the legal case, the usage of anti-human
trafficking provisions in the criminal law investigation, the media
presentation of the case, as well as contestations around the usage of
anti-human trafficking perspectives within the campaign.

Several possible legal strategies were discussed and eventually
pursued by lawyers and others involved in the core campaign
group. These corresponded to some of the campaign's main aims –
the prosecution of the individuals and companies abusing the tree
workers and financial compensation for the workers. The support for
a criminal inquiry into fraud, human trafficking and other crimes
was one of the most important strategies, along with some civil law
approaches. The criminal complaint on behalf of the first group of
workers was submitted in June 2010. Several police units investigated
the case from 2010 based on their specialisations. The legal classifica-
tion of the tree workers as a human trafficking case was disregarded
by the police and the state prosecutors. They mostly interpreted
the definition of human trafficking in the Czech Criminal Code as
including violence, threats of violence, imposing a ban on leaving
the workplace or confiscating passports, an interpretation that
was criticised as too narrow a definition of human trafficking for
purposes of labour exploitation by the workers' attorney (letter by
Prague Attorneys, 22 June 2010; Šmíd, 2013). The investigation was
later further fragmented into police units based on geographical areas
where the workers signed the contracts or worked. Eventually the
case did not make it to the criminal court despite several complaints
from the attorneys. Compensation for wages and other damages was
to be sought as auxiliary to the criminal case proceedings as well as
through filing an insolvency claim against Affumicata, neither of
which were successful.

The anti-human trafficking angle presented itself as 'an opportunity'
that had not been realised. The relatively cooperative relationship
established in 2010 between the attorneys and a representative of the
Ministry of the Interior responsible for human trafficking issues did
not continue after this person left the position. Although there were
some exceptions, generally the representatives of state institutions,
including the police, adopted a 'defensive' position against what

they saw as attacks from organisations and lawyers involved in the campaign (Matouš Jíra, personal communication, 18 July 2014). International pressure on the Czech state based on the transnational activities of organisations like La Strada resulted in the downgrading of the Czech Republic's standing in the *US Trafficking in Persons Report 2011* (US Department of State, 2011). However, it did not have any positive results for the investigation of the case. Following the report's publication, 'the Head of the Government criticised the Minister of the Interior who in turn criticised the bosses of the Police Unit for Combating Organised Crime. Those who paid most for it were the ordinary policemen that worked intensively on the case' (Petra Kutálková, personal communication, 14 July 2014). The lawyers did not wish to be seen to be those publicly attacking the police or the state prosecutors, which was supposed to be the task of the non-formalised initiatives within the campaign. The state authorities, however, were usually unable to make such distinctions between the activities of lawyers and informal initiatives (Matouš Jíra, personal communication, 18 July 2014).

The aim of the tree workers campaign was to recognise these workers as subjects with economic rights, and therefore as entitled to fair remuneration. But when 'illegality' is made visible in such campaigns it creates dilemmas (Chauvin, 2009). This issue was attenuated due to the recruitment of mostly EU citizens by subcontractors in the second half of 2009. However, an important question remained, regarding the Vietnamese workers who faced a ban on their stay in the Czech Republic due to their previous illegal employment in forestry. Here again, one way to legalise the stay was to use the measures to support victims of human trafficking. However, the number of individuals interested was low, as they would have been restricted in their right to work, and there was also the negative experience of a Vietnamese migrant who unsuccessfully applied to the State Programme.

The human trafficking framework, however, was not shared by one of the lawyers involved in the case, who said:

I do not insist that [the representatives of Affumicata] should be sentenced as human traffickers. They should be sentenced as perpetrators of a fraud and the state should help the victims in some way in its own interest. This could help close the case as well as ... encourage other migrants in the future that it is possible and sometimes even advantageous to defend oneself. However, the reality is such that the state does not wish to do this. Both the [State Programme] and the institute of long-term residence for the purpose of protection is just a play to perform that something is being done. (Pavel Čižinský, personal communication, 11 November 2010)

The representation of the case in the media was also discussed within the campaign. The human trafficking discourse was often visible in simplified ways. Thus the La Strada representative became 'allergic about the stories of new slavery' (Petra Kutálková, personal communication, 14 July 2014). She also criticised the publication of photos of one Vietnamese worker, which was allowed by other people in the campaign, contesting claims that the worker knowingly approved of it (Nguyenová, 2014).

Framing the tree workers case as one involving human trafficking, criminal activities and ethnicised/non-Czech workers facilitated access to the Czech media. After the first long investigative article was published in the street magazine *Nový Prostor*, other national and international media started to report on it (Křížková and Čaněk, 2011). The media coverage had only a limited effect in creating pressure on most of the companies involved or on the investigation. But the campaign did successfully make the public tender chain visible. This at least obliged Less & Forest and the SFCR to respond through press releases, and led to negotiations between the Ministry of the Interior and the Ministry of Agriculture on the risks involved in organising public bids.

TEMPORARY CONSENSUS AMONG DIFFERENT KINDS OF POLITICAL ACTIVISM

The campaign comprised various kinds of political activism. Old (trade unions), new (migration and migrant rights NGOs) and radical (informal anti-racist and migrant rights groups) kinds of political activism (Císař et al., 2011), with their different aims, strategies, organisational structures and repertoires of action, were represented. The new and radical kinds of political activism tend not to cooperate with each other, as the mainstream activists 'do not wish to be seen as allies of the radicals' who strive for a transformation of society at large (Císař et al., 2011: 142).

The large political consensus among migration NGOs, informal IRMW (partly comprising representatives of migration NGOs) and INR was possible due to the fact that the critique of the condition of migrant workers in forestry was not a critique of the capitalist economy as such. The tree workers case was instead being described within the campaign as a structural failure of the various state policies described earlier. In 2014, a representative of the INR reflected on their collective's development:

> We started out as an apolitical anti-racist and anti-fascist group. We have been moving towards anti-capitalist activities ... The kind of exploitation [in the tree workers case] has been enabled by the economic and political conditions, which have been set here. ... If the campaign was organised today, its main points would be framed a bit differently. This might have been problematic for other people in the campaign. (personal communication, 7 July 2014)

The involvement of radical political activism in the campaign was thus mostly limited to the enlargement of the repertoire of protest actions, to include demonstrations and other kinds of public protest that have not been very common in the Czech Republic's new kind of political activism (Císař et al., 2011).

CONCLUSION

The tree workers campaign was an important migrant rights campaign in the Czech but also Central European post-socialist context. A consensus reached within the campaign enabled the inclusion of a large variety of organisations, encompassing old, new and radical kinds of political activism with their varied repertoire of actions. A division of labour was organised among them. However, the loose network also had its disadvantages, in that it did not build up an organisational base that could pursue some of the more structural issues such as the undercutting of costs in public bids or the regulation of seasonal work. Due to the relatively short history of international migration and low levels of politicisation of this topic, it was a temporary consensus that could be harder to reach today. Although successful in raising the case and pointing to its structural causes, the campaign was not able to reach many of its goals in a political and media environment that is not very responsive to cases of labour rights violations. Neither was the human trafficking discourse helpful, apart from gaining international and some domestic support for the case, which confirmed the thesis of the sceptics in the campaign that the human trafficking framework is there to give the impression that the state is doing something to tackle the exploitation of migrant workers. Finally, the most troubling conclusion from the campaign is that even a relatively sustained effort over several years may not lead to justice for migrant workers.

NOTES

1. This chapter was partly supported by a grant entitled 'Testing EU Citizenship as Labour Citizenship: From Cases of Labour Rights Violations to a Strengthened Labour-Rights Regime' from the European Commission's Europe for Citizens programme. Responsibility for the information and views shared here lie entirely with the author. I would like to thank Luba Kobová for her comments and suggestions.
2. A total of 283 Vietnamese citizens took part in the 'voluntary returns' programme in 2009 (Ministry of the Interior, 2009b).

REFERENCES

Anderson, B. (2010). 'Migration, Immigration Controls and the Fashioning of Precarious Workers'. *Work, Employment and Society*, 24(2), 300–17.
Burawoy, M. (1976). 'The Functions and Reproduction of Migrant Labor: Comparative Material from Southern Africa and the United States'. *American Journal of Sociology*, 81(5), 1050–87.
Čaněk, M. (2011). 'Když se sází les, létají třísky: O zaměstnávání pracovních migrantů ve státních lesích'. *Migraceonline.cz*. www.migraceonline.cz/e-knihovna/?x= 2279186 (accessed August 2015).

—— (2014). 'The Social and Political Regulation of Labour Migration in the Czech Republic: The Case of the Czech Republic'. Unpublished doctoral dissertation, Charles University, Prague.

Chauvin, S. (2009). 'Des mobilisations bridées: Le syndicalisme informel des travailleurs journaliers aux États-Unis'. In Béroud, S. and Bouffartigue, P. (Eds), *Quand le travail se précarise, quelles résistances collectives?* (pp. 253–70). Paris: La Dispute.

Císař, O., Navrátil, J. and Vráblíková, K. (2011). 'Staří, noví, radikální: politický aktivismus v České republice očima teorie sociálních hnutí'. *Czech Sociological Review,* 47(1), 137–67.

Ciupijus, Z. (2011). 'Mobile Central Eastern Europeans in Britain: Successful European Union Citizens and Disadvantaged Labour Migrants?'. *Work, Employment and Society,* 25(3), 540–50.

Czarzasty, J. and Mrozowicki, A. (2014). *Organizowanie związków zawodowych w Europie: Badania i praktyka.* Warszawa: Wydawnictwo Naukowe Scholar.

Daniel, M. (2010). 'Podnikání jako strategie pro udržení legálního statusu pracovních migrantů'. *Migraceonline.cz,* 12 February. www.migraceonline.cz/cz/e-knihovna/ podnikani-jako-strategie-pro-udrzeni-legalniho-statusu-pracovnich-migrantu (accessed August 2015).

Fine, J. (2006). *Worker Centers: Organizing Communities at the Edge of the Dream.* Ithaca, NY: ILR Press/Cornell University Press.

iDNES.cz (2009). 'Veřejné práce by byly drahé, hájil šéf azylového odboru návrat cizinců'. *iDNES.cz,* 17 February. http://ekonomika.idnes.cz/verejne-prace-by-byly-drahe-hajil-sef-azyloveho-odboru-navrat-cizincu-1kf-/ekonomika. aspx?c=A090217_162053_ekonomika_ven (accessed August 2015).

Iniciativa Za práva pracovních migrantů a migrantek (2010). 'První pochod za práva migrantů'. *Migraceonline.cz,* 3 June. http://migraceonline.cz/cz/e-knihovna/prvni-pochod-za-prava-migrantu-tiskova-zprava-iniciativy-za-prava-migrantu (accessed August 2015).

Křížková, M. and Čaněk, M. (2011). 'Obchodníci mezi stromy'. *Nový Prostor,* 367. www.novyprostor.cz/clanky/367/obchodnici-mezi-stromy.html (accessed August 2015).

Kutálková, P., Pluhařová, D., Šimonová, T. and Otáhalová, L. (2013). 'Strategické zastupování: od teorie k praxi'. In Střítecký, V. and Topinka, D. (Eds), *Obchodování s lidmi za účelem pracovního vykořisťování v teorii a praxi* (pp. 107–55). Praha: Ústav mezinárodních vztahů, v.v.i. and La Strada Česká republika, o.p.s.

Ministry of the Interior. (2008). *Propouštění zahraničních pracovníků v důsledku hospodářské krize – rizika a možné dopady na bezpečnostní situaci v České republice.* Czech Republic: Ministry of the Interior.

—— (2009a). *Analýza bezpečnostních rizik spojených s propouštěním zahraničních pracovníků.* Czech Republic: Ministry of the Interior.

—— (2009b). *Informace o projektu dobrovolných návratů.* Czech Republic: Ministry of the Interior.

Nguyenová, T. L. (2014). 'Spolupráce médií s neziskovými organizacemi na příkladu kauzy, Stromkaři' a mediální zpracování případu'. Published bachelor's thesis, Charles University, Prague. https://is.cuni.cz/webapps/zzp/download/130130144 (accessed August 2015).

Overbeek, H. (Ed.) (2003). *The Political Economy of European Employment: European Integration and the Transnationalization of the (Un)employment Question.* London and New York: Routledge.

Pijpers, R. (2010). 'International Employment Agencies and Migrant Flexiwork in an Enlarged European Union'. *Journal of Ethnic and Migration Studies*, 36(7), 1079–97.

Polanyi, K. (2001). *The Great Transformation: The Political and Economic Origins of Our Time.* Boston, MA: Beacon Press.

Pun, N. and Lu, H. (2010). 'A Culture of Violence: The Labor Subcontracting System and Collective Action by Construction Workers in Post-Socialist China'. *The China Journal*, 64, 143–58.

Rogaly, B. (2008). 'Intensification of Workplace Regimes in British Horticulture: The Role of Migrant Workers'. *Population, Space and Place*, 14(6), 497–510.

Šafránková-Pavlíčková, L. (2009). 'Otevření Pandořiny skříňky: Mediální obraz cizinců pracujících v ČR'. *Migraceonline.cz.* http://migraceonline.cz/e-knihovna/?x=2192178 (accessed August 2015).

Slavnic, Z. (2010). 'Political Economy of Informalization'. *European Societies*, 12(1), 3–23.

Šmíd, M. (2013). 'Komparativní analýza evropských rozsudků v oblasti obchodování s lidmi za účelem pracovního vykořisťování'. In Střítecký, V. and Topinka, D. (Eds), *Obchodování s lidmi za účelem pracovního vykořisťování v teorii a praxi* (pp. 107–55). Praha: Ústav mezinárodních vztahů, v.v.i. and La Strada Česká republika, o.p.s.

Szczepaniková, A. (2010). 'Performing Refugeeness in the Czech Republic: Gendered Depoliticisation through NGO Assistance'. *Gender, Place and Culture*, 17(4), 461–77.

Transparency International Czech Republic. (2011a). *Rizika ztrát v lesním hospodářství.* www.transparency.cz/doc/aktuality/Rizika_ztrat_v_lesnim_hospodarstvi___TIC.docx (accessed August 2015).

—— (2011b). *Poznámky TIC k rizikům ztrát v lesním hospodářství LČR.* http://transint.xred.cz/doc/Poznamky_TIC_ke_korupnim_rizikm_FIN.pdf (accessed August 2015).

US Department of State. (2011). *Trafficking in Persons Report 2011.* Washington, DC: US Department of State. www.state.gov/j/tip/rls/tiprpt/2011/ (accessed August 2015).

Vosko, L. F. (2010). *Managing the Margins: Gender, Citizenship, and the International Regulation of Precarious Employment.* Oxford: Oxford University Press.

6

Towards a History of the Latin American Workers Association 2002–12

Jake Lagnado

This chapter charts the life of the Latin American Workers Association (LAWAS),[1] which organised chiefly among contract cleaners in London between 2002 and 2012. After looking briefly at a historical precedent, the first such association in the early 1980s, it turns to the early days of LAWAS' second incarnation in 2002, and its subsequent partnership with leading British union T&G/Unite,[2] during the high point of the latter's Justice for Cleaners (J4C) campaign in London. Finally, I discuss the breakdown of this relationship in 2009 over workplace issues and support for undocumented workers, and the newly independent LAWAS that emerged. My aim is to bring together some strands of a story which, as with much grassroots worker history, has not been told elsewhere, and which I hope my fellow participants in that story will continue to enrich with their own perspectives and detail in the future.

BACKGROUND: THE 1980S

Latin American emigration to Britain increased in the 1970s, notwithstanding much older historical connections by way of economic colonisation and wars of independence. For present purposes this emigration featured two key groups.[3] There were those fleeing the right wing dictatorships of the period, of which Chileans escaping the Pinochet regime formed the largest group. The Chileans arrived in a relatively organised fashion thanks to the support of what was then a strong British trade union movement, forming communities in industrial towns such as Glasgow and Sheffield, as well as London. Meanwhile, other Latin American migrants came on work visas for service sector jobs, among whom Colombians were the most prominent (Sassen, 2001). When the British government ended the work visa option in 1979, some of this latter group applied for residence, while others became undocumented. So too did many who followed in their footsteps throughout the 1980s, as Colombia was hit by commodity price crashes, manufacturing decline and, conversely, increased mobility resulting from the growing drugs trade. In this decade a new group of Colombians also began to arrive – political exiles escaping an incipient dirty war against the left and trade unions.

Hospitality and contract cleaning were the main areas of employment open to most new arrivals in the 1980s. Already in previous years the likes of the Cleaning Action Group and the T&G's International Catering Workers Branch had begun trying to organise in these sectors (Alberti, 2013; B, 2009). Then, in 1981, a group of workers in London set up the first Latin American Workers Association. As a result, several hundred Latin Americans joined the T&G, one of Britain's largest unions with a largely private sector membership concentrated in transport and industry. In the union, these workers continued to be represented through the Association. With T&G backing, they achieved union recognised agreements in a number of cleaning contracts. But their efforts were undermined by the companies, who undercut each other during tendering processes by eroding hard-won terms and conditions. Immigration raids which served to undermine organising efforts were another problem, notably one on the prestigious department store Selfridges, which had become one of the main organising focal points for the cleaners. This unsettled LAWAS's relationship with the union and led to its demise. But worse was to follow when a young Colombian organiser, Hebert Marin, was murdered in Colombia in 1986 just one day before he was due to return to London (Ardill and Cross, 1987).

2002-4: REFOUNDATION, THE COLOMBIAN YEARS

Some 15 years later, in 2001, a London memorial meeting was held for Marin. One of those present was Julio Mayor, a Colombian trade unionist who had come to London in the late 1990s – a high point of emigration from Colombia to the UK as war and recession took their toll. Upon his arrival, Mayor became active in the Colombian Refugee Association (CORAS), where many workers came in search of support for workplace problems. Even where they were members of existing unions, language difficulties and lack of union recognition made accessing support difficult. Mayor's interest in providing support in this area led a Chilean member of the original LAWAS employed by CORAS to put him in touch with Bob Tennant, secretary of a local government branch of the T&G. Tennant was receptive to Mayor's concerns, and invited him to the memorial meeting.[4] There, Mayor met Ernesto Leal, a Chilean trade unionist exile who had moved to London from Scotland in the late 1980s. Like others, Leal had arrived in Scotland with the support of the British trade union movement, and immersed himself in the movement there (Anon, 2009; Silver, 2011). But when he moved to London and began working as a cleaning supervisor, he found a newer generation of Latin Americans working in deunionised conditions and in need of support. Together, Leal and Mayor, two Latin American trade unionists of different generations and nationalities, who had arrived in different periods and under different conditions, made common cause and set to work building a new Latin American Workers Association.

Notwithstanding the links between them, the new LAWAS faced a tougher environment than that faced by its 1980s predecessor, and this was to affect its *modus operandi*. This tough new environment was defined by three key features: the nature of Latin American emigration in this period, a quarter century of Britain's new neoliberal economic model, and the re-emergence of immigration and asylum as political issues.

First, the Colombian emigration of the 1990s was on a different scale from that of the Chileans in the 1970s, in that it formed part of a mass exodus of which union, left and social movement activists were but one component. Unlike their Chilean counterparts, these activists rarely left with any kind of organisational support, but rather had to make their own way in the face of heightened immigration controls. Thus, for this new group of exiles there was no natural meeting point with the UK labour movement, whose vision of Latin America remained rooted in the romanticism of a previous era. But they could find some support and make contacts through a number of small community organisations and NGOs providing general advice to Latin Americans in London. These NGOs had benefitted from the ethnic minority grants awarded by left wing local authorities of the 1980s, notably the Greater London Council. Indeed, at the outset some had been more overtly political, but found themselves increasingly restricted to assisting a growing and needy population within the confines of the caseworker–client relationship. Ironically, this relationship mirrored the 'servicing' model with which Britain's unions had sought to stem their decline in the 1980s by refocusing away from collective action and towards offering individual services to members, from resolving individual workplace grievances to offering cheap insurance policies.

These new arrivals found work at the bottom end of the service sector, notably in contract cleaning. This sector benefitted from the neoliberal turn in the world economy, as championed in Britain by the Conservative governments of 1979–97 (and New Labour thereafter) in two ways. This occurred due to two factors: first, the transfer of jobs from the public to the private sector through privatisation and outsourcing; and second, the rise of London as a global financial centre, as epitomised by the Canary Wharf office complex in east London. The governments of the day helped ensure that it was a deunionised, low-wage workforce which stepped in to provide cleaning, cooking, security and other services for both the public sector and the world of finance by abolishing wage controls and curtailing trade union rights. These policies were central to a class offensive aimed at rolling back the terms and conditions won and defended by a hitherto highly unionised workforce, especially in the public sector.

Newly arrived migrants such as the Colombians, often in a vulnerable legal situation due to their immigration status, and with less chance of getting work quickly in other sectors, were among those who came to make up this new workforce. But by the 1990s Britain had become increasingly hostile to immigrants. In particular, during this period the media scapegoated the refugees arriving in increasing numbers to escape the wars raging across the post-Cold War world. At the same time, the closing down of other legal routes of migration to the UK had left political asylum as one of the few options left. For many, arrival in the UK was just the start of a process lasting many years to achieve the right to work and residency. Meanwhile they would be vulnerable to myriad employment abuses.

Figure 6.1 Advert for first public meeting of what was to become the relaunched LAWAS, published alongside accompanying interview in Anon (2002).

It was in this context that, with the support of Tennant's union branch, Leal and Mayor held an initial public meeting on 9 February 2002 at London's Conway Hall, a historic meeting point for both the British and exiled left (Anon, 2002: 11). To attract attendance they advertised a screening of the film *Bread and Roses* in London's Latin American press, inspired by the Latino-led Justice for Janitors campaign in the US (Figure 6.1). As Mayor recalls, at first their efforts seemed to have been wasted, as only a handful of people had arrived when they began to play the film. But by the time the lights came on at the end there were several dozen – out of whom a provisional committee was formed. This committee began to meet fortnightly and adopted the name Latin American Workers Association:[5]

> Desde el día del primer encuentro [...] formamos una Junta directiva para darle forma como una organización comunitaria, afortunadamente todos los que integramos esta Junta Directiva teníamos una amplia trayectoria sindical en nuestros países de origen. Empezamos a tratar de buscar solución a los problemas laborales que tenia nuestra comunidad, pero no teníamos donde atenderlos y lo hacíamos regularmente en cafés, McDonalds, restaurantes o simplemente en un parque a falta de sitio estable para atenderlos.
>
> At our first gathering [...] we formed a management committee in order to set ourselves up properly as a community organisation. Fortunately all of us who joined this committee had a great deal of trade union experience in our countries of origin. We began trying to resolve the workplace problems faced by our community, but had nowhere to attend people and so ended up attending them in cafes, McDonalds, restaurants or just in a park. (May 2005 letter from LAWAS Management Committee to T&G Region One)

From then on more Latin American workers came into their orbit, some of whom had been active in the left and in trade unions back home. For the Colombians among this latter group CORAS was an important point of contact. So too were other Latin American NGOs and community organisations such as the Indo-American Rights for Migrants Organisation, who let an itinerant LAWAS meet on their premises.

For the newly born Association this lack of a base was a major hindrance to their work, and Leal worked his trade union contacts to try and get one. In May 2003 he secured the use of Dalston Cross Community Centre, run by an Anglo-Cuban couple in east London. From these cold and spartan premises, Leal and Mayor began giving advice to workers on a daily basis. LAWAS started taking shape on other fronts too – a summer coach trip to the south coast helped raise the funds to open the Association's first bank account, and a local health NGO helped draft statutes with a view to applying for charitable status.

Having built up this momentum, the Association decided to hold its first assembly on 27 September 2003 at Dalston Cross Community Centre. This meeting officially inaugurated the Association, elected a new management committee and expressed its goal to 'defend the rights of Latino workers whatever their status in the United Kingdom'. Thus, from the start, LAWAS put the question of immigration status and its impact on workers' rights centre stage in its desire to put principles into practice. The predominantly Colombian background of those present and the subjects they discussed gives a clear sense that they felt engaged in a battle for trade union and human rights on two fronts – back home and in the UK.

At this stage LAWAS activists were still sceptical about the usefulness of existing UK unions as a vehicle to support Latin American workers locally, fearing that they might just use LAWAS as a recruiting machine to get more dues, rather than provide real practical support on the issues that mattered to Latin American workers, especially for those who were 'illegal'. (Indeed, one of the first collective issues LAWAS faced was an immigration raid on a north London industrial launderette.) They felt that the Association needed to be on a more stable footing before entering into any partnerships. But how to achieve that was a matter of debate. Some thought LAWAS should eventually become a union for all cleaners, while others thought it should focus on the Latin American community which it knew best, and should seek local government funding available to so-called ethnic minority community organisations.[6] This debate would continue throughout the Association's existence, but in the short term, events soon overtook it.

2004–9: FROM HEROES TO PARIAHS

By April 2004 internal issues at the Dalston Cross Centre meant LAWAS could no longer use it, and the Association was once again homeless. But Leal's efforts to find a more permanent home paid off when T&G agreed to enter into a partnership, providing LAWAS with a room and a computer at its north London office. Although LAWAS members were still wary of throwing their lot in with the union, the offer was seen as a major step forwards. A volunteer rota was hastily arranged and the office was officially inaugurated on 8 July 2004 with speeches, dances and food (Figure 6.2). At the same time, a rolling publicity campaign began in the Latin American community, taking in radio, newspapers, churches, embassies, public meetings and the annual Carnaval del Pueblo. A Trades Union Congress (TUC) pamphlet on employment rights and a leaflet advertising the new office's advice service proved to be highly effective Spanish-language tools in this campaign.

Figure 6.2 Inauguration of LAWAS–T&G partnership, summer 2004; (left to right) Julio Mayor, Ernesto Leal, the author (interpreting), Pat O'Keefe (T&G), Jenny Mayor (interpreting). Photo courtesy of Julio Mayor.

Once word got around, the community response was overwhelming, as from its small room in the T&G's offices LAWAS combined advice and representation by workers for workers with a huge recruitment drive into the union. Membership of LAWAS was automatic upon coming into contact with the Association and soon approached a list of nearly 1,000, concentrated above all in contract cleaning, the majority of whom were signed up to the T&G.[7] LAWAS became known colloquially in the community as the *sindicato latino*. Nevertheless, in the words of the first Unite organiser assigned to the Association, its work remained largely 'under the radar'. Issues ranged from wage theft and dismissals, through to sexual and racial harassment. What made LAWAS's work especially challenging was the way employers used the language barrier and immigration status, with the connivance of local managers in an increasingly decentralised command structure, to try and deny workers their basic rights and maximise profits. It is ultimately to the employers' advantage that under British employment law, if a contract is known to be illegal (because, for example, an employee's immigration status means they are not legally entitled to work), a claim cannot be brought in an employment tribunal. In this respect, employment and immigration law are tied together in the UK in a particularly pernicious way.

At the same time the union was kick-starting its Justice for Cleaners (J4C) campaign along the lines of the US-influenced 'organising model', with its twin goals of union recognition and the London 'living wage' at strategically chosen sites, and in partnership with London Citizens, a campaigning alliance of faith groups and other 'civil society' groups influenced by Saul Alinsky in the US. At first it seemed LAWAS's efforts might feed into the campaign. Indeed, LAWAS initially developed a strong working relationship with J4C organisers, helping cleaners to organise at work, arranging weekend activities such as English classes, and in general promoting J4C in the Latin American community.

However, for the many Latin American cleaners who joined the T&G through LAWAS but did *not* work in the buildings targeted by J4C, it was impossible to take part in their new union. The rigidity of the organising model meant that the union could often not assist when workers wanted to organise, because the size or location of the workplace did not fit the plan. This also had a lot to do with the fragmented nature of contract cleaning, with employers always seeking to increase the rate of exploitation and undermine collective organisation through shorter shifts and smaller workforces. Lacking a functional union branch, LAWAS became the de facto branch of the members it recruited, who constituted informal union cells in unorganised workplaces and fought workplace disputes as best they could with the support of LAWAS activists. This lack of a place in the union's democratic structures was to later prove fatal.

Operating without the structure and facilities of a formal union branch put LAWAS under an intolerable strain, which in turn tested relations with the wider union. At its third assembly in February 2006, activists complained vociferously that it often felt like LAWAS was just there to increase union membership and take the strain alone of new members with all their problems, as had originally been feared. As a result, LAWAS struggled to develop independently, and in the absence of an active committee, its office volunteers to a large extent effectively came to represent the organisation.

Despite these difficulties, LAWAS plunged into activity around migrant rights which would have major longer-term significance for its future. The intense work of 2004–6 had brought in new volunteers from the 1,000-odd paper members – among them workers who had received support from LAWAS and were keen to put something back into the organisation. In 2006 these new recruits in particular brought LAWAS into a coalition with J4C organisers, shop stewards and radical migrant rights groups such as No Borders in promoting a march 'for freedom of movement and the right to stay' as part of the 3rd International Day of Action on Migration called by the European Social Forum.

Organising this march was to prove a high point of LAWAS's joint work with the T&G. One of the biggest issues facing them both was the workplace checks and raids increasingly being used by employers and the British immigration service to undermine organising and target activists. This situation was soon to be exacerbated by new legislation from the then Labour government in the form of the employer sanctions for hiring undocumented workers envisaged by the 2006 Immigration, Asylum and Nationality Act. To build for the march, LAWAS worked its contacts, including those made through the campaign in support of Jean Charles de Menezes, a young Brazilian shot dead by police in 2005. As a result, LAWAS was soon building for the march with other Latin American solidarity and community groups starting to organise in tandem with social movements back home, such as Bolivians and Ecuadorians. Together they targeted Latin American churches, radio stations and shopping centres. The *Todas las Voces* radio show, run by LAWAS activists, played a crucial role. This process was to diversify LAWAS's activist base. It also set a precedent for joint work between Latin American left and solidarity groups in London under the umbrella of the Coordinadora Latinoamericana.

Links were forged not just with other Latin American groups but with a variety of other organisations. These included the hospitality and domestic workers branches of T&G (now Unite), other unions and TUC-backed initiatives such as the Vulnerable Workers Project and local trades' councils. Community law centres became vital allies, assisting in legal cases where union lawyers or officers had failed to support members. LAWAS worked with cleaners to try to organise around workplace issues at various sites including the BBC, Kew Gardens, Fitness First gyms and the prestigious Tower 42 building in the heart of London's financial district (see, for example, Anon (2007) on the BBC and Uribe Marin (2009) on Fitness First). At Tower 42, the union eventually agreed to get involved, representing a large workforce in J4C's target zone which had already started to self-organise. But elsewhere it was impossible to get serious backing. Activity continued on the immigration issue, as highlighted by a press release put out at the time (Latin American Workers Association, 2007), and involvement in a series of national Trade Union and Community Conferences against Immigration Controls initiated by the group No One is Illegal.

Besides organising and casework, member education was always a priority for LAWAS. From the start it had organised English and workplace rights classes, both alone and in partnership with the College of North East London and the London Coalition Against Poverty. Finally, in late 2006, LAWAS and J4C organisers got Unite to arrange a pilot English course. LAWAS found a teacher and enough students to make the pilot project such a success that a large-scale education programme was then provided for migrant workers. This programme later developed into the United Migrant Workers Educational Project (UMWEP) – a major union showpiece to this day. Similarly, when a pilot immigration law course was arranged for J4C and other cleaner activists in response to workplace immigration checks and raids, LAWAS drew on its pool of Latin American activists to provide services to half the students. Again, the success of the pilot course led to it being rolled out nationally.

One reason for the emphasis on education was the ongoing disruption caused by the revolving door syndrome whereby LAWAS activists would soon be 'talent spotted' and recruited to positions in the union/NGO world. The recruitment of LAWAS's first office volunteer as a T&G organiser was followed by another being recruited by London Citizens as their West London organiser. A Brazilian volunteer also left LAWAS to devote herself to the role of secretary of the T&G's hospitality branch. Hence there was a constant need to train new activists as replacements. To help provide some minimal stability, the union, to its credit, accepted a petition to fund the Association's office work by providing a nominal daily payment in lieu of lost wages and invited LAWAS volunteers on to shop steward courses in recognition of the role they effectively played as roving shop stewards for a sector of the union membership that still had no place in the union's structures.

2008–11: THE SECOND INDEPENDENCE

From late 2008, three key developments led to a 'perfect storm' which was to determine the Association's fortunes over the next period, namely, a turn to militant, independent protest among Latin American cleaners, the campaign for an amnesty for undocumented workers, and the growing unity of different left wing Latin American groups in London.

Starting with the 2006 migrants' rights march, LAWAS had sought to revitalise and expand its work by strengthening links with different left wing migrant groups, a process which continued with a fourth assembly in November 2007 and a large-scale training session in September 2008. These groups already included the Bolivia and Colombia Solidarity Campaigns and Ecuadorian Movement in the UK (MERU), and in 2008 they were joined by Polo UK, the London chapter of the new Colombian party of the left, Polo Democratico.

Together they reflected the growth of social movements and left parties in Latin America, with the Bolivians and Ecuadorians reflecting the arrival of newer groups of migrants to the UK.[8] Unlike the established Latin American solidarity campaigns supported by British unions, they engaged with Latin American communities in London. Unlike most pre-existing Latin American NGOs and community organisations, they sought to mobilise those communities. This meant not only supporting processes back home but addressing people's actual problems in the UK. In 2008 they started coordinating activities under the umbrella name of the Coordinadora Latinoamericana, providing new blood and a set of allies for LAWAS.

Both inside and outside Unite's Justice for Cleaners campaign, Latin American cleaners' campaigns had gathered pace. In September 2008, five members of a LAWAS cell at the government's National Physical Laboratory (NPL) in south-west London were dismissed for circulating a leaflet complaining of their treatment by bosses. This was the latest episode of a long-running dispute dating back to a large-scale immigration raid at NPL the previous year. The raid had been used to reduce the numbers of the 30-odd cleaning staff, typifying how attacks on employment and immigration rights went hand in hand. While the workers' unions (Unite and civil service union Prospect) restricted themselves to legal advice and representation, the support campaign, formally launched by the newly formed coalition Campaign Against Immigration Controls (CAIC), was characterised by noisy pickets of high-visibility targets. This change marked a major departure in LAWAS's approach to campaigning – one that moved away from an office-based approach and dependence on Unite (undercurrentspaulo, 2009).

For the union, however, such a departure was a matter of concern. Having initially ignored the campaigning, Unite's Regional Secretary Steve Hart warned one of the sacked NPL cleaners that their campaign was being backed by 'extreme groups' – a clear allusion to the CAIC that came out of the second Trade Union and Community Conference against Immigration Controls in April 2008, and which had launched the campaign in support of the sacked NPL cleaners after the immigration raid there was exposed at the conference. Still, not all support was withheld – one union official famously counted picket whistles one by one before handing them over to one of the sacked cleaners for use at a protest.

Perhaps equally worrying for the union leadership was the fear of contagion of a group of cleaners initiating their own actions. This fear was borne out by the response of cleaners at Schroders investment bank who *were* officially organised under the umbrella of J4C when faced with the threat of redundancies as 'payback' for securing the living wage. They heard about the NPL pickets, and were inspired to call their own demonstration, initially without union authorisation. The shop steward at Schroders at the time was a veteran of the 1980s LAWAS, but was not the only one to provide a living link during this period between the old and new LAWAS.

Elsewhere at the University of London's School of Oriental and African Studies (SOAS), a group of Latin American cleaners, including a number linked to MERU, had joined a left wing branch of the public service union Unison in a fight for union recognition, the living wage and against victimisation (Bergos and Hearn, 2010). Unlike at NPL and Schroders, this was the one case of the workers' union branch actively supporting its members.

In November 2008, a watershed moment arrived in terms of links across these three previously isolated campaigns when workers from each of them shared a platform at a public meeting in Elephant and Castle, the traditional heart of London's Latin American community, organised by LAWAS and the Coordinadora with the support of CAIC and London No Borders (Anon, 2011: 11). The meeting celebrated the gains made through worker-led, grassroots action, while reflecting on the challenge of working with mainstream unions. This challenge now extended to the issue of a government amnesty for undocumented workers. Unite had by now decided at the highest level to support London Citizens' 'Strangers into Citizens' campaign for a limited amnesty. The Coordinadora's position on the other hand was that a partial amnesty would divide the community, making some even more vulnerable (Coordinadora Latinoamericana, 2009).

In the New Year, tensions came to a head between LAWAS and Unite. The trigger was a dispute which followed an increasingly familiar pattern: a living wage victory by cleaners at the Willis insurance company in the City of London was followed by a counterattack by the employer on jobs and conditions in the context of a move to a prestigious new building, smashing union organisation in the process. When the shop steward and four others were abruptly made redundant in the middle of relocation negotiations, they held a series of noisy weekly protests against Willis and its cleaning contractor Mitie outside the new building for six months, attracting cleaners from nearby sites and others from LAWAS's support networks (IWGB Cleaners and Facilities Branch, 2009).

LAWAS's new campaigning approach, as typified by the NPL, Willis and later disputes, relied heavily on forging new alliances and generating its own publicity. As a result the organisation became much more visible. Every dispute where the LAWAS banner appeared in support was covered by press releases, interviews and video documentaries. The *Morning Star*, the daily paper supported by the Communist Party of Britain and a number of mainstream unions, carried extensive coverage of the Willis struggle thanks largely to one maverick journalist. In the Spanish-language media, the newspaper *Noticias Latin America* and its successor *The Prisma* provided the most in-depth coverage for years to come, while the bilingual *Frontline Latin America* drew the links between workers' struggles at home and abroad.

Meanwhile the Coordinadora tried to use its collective voice to get the union back on board in the Willis dispute, but the differences between LAWAS and the union over the amnesty issue put paid to this. In the build-up to the May 2009 Strangers into Citizens march in central London, the Coordinadora set out its critique of the partial amnesty proposal through public meetings in the Latin American community and a booklet it published and distributed. A meeting between the Coordinadora and the union to resolve differences over the Willis dispute ended with a union offer to try to restart negotiations on behalf of the sacked cleaners in exchange for the Coordinadora forming part of the union's block on the amnesty march. This deal was not accepted – the Coordinadora marched as planned as part of an independent 'papers for all' block. On 1 May 2009, days prior to the amnesty march, the national union leadership sent a final letter to the Willis cleaners containing a final refusal of support for their cause.

Despite this, the weekly pickets continued, and in the face of ongoing publicity around the dispute, Unite officials decided to launch their own very public counter-campaign. Although this was hardly the first time in the union's history that members had criticised official positions or held unofficial protests, the problem was that Justice for Cleaners was a flagship campaign which was tightly controlled from the top since its inception. Inside the union, this campaign united moderates with key figures in the United Left caucus.[9] As previously, officials developed the theme of extremists trying to rock the boat: 'People need to decide whose side they are on' wrote Regional Secretary Steve Hart in a briefing, contrasting the 'mass of the cleaners' with 'tiny groups seeking to undermine our united campaign'.[10] This did not stop the Willis shop steward achieving a credible 29 out of 80 votes at the inaugural elections of the Justice for Cleaners union branch. The Willis cleaners and their supporters persisted in trying to win the union over. In May 2009 the workers and their supporters were filmed by the union as they delivered a petition at Unite House headquarters in response to the final refusal of support, although not without being challenged by those present.

As LAWAS flexed its new sense of independence, it faced down both the cleaning companies and the union. One leading J4C and LAWAS activist was arrested by immigration officials in a trap sprung by his employer, Lancaster, furious that as a cleaning manager at Schroders he had covertly supported the cleaners' campaign there. He was eventually freed without charges but dismissed from his job. But when a picket was held outside the appeal against his dismissal, union officials reacted by ordering an 'investigation' into him and refusing him access to educational courses (Durango, 2009). Meanwhile, employers and the government continued to combine forces to use immigration raids to terrify cleaning workers, in particular where they were organising. In June 2009, SOAS was hit by a raid which saw nine cleaners detained. A vibrant campaign was mounted in support of them, with students occupying the vice-chancellor's office for several days. The Willis building itself was hit shortly after, provoking an energetic show of solidarity from SOAS cleaners and others. But rather than express solidarity, Unite officers resorted to increasingly outlandish attacks, such as claiming that activists raising the possibility of non-cooperation with immigration checks were being 'paid by the Cleaning Bosses to attack the cleaners'. They also claimed that other unions such as Unison and the transport union RMT (Rail, Maritime and Transport Workers) had brought immigration raids upon their members by not organising properly (Kane, 2009). It later emerged that they were anxious to play down the raids for fear of losing potential members. But for Latin American and other migrant workers, the fear was real enough.

Ironically, despite these problems, the campaigns that LAWAS had supported breathed new life into the organisation, winning it friends across different unions and the Latin American community. It had not run the campaigns, but they became a symbolic point of unity for them. Nowhere was this better expressed than at LAWAS's fifth assembly, held in August 2009. The largest yet, it elected a new committee that for the first time represented almost all the main Latin American nationalities in London, as well as the largest ever female participation. The role of women would stand out in the intense years of activity that followed. During this tumultuous period, LAWAS had continued to operate its office out of Unite, where it continued to recruit into the union. Despite everything, the tactic remained to continue the fight from within. But as was clear at the 2009 assembly, the relationship with the union's regional administration was on a knife edge. Not only did the union want out but so did voices within LAWAS, and the inevitable loss of its office in September 2009 was met with anger but also perhaps some relief. Another somewhat greater loss was experienced at the same time with the death of co-founder Ernesto Leal, who since 2005 had been too ill to take part (Anon, 2009; Latin American Workers Association, 2009).

Over the next two years, the Association focused on combining workplace protests with educational and cultural events. Individual casework was given less priority than maintaining and building a vibrant activist base. New partnerships were built, with the Ecuadorian government to provide an advice surgery, and the Workers Educational Association for basic skills and language courses. The National Union of Journalists provided a temporary new office. For those involved this was an intense period full of innovation. A pop-up centre was set up in the Elephant and Castle shopping centre, a traditional hub of Latin American life in south London. The language classes led to an autonomous language exchange around the corner at South Bank University – LAWAS's new weekend base. LAWAS also helped set up the Latin American Coalition Against the Cuts (COLACOR), which among other things supported the fight to save the Golden Years day centre for Latin American pensioners, and worked with Black Activists Rising Against Cuts and local anti-cuts groups in south London as part of the then burgeoning movement against the austerity measures of the recently elected Coalition government.[11] Its activist base also crossed over with the newly formed Latin American Recognition Campaign in support of ethnic minority recognition (Però, 2014).

Nevertheless, the thorny issue of how LAWAS should organise and relate to trade unions remained unresolved. At University College London and UBS bank, leading activists were victimised and the support campaigns brought unprecedented levels of solidarity from the student movement and the wider trade union movement respectively, while again testing relations with Unite. In April 2010, LAWAS members made a concerted attempt to stand for election in Unite's new Cleaners Branch, but were refused on procedural grounds. They walked out en masse with their supporters.

There was little thirst left for combating such bureaucratic manoeuvres, and so LAWAS began to discuss alternative ways to organise workers who might otherwise have joined Unite. An organised debate was held between those who proposed creating a branch of the small, direct action-oriented Industrial Workers of the World (IWW), and others who proposed setting up a new union open to all migrant workers. The former carried the day, in part because the IWW offered an existing organisational framework. The new IWW Cleaners Branch had its baptism of fire six months later in mid-2011, when it supported workers engaged in a series of wildcat strikes over unpaid wages at London's prestigious Guildhall complex, home to the City of London Corporation which governs the capital's financial district.

Several of the Latin American worker-activists in the Guildhall dispute had arrived recently from Spain. They represented a new group present in the struggles of London's Latin American workforce in London – those escaping the Southern European countries worst hit by the 2008 global economic crisis. As European Union citizens with the right to work, they were not hampered by problems of immigration status and sometimes came with experiences of a more combative approach to labour relations. Notwithstanding the desperate conditions in which they sometimes arrived, having lost employment, and then often their own homes due to repossession by the banks in Spain, their arrival would energise the movement for years to come.

A full discussion of the subsequent history of LAWAS and its offshoots remains outside the scope of this chapter and has been partially addressed elsewhere (for example, B, 2009; Kirkpatrick, 2014), so I shall provide only the briefest of summaries here. From mid-2011 a series of internal divisions meant its core activists, having to some extent learned their art in LAWAS, went on to work on different projects. Notable among these was the IWW cleaners' branch, which on the heels of the Guildhall dispute exploded in terms of growth and activity, drawing on years of potential and frustration among Latin American workers in London and energised by the new arrivals from Spain. This branch eventually went solo to form a new union, the Independent Workers of Great Britain (IWGB), as if reverting to the original alternative proposal for LAWAS to convert itself into an independent union. Elsewhere LAWAS activists with personal experience of the use of immigration powers against migrant workers felt that after years of marches and conferences it was time to take direct action, and helped set up the Anti Raids Network – a practical project to resist immigration raids in the workplace and the community (Cuervo, 2014; Jones, 2012). Other ex-LAWAS members became active on other fronts, including a variety of trade unions, with some returning to work with Unite or staying with the IWW. Others still began working with organisations supporting female victims of domestic violence in the Latin American community. A reduced core group continued to manage extremely popular weekly Saturday sessions in London's Southbank University, mixing the language exchange with employment rights workshops. These sessions continued until the university chose to restrict community access to its facilities, and most activities ceased in 2012.

CONCLUSION

Unlike its predecessor, the LAWAS of 2002 onwards was born after two decades of sustained attacks on workers' rights in the UK, and its members faced precarious conditions in the cut-throat world of outsourced contract cleaning. But they brought with them a trajectory of struggle against such attacks in their own countries, and LAWAS got much of its initial energy from those who had come from that most risky of environments for any trade unionist – Colombia. On one level, the trade union movement which LAWAS members encountered in the UK embraced them: it had its own traditions of international solidarity and in theory at least the new organising approach was, as in the US, prepared to engage with deunionised sectors in which migrant workers played a major part. But this approach contained its own orthodoxies which sometimes prevented it from responding positively when workers themselves took the lead. The approach was also taken up at a time when both policy and practice were in many ways much more timid than those of the 1970s.[12]

The Association relied during its existence on the sheer willpower of a revolving door of worker-activists, and often lived on the brink of self-destruction, but at its best remained a *sui generis* organisation by the workers, for the workers. Ultimately it was never institutionalised, although this was mainly a result of not resolving the debate around how to put it on a firmer footing. What is certain is that it gained a reputation which belied its fragile structures, and maybe lasted longer than anyone would imagine under such circumstances.

NOTES

1. There have been several variations on the name since 2002. On early publications it has also appeared as Asociacion de Trabajadores Latinoamericanos (ASTRAL), and sometimes called informally Asociacion Latinoamericana de Trabajadores. It was popularly known as the *sindicato latino* among workers. In English it was often informally called LAWA, but in 2006 the Association decided to officially use the abbreviation LAWAS, in order for it not to be confused with LAWA (Latin American Women's Aid).
2. T&G refers to the Transport and General Workers Union, sometimes also abbreviated as TGWU. In 2007 it merged with leading white collar union

Amicus to form Unite. The union is especially strong in the private sector and is Britain's largest union alongside Unison, which represents public sector workers. In this article I have referred to both the T&G and Unite depending on the period being discussed.

3. The late 1970s also saw the start of significant emigration from Brazil, but LAWAS appears to have remained a largely Spanish-language affair in both its 1980s and 2000s versions.

4. For an overview of Tennant's wider activity see GLATUC (2014).

5. My own first experience of LAWAS in action was when asked by one activist to interpret at a meeting between cleaners and local management at London's Royal College of Surgeons, because the employer, like many others at the time, was exploiting a loophole in the law to subtract national holidays from the minimum annual entitlement.

6. Author's interview with Julio Mayor and Mario Patino (2003).

7. These figures were disputed by the union. This was mainly because when LAWAS made contact with workers in a building which then led to an organising effort, the names of the broader group were recorded and approached via mail-outs and telephone calls to take part in LAWAS events. A formal membership system was never implemented.

8. A fuller discussion of the makeup of the Coordinadora, and the difference between the Latin American solidarity campaigns which joined it (Colombia Solidarity Campaign, Hands Off Venezuela) and their well-funded counterparts operating in the mainstream of the British trade union movement is outside the scope of this chapter .

9. The United Left is a caucus within Unite. The division mirrored that in union leadership elections that year, when the United Left provided the main backing for the successful candidacy of long-serving official Len McCluskey against others, including runner-up Jerry Hicks, who ran on a grassroots, pro-direct action platform and supported LAWAS during the UBS dispute. Some Unite branches remained supportive of LAWAS.

10. Letter from Steve Hart, Regional Secretary of Unite Region 1 to union officers, 26 June 2009, forwarded to the author's union branch.

11. See for example, Jimenez (2011), and an excellent documentary on COLACOR produced by a LAWAS video activist (IWGB Cleaners and Facilities Branch, 2011).

12. For a critical discussion of the organising approach, see Cohen (2009).

REFERENCES

Alberti, G. (2013). 'Transient Working Lives: Migrant Women's Everyday Politics in London's Hospitality Industry'. Unpublished doctoral dissertation, School of Social Sciences, Cardiff University.

Anon. (2002). 'Latinos en Londres se unen'. *Express News*, 30 January, 11.

Anon. (2007). '£60m Surplus at the BBC, So Why Aren't Cleaners Getting a Living Wage?'. *Hammersmith and Shepherds Bush Gazette*, June 29, 5.

Anon. (2009). 'Ernesto Leal, Political Activist'. *The Scotsman*, 29 November. www. scotsman.com/news/obituaries/ernesto-leal-political-activist-1–770168 (accessed August 2015).

Anon. (2011). 'Meeting en el Pullens Centre de Elephant and Castle: Cleners [*sic*] despedidos callan por temor de retorsiones'. *Expreso Latino*, December, 11.

Ardill, N. and Cross, N. (1987). *Undocumented Lives: Britain's Unauthorized Migrant Workers*. London: Runnymede Trust.

B, R. (2009). 'Crisis in the Cleaning Sector'. *Mute*. www.metamute.org/editorial/ articles/crisis-cleaning-sector (accessed August 2015).

Bergos, M. and Hearn, J. (2010). 'Learning from the Cleaners? Trade Union Activism among Low Paid Latin American Migrant Workers at the University of London'. Working Paper No. 7, Identity, Citizenship and Migration Centre, University of Nottingham.

Cohen, S. (2009). 'Opening Pandora's Box: The Paradox of Institutionalised Organising'. In Gall, G. (Ed.), *The Future of Union Organising: Building for Tomorrow*. London: Palgrave Macmillan.

Coordinadora Latinoamericana. (2009). *Amnistia para algunos o papeles para todos?* London: Coordinadora Latinoamericana. https://lacomunauk.wordpress. com/2009/10/24/amnistia-para-unos-o-papeles-para-todos/ and https:// thecommune.wordpress.com/2009/10/18/amnesty-for-some-or-papers-for-all/ (accessed August 2015).

Cuervo, J. C. (2014). 'José Luís Sánchez Arancibia: The True Story of a Battle Won'. *The Prisma*, 6 September. www.theprisma.co.uk/2014/09/06/jose-luis-sanchez-arancibia-story-of-a-battle-won/ (accessed August 2015).

Durango, A. (2009). 'Alberto Durango: 'I am for Justice and the Truth'. *The Commune*. http://thecommune.wordpress.com/2009/07/02/alberto-durango-i-am-for-justice-and-the-truth (accessed August 2015).

GLATUC (Greater London Association of Trade Union Councils). (2014). 'BOB TENNANT died on Monday, 6 January, his 65th birthday (6/1/1949–6/1/2014)'. Obituary. www.glatuc.org.uk/news_detail1.php?id=223 (accessed August 2015).

IWGB Cleaners and Facilities Branch. (2009). Willis demo1, 13 November. www. youtube.com/watch?v=Hvnq38sYsxQ (accessed August 2015).

—— (2011,). *COLACOR*, 3 March. www.youtube.com/watch?v=9CqqfVLsqsg (accessed August 2015).

Jimenez, M. (2011). 'LAWA reports on 26th March'. *Lambeth Save Our Services*. http:// lambethsaveourservices.org/2011/04/04/lawa-reports-on-26th-march/ (accessed August 2015).

Jones, S. (2012). 'How London's Latin Americans are Fighting Back'. *The Guardian*, 22 June. www.theguardian.com/uk/2012/jun/22/london-latin-americans (accessed August 2015).

Kane, C. (2009). 'Exposed: SOAS Unison, RMT and Unite Cleaner Activists in the Pay of the Bosses'. *The Commune.* http://thecommune.wordpress.com/2009/08/19/exposed-soas-unison-rmt-and-unite-cleaner-activists-in-the-pay-of-the-bosses/ (accessed August 2015).

Kirkpatrick, J. (2014). 'The IWW Cleaners Branch Union in the United Kingdom'. In Ness, I. (Ed.), *New Forms of Worker Organization: The Syndicalist and Autonomist Restoration of Class Struggle Unionism,* (pp. 233–57). Oakland, CA: PM Press.

Latin American Workers Association. (2007). *Latin American Migrant Workers Detained.* Press release. http://london.noborders.org.uk/news/latin-american-migrant-workers-detained (accessed August 2015).

—— (2009). 'Tribute to Ernesto Leal and More Unite Attacks on Latin American Workers Association'. *The Commune.* http://thecommune.wordpress.com/2009/11/15/tribute-to-ernesto-leal-and-more-unite-attacks-on-latin-american-workers-association/ (accessed August 2015).

Però, D. (2014). 'Class Politics and Migrants: Collective Action among New Migrant Workers'. *Sociology,* 48(6), 1156–72.

Sassen, S. (2001). *The Global City: New York, London, Tokyo.* Princeton, NJ: Princeton University Press.

Silver, S. (2011). 'Chilean Fascism: An Interview with Ernesto Leal'. http://stevesilver.org.uk/blog/chilean-fascism-an-interview-with-ernesto-leal/ (accessed August 2015).

undercurrentspaulo. (2009,). *Amey, Julio and Pedro,* 3 Januar. www.youtube.com/watch?v=ho7W4-RBhKc (accessed August 2015).

Uribe Marin, M. del P. (2009). 'David contra Golia'. *Noticias Latin America,* 17.

Vicente, G. (1996), 'Latin Americans in London: Migration and the Politics of Not Belonging'. Unpublished masters dissertation for Institute of Latin American Studies, London.

FURTHER READING

For long-term ethnographic work on LAWAS and its relationship with T&G/Unite and other community organisations, see the work of Davide Però.

An unofficial online repository of LAWAS statements and interviews covering the events of 2009–10, most of which LAWAS only published in email bulletins or leaflets, can be accessed at https://thecommune.wordpress.com/ and its Spanish sister site http://lacomunauk.wordpress.com (accessed August 2015).

The LAWAS Facebook page documents some of its activity in the 2010–12 period: www.facebook.com/LatinAmericanWorkersAssociation?fref=ts (accessed August 2015).

7

Lessons from Migrant Workers' Organisation and Mobilisation in Switzerland

Vasco Pedrina

To understand the Swiss trade union experience in migrant workers' organising and mobilising, it is necessary first to describe the context. Thus, this chapter begins by describing the developments that, in the 1960s, led the building and wood workers' union of the time – as the first union in Switzerland and one of the first in Europe – to organise migrant workers on a large scale. It also examines the structures put in place and the political campaigns that were carried out to achieve that goal. In addition, emphasis will be placed on the impact that the integration of migrant workers into the unions has had on the orientation of trade union policies. Finally, a look at the result of the latest Swiss referendum ballot on immigration policy, of 2 September 2014, unfortunately shows that nothing is ever definitively won in the struggle against xenophobia and for equal rights.

ROLE OF MIGRANT WORKERS IN THE ECONOMY AND EVOLUTION OF MIGRATION POLICY

Behind only Luxembourg, Switzerland's migrant density is the second highest in Europe: 24 per cent of a total population of eight million. That is twice as high as in Germany, Italy and Austria or four times as high as in France. More than a third of the hours worked in the country are performed by migrant workers. Entire branches of the economy could not operate without them. This also reflects highly restrictive naturalisation policies.[1]

At the beginning of the twentieth century, Switzerland was still a country of emigration. But since the end of the Second World War, hardly any Swiss have had to emigrate out of necessity. Thanks to its still intact industry, Switzerland's growth in the 40 years of post-war prosperity was such that the country had an ever more massive recourse to immigrant labour. At the end of the war, there were large reserves of job-seeking workers in Southern Europe. As a result, successive waves of hundreds of thousands of Italians, then Spanish and Turkish workers, and still later Yugoslavs and Portuguese, came to work in Switzerland (Wicker et al., 2003).

The Swiss authorities' policies to regulate immigration have gone through different phases. After the democratic revolution of 1848 and until the early twentieth century, a period marked by the country's industrial take-off, official immigration policy was characterised by openness. Switzerland was at the time a country of refuge for many of the trade union activists and political refugees who had an impact on the history of the Swiss labour movement. The policy of restricting immigration by quotas began during the First World War and continued after it, under the influence of unemployment, conservative movements, and Nazism-Fascism. A return to an open immigration policy, at least in relation to the citizens of the European Union (EU), coincided with the entry into force in 2000 of the bilateral agreements between Switzerland and the EU. As a result of a popular initiative launched by the populist and xenophobic right, the Swiss people decided in a vote on 9 February 2014 to call into question the Switzerland-EU agreement on the free movement of persons, not without provoking a crisis in the country's relations with the EU, the outcome of which is still uncertain.[2]

The trade union movement is based on the principles of equality and solidarity. But the history of the relations between national and immigrant workers shows that in practice the application of these principles is not at all simple. Although, in its origins, the trade union movement saw itself as internationalist, the 'age of extremes' (Hobsbawm, 1994) – the period of the two world wars, and the Cold

War and its influence on society – led it to yield to the destructive temptations of nationalism.

In the period of large-scale immigration during the 1950s and 1960s, not only did xenophobic forces call on the Swiss authorities to implement a more restrictive immigration policy, but so did trade unions, under pressure from their national base. National workers regarded the new labour force from outside the country as a threat to wages and jobs, and were receptive to the lure of xenophobic voices. In any capitalist system, some employers have no qualms about using migrant workers to put downward pressure on wages. There are two ways to resist that pressure: either a common, national-immigrant struggle against wage and social dumping, or a demand for quotas in the hope that the shortage of labour thus created will automatically lead to an upward pressure on wages. History has proven the second path to be a dead end. For one thing, any quota system is inevitably accompanied by a discriminatory status for migrant workers. And discriminatory situations lead to deteriorated wages and working conditions, in a wage dumping dynamic. Moreover, in economic booms, employers circumvent the quota system in order to hire undocumented migrant workers, under deplorable conditions. Lastly, such discrimination is a source of division among workers, undermining the capacity for trade union struggle and bargaining (Alleva, 2001).

One of the main goals of the quota system, with its discriminatory rules, was to do everything possible to prevent a majority of the migrant workers from staying permanently in the country. The status supposed to best serve the purpose of realising the principle of a constant rotation of migrants was that of the seasonal worker. In its first phase, seasonal workers were throughout their lives unable to acquire even an annual residence permit. From a human rights perspective, the seasonal workers' status was a disgrace for Switzerland: demeaning 'border medical examinations', prohibition to change jobs, inhumane prohibition of family reunification and tens of thousands of hidden children. In sum, a system that is reminiscent of yesterday's South African apartheid or the *kafala* system for migrant workers in today's Qatar (see Chapter 3).

ORGANISING MIGRANT WORKERS INTO
SWISS TRADE UNIONS IN THE 1960S

The history of the international trade union movement shows that, more often than not, national unions have missed the boat of integrating migrant workers into their ranks. Yet the Swiss trade union movement was among the forerunners in this endeavour, and among those that have been most successful in it. Among the key factors was the foresight both of a number of open-minded national trade union leaders and of politically mature migrant workers. That foresight lay not just in the conviction that only in unity is there strength, but also in the recognition – against the conventional wisdom – that labour immigration was not a passing phenomenon and that despite all the discriminatory rules to impose rotation, even seasonal workers would one day be able to stay in the country with their families.[3]

Although of moderate social democratic outlook, in the mid-1960s the leaders of the building and wood workers' union already made the strategic choice to actively organise migrant workers, given the huge growth in immigrant labour on building sites. They did that despite the 'risk' of there being Italian or Spanish Communist Party activists among the migrants. For their part, those parties made their contribution by calling on their members to join the Swiss unions. It must be said this was far from being possible in all the country's unions because in the midst of the Cold War, the 'red, Stalinist scare' was deeply rooted among some of them. As a result, other unions opened their doors to migrants only 10–15 years later than the building workers did. This was not without consequences. Today, immigrants are under-represented in some of those unions. By contrast, 20 years later, the membership of the building workers' union, thanks to its immigrant members, has exceeded that of the metal workers' union to make it Switzerland's largest trade union (Schweizerischer Gewerkschaftsbund, 2007).

The foresight mentioned earlier related also, and especially, to the modalities applied to achieve the organisation of migrant workers and to ensure that the trade union would truly become their organisation, their new homeland. Two key elements of the chosen strategy proved decisive in achieving the desired breakthrough. The first of these was the decision to appoint, as union officials, nationals of the countries of origin for the tasks of member recruitment and worker organising. A great advantage was that in the pool of newcomers there were many socialist and Communist Party activists with experience in social struggles. The earlier mentioned problem of the so-called 'red scare' was resolved pragmatically by the foremost Swiss trade union leader at the time, Ezio Canonica. The deal offered to the communist activists was as follows: 'We are appointing you as trade union officials although you are communist party members, but you have to promise us to refrain from any active engagement for your party here in Switzerland'.[4] The second element was the decision to create special structures for migrant workers within the union, allowing them to organise themselves into 'interest groups', either according to nationality, language or on an intercultural basis.

By recruiting Italian, and then Spanish, Turkish, Portuguese and Yugoslav migrants as union officials, the trade union resolved, first of all, the problem of communicating with the newcomers. Moreover, it was made much easier for the migrant workers to establish relations of confidence and identification with the union. And the creation of the 'interest groups' made it possible for the migrants to operate together in their own culture and thereby to articulate, without insurmountable obstacles, their demands.

In retrospect, it can be said that history has vindicated those who dared to leave the beaten path of 'structural conservatism', which is widely rooted in trade union traditions, and in other European countries has to this day often prevented the large-scale organisation of migrant workers. By the end of the 1980s, the building and wood workers' union had 130,000 members, of whom two-thirds were immigrants (Fluder et al., 1991).

THE ORGANISATION OF MIGRANT WORKERS
IN TODAY'S TRADE UNION STRUCTURES

Before looking at trade union policy issues, it is useful to outline the present union organisation of immigrants, on the basis of the example of the country's largest trade union, Unia. The union was created through the merger in 2004 of four private sector unions, including the building and metal workers' unions. It organises some 200,000 workers, half of whom are of immigrant origin (Rieger et al., 2008; Schweizerischer Gewerkschaftsbund, 2007). Their nationalities vary according to the successive cycles of immigration, and their total share of the union's membership increases year by year.

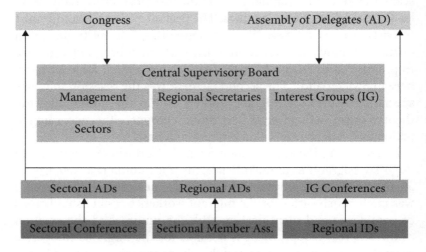

Figure 7.1   Migrant workers' organisation into 'interest groups' within the union.

Language-based interest groups (IGs) – for Portuguese, Serbians, Albanians, etc. – now exist only in the German-speaking part of Switzerland on a local basis (see Figure 7.1). Elsewhere, the IGs are structured more regionally and on an intercultural basis, which does not prevent them from occasionally holding special meetings in order to address an issue that concerns a single nationality. The IGs are statutory bodies, with representation rights at the levels of the sectoral, regional and national committees. They naturally have the right to present proposals at assembly and congress meetings, as shown in Figure 7.2.

Immigrant union members receive – in addition to the services and benefits offered to all members – a range of specific services. Information is disseminated in several languages. Depending on requirements, leaflets can be translated into eight or more languages[5]

Unia – migrant workers' structures as trade union bodies

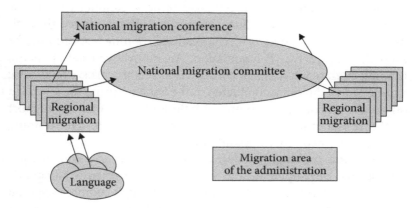

Figure 7.2   Unia structures.

and distributed in workplaces and neighbourhoods, or at meetings of immigrant associations. Alongside the regular union journals in Italian, French and German, published every week or two weeks, a newsletter in Spanish, Portuguese, Serbo-Croatian and Albanian is published every two to three months. Thematic brochures are produced in different languages and adapted to the needs of each nationality. There is a regular use of immigrant media to disseminate trade union messages. Immigrant associations are an important contact channel. But there is close collaboration also with the consular sections of embassies. Finally, increasingly close cooperation with the trade unions in the countries of origin has helped to develop an information system aimed at migrants before they leave their countries. The information for seasonal workers coming to Switzerland for the first time – particularly through meetings before the season starts – has rendered valuable services. In Switzerland's frontier zones, full-time union services have been set up in the offices of the unions of the countries of origin. As unionised immigrants participate also in Switzerland's regular union structures, such as the occupational groups, the union is obliged to provide interpretation services at those meetings, which represents a substantial investment. But that is the price to be paid for effectively promoting participation and integration.

A large effort is made in training, both in language courses to promote integration and in remedial basic vocational training or professional development. Such courses are often arranged through joint or cooperation bodies with specialised training institutions, like the Italian-based ECAP Foundation. An innovative example is the training courses for seasonal construction sector workers to acquire a professional diploma, conducted in the winter, during the so-called off season, and organised jointly with the employers with the support of the labour ministries of the countries of origin. The training courses have allowed thousands of unskilled seasonal workers to acquire basic training, to advance both in their pay and in their professional development, and to become permanently integrated in Switzerland. As regards trade union training, it comprises special courses by language group or on a multicultural basis for immigrant trade union members.

THE BIG BATTLES FOR EQUAL RIGHTS

To ensure success in the trade union organising of migrant workers, it is essential to offer the services they need most, such as information and levers for the defence of their rights in relation to their employers, for their everyday life in the host country, for everything concerning their social security, etc. But in attaining visibility and the media and political impact needed to be recognised as an attractive partner, trade union campaigns for equal rights are decisive.

When in the 1960s and 1970s, the building workers as the first Swiss union began the long march to organise migrant workers, the union centred its priorities on the struggle against seasonal worker status. As those workers were crammed into unsanitary barracks on the fringes of cities or large construction sites, the first objective was the battle to improve their housing conditions. As they were subjected to pay discrimination, the union used collective agreement renewal negotiations to mobilise these migrant workers for pay parity. On the political front, the union fought against the border medical examinations imposed on entering the country at the beginning of each season. It also challenged the rules that stipulated that even after several seasons of work they were still ineligible for an annual permit allowing them to bring their families to Switzerland and that they were forbidden to change jobs, making them totally dependent on the employer's goodwill. Those battles led the union, from the late 1970s onwards, to demand the abolition of seasonal worker status, to organise the first national demonstration on the matter in 1980, and to support a popular initiative to that end, which, however, was rejected by voters in a 1981 ballot. The employers' propaganda – with warnings of economic catastrophe if seasonal worker status was abolished – had had its effects. It was not until the end of the 1980s that the objective was attained, in a new trade union offensive conducted during the political debate on how to regulate Switzerland's bilateral relations with the EU. That offensive consisted of three elements. The first of these was developing arguments that, while being based on human rights, also included a line of economic reasoning that was able to respond to the fears that had led to failure in the vote ten years before. Second, this involved persuading the governments of the migrant workers' countries of origin, especially Italy, Spain and Portugal, to put political pressure on Switzerland. Third, it included mobilising workers in Switzerland within a dynamic of equal rights and unity, raising their awareness that the one does not go without the other (Schweizerischer Gewerkschaftsbund, 2004; Unia, 2008, 2014).

In September 1990, the building workers' union staged a national demonstration for the abolition of seasonal worker status. The demonstration went into the country's labour history not only because of its size (20,000 demonstrators), but because it marked the beginning of a shift to combative trade unionism, refocusing on workers' mobilisation.

The trade union campaign, which could have succeeded in 1992 had the Swiss people not narrowly rejected the European Economic Area agreement with the EU, finally led to the abolition of seasonal worker status, with the entry into force in 2000 of the Switzerland-EU bilateral agreements. This campaign has served as a point of reference for all the campaigns that the unions have carried out in many fields over the past 30 years. These campaigns include ones to address the particular needs of different nationalities. Examples from the 1990s include: a campaign for equal rights for workers from the former Yugoslavia as compared to the treatment of workers from the EU; a struggle for new eligibility rules for seasonal workers on unemployment benefit in Portugal during the off season; and EU citizens' pension fund rights. The 2000s saw the long and successful battle to end visa requirements in the Dublin/Schengen area (ensuring free movement within the EU, but imposing an 'iron curtain' at its borders) for migrant workers from non-EU member former Yugoslav countries; and the still ongoing battle for the reintroduction of a bilateral social security agreement with Kosovo. Other campaigns have addressed the particular needs of migrant workers within the context of sectoral collective bargaining battles as well as within lawmaking processes. In that connection, one can refer to the two campaigns, in the 2000s, for a minimum wage of 3,000 Swiss Francs (CHF) and, starting in the 2010s, for a minimum wage of CHF4,000. Those campaigns opened the way for a significant increase in lower wages, which was especially beneficial to migrant workers – even despite the Swiss electorate's rejection of a statutory minimum wage in May 2014. Mention should also be made of the two political campaigns of the 1990s and the 2010s for the regularisation of undocumented migrant workers, which were only partly successful (like the right to school education for the 'clandestine children' of seasonal or undocumented workers, and the right to health insurance for all, including 'undocumented' migrants); and finally those campaigns – unfortunately unsuccessful – to obtain the right to vote at least at communal and cantonal levels, and the right to facilitated naturalisation (with, as partial successes, the introduction of the possibility of dual nationality and the abolition of a very high naturalisation tax).[6]

The campaigns are carried out through the use of petitions, referendums (for example, against tightening asylum law), popular initiatives (for example, for the right to vote), symbolic actions or demonstrations accompanying political pressure on the Swiss authorities and those of the countries of origin. In short, in the words of Vania Alleva, co-president of Unia:

Equality of opportunity, participation and residence permit security are the essential levers for all forms of integration. Their promotion must go beyond the world of work and encompass all spheres of action, also at the political level. In that action in Switzerland, the trade unions have a central role to play ... The Swiss industrial unions are among the only ones in the world where from one third to two thirds of the workers the unions organise are without political rights. The trade unions are, in effect, the only place where migrant workers can – at least indirectly – assert political influence. (Alleva, 2001)

THE BIG BATTLES TO ENSURE UNITY BETWEEN
NATIONALS AND IMMIGRANTS

A logic of unity between nationals and immigrants can never be assumed, even in a country where there is a long tradition of fighting for equal rights. It is not even sure to exist between long-time immigrant residents and newly arrived migrants. This effort will always be marked by ups and downs.

Even within unions, tensions can run high, especially at times when trade union policy is undergoing change. For example, the decision to fight for the abolition of seasonal worker status was at the time contested by a conservative tendency among Swiss trade unionists, which saw the move as a threat to the material benefits that the union had gradually acquired during the years through the quotas system. Indeed, the flat-rate contributions paid to the union by the companies for seasonal workers, through the joint fund[7] provided by the collective agreement for the construction industry, did in fact bring in quite a lot of money. It was of course used to deliver services to that category of migrant workers, but it also helped to finance trade union structures.

Those tensions have regularly resurfaced, especially on the occasion of the many national votes on popular initiatives directed, since 1970, against immigrants, and then, especially since the mid-1990s, against asylum seekers, initiatives that have marked the country's political agenda. On each occasion, the xenophobic right has sought to challenge the legitimacy of the unions in defending national workers. Beyond persuasion through information and campaigns, the best antidote against such xenophobic venom remains a united struggle for common objectives. The 1990s and 2000s have been character-ised by many political battles and company-level (and industry-level) strikes in which such unity was obviously the key to what has been successfully achieved. In a cycle of actions, which began in 1992 with the one-week strike in the marble and granite sector against the dismantling of the collective agreement and has continued since then with numerous company-level strikes in various other sectors, a climax was reached in 2001–2, with the construction industry's first national strike in 50 years. While in the political arena a rise in retirement age was being contemplated, thanks to determined mobilisation and unity actions, in which immigrant workers played a big role, it was possible to win an early retirement scheme that rapidly lowered the retirement age for building workers from 65 to 60 years, with a pension at 90 per cent of their wages (Baumann and Zenth, 2002).

Integrating migrant workers into trade union structures is not like going on a Sunday stroll. It is not enough to offer them space in their own structures, as in Unia's IGs. The biggest challenge is their integration into a union's ordinary structures and especially into executive committees and bodies at all levels. There is not only the language barrier, but also cultural differences – and the 'home advantage' of nationals plays a role too. It's a long process, taking more than just a few years, to arrive at a point of balanced representation. And as in the struggle for gender equality, without lasting promotional measures, there is a permanent danger of regression, all the more so since the rotation of migration flows continually raises new integration challenges. That today five of the nine members of Unia's board are *secondos* (second-generation foreigners), several the sons of former seasonal workers, and that about half the union's officials are of immigrant origin or of dual nationality, nonetheless represents an achievement that the union can legitimately be proud of.

In Switzerland, trade unions have become the civil society organisation that plays the biggest role in immigrants' integration and in preventing tensions between national groups. Naturally, that also applies to immigrants among each other. In that respect, the toughest test was posed by the Balkan wars during the 1990s. At the time, the building and industrial workers' union alone organised more than

15,000 Serbian, Croatian and Kosovo-Albanian workers. Even within its own ranks there were acute tensions between these nationalities. Suddenly, each national group felt it was being disadvantaged. Protest letters and petitions were circulated and threats of mass resignations from the union were quite frequent. Trade union leaders were even confronted by death threats on the appointment of a trade union official who was not of some group's desired nationality. In such a context, preserving unity becomes an extremely difficult balancing act. But the union succeeded without the loss of members, thanks to several measures. These included an exclusive focus on defending the interests of workers in Switzerland, regardless of their ethnic origins. Further, by maintaining strict political neutrality, the union refused to allow itself to become involved in the conflicts in former Yugoslavia, a stance that didn't prevent humanitarian support. To that end, the union successfully committed itself to making it possible for Kosovo-Albanian seasonal workers – when the war was at its worst – to bring their families to Switzerland. It also stopped any measures that might lead to interethnic conflicts, like the refusal to yield to any mafia-type pressure, which could corrupt the organisation. Opting for those measures was predictably criticised as opportunistic by some activists, but they helped to preserve unity within the movement. This contribution of trade unions to their communities, their role as a force integrating immigrants into host country societies, is still greatly underestimated.

THE IMPACT OF MIGRANT WORKERS' INTEGRATION ON TRADE UNION POLICY ORIENTATIONS

The integration of a large number of migrant workers into our ranks has enabled us not only to avoid the decline in union membership experienced by the unions in Europe that missed the boat. It has also, over time, changed the union's culture in the sense of 'unity in diversity', and it has, above all, contributed to increasing its combativeness.

On the world stage, Swiss trade unionism had for a long time the reputation of being a rather conservative movement in an economically privileged country. Today, although Switzerland remains a country with a high standard of living, its unions – in particular, the inter-industrial union Unia and the Swiss Federation of Trade Unions (USS) – are considered among the most innovative and combative in the European trade union movement. Much of the credit for that must go to the unionised immigrants. How did that happen? From the second half of the 1960s onwards, by opening the doors to activists of immigrant origin from diverse political backgrounds, and selecting union officials from among them, the building workers' union of those years laid in a timely manner the foundation for the trade union development that took place during the period of the largest inflow of migrants. That opening also facilitated, from the 1980s onwards, the integration, into a trade union movement hitherto controlled by conservative social democrats, of a new generation of activists from the extra-parliamentary leftist movements launched in 1968.

The combination of those two new forces with what remained of the combative tradition of the national trade unionists formed during the post-war struggles made it possible, starting in the early 1990s and based on the building workers' union, to launch a general movement for a reorientation of trade union strategy towards dynamic and combative trade unionism. The same forces also at last cleared the way for the first steps in a profound reorganisation of trade union structures towards inter-industrial trade unionism, capable of bringing about the envisaged new policy orientations. None too soon, as the decades of post-war growth and of union strategy being increasingly limited to backroom negotiations with the employers (that is, in the absence of the pressure of collective action) had terribly weakened trade union workplace networks and therefore also the unions' mobilisation capability on both the collective bargaining and political fields. The long Swiss crisis of the 1990s and the breakthrough of anti-union neoliberalism dramatically exposed those deficiencies.

Consequently, a race against time was launched: regaining the will and power to strike in the social field and building a renewed referendum capacity in the political arena had become a matter of life or death. In the end, the race was won. Owing to successive mergers starting in 1992 – first in the private sector, then in the public sector – within the two main trade union confederations, a policy of openness at the confederal level to originally professional-type associations, and the gradual rediscovery of strike action and the anchoring of the right to strike in the Federal Constitution in 2000, it has been possible to revive a movement that had almost slipped into political insignificance. That turnaround would almost certainly have been impossible without the input of immigrant activists and officials. Still today, although the new generations of immigrants no longer share the history of the party activists that emerged from the anti-fascist struggles, the immigrant component remains a force for progress and dynamism within the Swiss unions.

CRISIS IN EUROPE, SOCIAL DUMPING AND THE RISE OF XENOPHOBIA: YET ANOTHER CHALLENGE TO WORKING CLASS UNITY

On 9 February 2014, the Swiss people said 'Yes' – in a very close vote – to a popular initiative, launched by the party of the populist and xenophobic right, demanding the removal of the free movement of persons between Switzerland and the EU, through the reintroduction of a quota system. This amounts to a deep rift, with serious implications for the Swiss economy and labour market, as well as for the trade unions and their strategic stance. A fresh surge in immigration over the past ten years, linked both to the health of the Swiss economy and to the crisis in Europe, has played its role. But there are other reasons for the voting result, which, among other things, relate to the refusal of the employers and the political authorities to accept a further reinforcement of the social measures flanking the free movement of persons (see below). The EU's fading attractiveness as a project for peace and social progress, after five years of brutal austerity policies, was the final straw. But if the new constitutional article is applied to the letter, it will have the effect of fundamentally calling into question all the agreements and relations between Switzerland and the EU, which with 58 per cent of Swiss exports and 75 per cent of its imports is the country's principal economic partner. It will also reintroduce, via quotas, a system of discriminatory statuses for immigrants that would sooner or later eliminate most of our equal rights gains in the fields of wages and social benefits, hard won over three decades of struggle (Alleva and Pedrina, 2014).

As far as the trade unions are concerned, there can be no question of accepting such consequences. That is why, with a view to the negotiations that have become inevitable between Switzerland and the EU,[8] the Swiss unions have defined three principles that must guide the resolution of the dispute. First of these is that the principle of non-discrimination, the basis of the free movement of persons between Switzerland and the EU, must continue to be preserved in the future. As there can be no quota system without discrimination, that means opposing any reintroduction of such a system. Second, there must be more, and not less, protection of wages and working conditions. Those who work in Switzerland, nationals or immigrants, must receive Swiss wages, and not, for example, Polish wages. Any practice of wage or social dumping must be resisted. The statutory instruments for the full application of the principle of 'for work of equal value, equal pay in the same place', namely in the country of destination, must be strengthened. Finally, the Switzerland-EU bilateral agreements must be maintained.

In exchange for the free movement of persons between Switzerland and the EU, and in preparation of the various direct democracy votes on Switzerland-EU relations, the trade unions have over 15 years managed to build a system of flanking social measures[9] to protect wages and working conditions that are among the best in Europe. Neoliberals and neoconservatives on the employers' side and in politics are working towards the abolition of this system and, at the same time, towards the country's isolation, in keeping with the nationalist logic of all populist, xenophobic and extreme right wing forces. To block their advance, Unia will draw on the rich experience accumulated in past battles, using the twin levers of mobilisation and alliances.

In terms of mobilisation strategies, Unia and USS will continue the campaign of denouncing and eliminating abusive cases of wage and benefits dumping, which we have been conducting for several years. That enables Unia to show – notably through strikes or work stoppages – that unity pays, and to increase pressure for the reinforcement of statutory and collectively agreed anti-dumping measures. The union will also raise awareness, in a broad campaign, of the negative consequences of the old quota system and of its most discriminatory status, that of the seasonal worker. This element is also a solidarity message to immigrants, who have been demoralised by the shocking popular vote.

STRIKES AND WORK STOPPAGES AGAINST WAGE AND SOCIAL DUMPING

The first of those strikes took place in 1994 on one of the large construction sites for the new Alpine railway crossings. South African miners had been hired on a wage that was well below that provided by the collective agreement. Such cases have proliferated since 2000 owing to the increase in the number of foreign companies that post their workers in Switzerland for a few weeks or months. In most cases they operate as subcontractors, which facilitates abuses. Two recent cases concern:

- The building site for the Zürich store of the Zara clothing multinational, in March 2014. A chain of subcontractors was using posted Spanish workers (staff being sent abroad by their employer for a project, see Cremers, 2010) on a working schedule of 60 hours (maximum allowed, 42 hours) for wages at a third to a half of those provided by the collective agreement. After a three-week work stoppage called by the union, the workers concerned secured the retroactive payment of the missing amounts. The main contractor agreed to contribute CHF150,000 to the aid organisation Solidar Switzerland, in order 'to demonstrate its social responsibility' as stated in the agreement.
- A big building site of the pharmaceutical multinational Roche, in Basel, where some 30 Polish posted workers were being paid a third of what the collective agreement has required since August 2013. After a one-week work stoppage in July 2014, they were compensated for an amount of more than CHF500,000.

With regard to alliances, Unia and USS intends to concentrate its efforts on the establishment of a coalition with company executives, employers' associations and forward-looking civil society movements, who are convinced that Switzerland and its inhabitants – with or without a Swiss passport – won't have a promising future without pursuing regulated relations with the EU, including the free movement of persons on a solid social basis. Also, in response to brutal austerity policies, we must at last make our proper contribution to the trade union struggle for changing the social and political course being taken in Europe. Only in that way can Switzerland escape from the dead end in which it is trapped, and the EU again become a source of hope – that in a spirit of a Switzerland showing solidarity and with the objective of a social, not a neoliberal, Europe.

GENERAL LESSONS FROM THE SWISS EXPERIENCE

This contribution might have led readers to believe that Swiss trade unionism is among the world's best. That is undoubtedly not the case. But with regard to migrant workers' organisation and mobilisation as well as the battles for equal rights, the Swiss experience can serve as a useful example for unions that are willing to face the challenge. In an increasingly globalised and interconnected world, where migratory flows will not cease to grow, any union is sooner or later sure to be confronted by the questions that we have had to address over the past few decades. In considering the key elements in the success of our approach, one can highlight the following points. First, without a clear commitment and a substantial, long-term investment of resources there is little chance of success. Second, if one accepts the premise that raising workers' awareness and organising are done primarily on the ground (in workplaces and where workers live and meet) and not in trade union offices, then the need to appoint nationals of the countries of origin as union officials for the tasks of member recruitment and worker organising is essential. Third, it is essential to create within the union special structures for migrant workers, enabling them to organise themselves into IGs, either according to nationality or language or on an intercultural basis. This will lead the union – even if the costs are high – to provide for translation services and for the development of an information system in several languages, and to multiply measures (e.g. training) to promote integration in the country of employment. Without such measures, it is inconceivable that the union will succeed in building the bridges needed to ensure mutual understanding between national and migrant workers, not only in society as a whole but also in each trade union. Finally, union campaigns and mobilisations for common aims (e.g. wages, working conditions, pensions), and also such actions for equal rights between nationals and migrants, are essential both for the organising dynamic and for the consolidation of unity between nationals and migrant workers. It's a job that needs to be pursued unceasingly and with determination; it goes against the tide of xenophobic and racist movements running through society and increasingly threatening – in these times of crisis – solidarity, even within trade unions. Unity between national and migrant workers, and equal rights: getting people to understand that the one does not go without the other remains a crucial challenge for the labour movement, regardless of history's ups and downs.

NOTES

1. In Switzerland, foreign residents have to wait twelve years before being eligible to apply for citizenship (compared to between four and ten years in EU states). Information on naturalisation available at: www.ch.ch
2. Consequences of the Swiss vote on free circulation of persons on 9 February 2014. See: www.europarl.europa.eu/RegData/etudes/briefing_note/join/2014/522327/EXPO-AFET_SP%282014%29522327_EN.pdf (accessed August 2015).
3. In fact some seasonal workers could change their status into a stable resident permit after several years. See Alleva and Pedrina (2014).
4. Of course, it was a restriction to their right to political affiliation. But the alternative at this time was only to exclude them from being able to become union secretaries.
5. In Italian, French, German, Spanish, Portuguese, Serbo-Croatian, Albanian, Turkish, Polish and sometimes also Tamil and English.
6. In the past, immigrants had to pay a fee of several thousand euros for naturalisation. This fee has been gradually lowered.
7. This joint or 'paritarian' fund is administered by a joint committee, composed of representatives of employers and trade unions.
8. The EU principles of free circulation of persons are incompatible with a system of quotas, which Switzerland wants to reintroduce.
9. Flanking measures to the free movement of persons means a couple of accompanying measures like a tripartite control system for minimum wages. For a good overview of the regulatory framework see Cremers (2011) and Baumann (2005).

REFERENCES

Alleva, V. (2001). 'Gewerkschaften und Nationalismus'. *Widerspruch*, 41, 103–9.
——and Pedrina, V. (2014). 'Personenfreizügigkeit und sozialer Schutz', *Widerspruch*, 65(41), 59–70.
Baumann, H. (2005). 'reier Personenverkehr und EU-Erweiterung. Genügen die flankierenden Schutzmassnahmen?'. *Widerspruch*, 48, 145–58.
—— and Zenth, D. (2002). 'Breakthrough for Early-Retirement Pensions in the Construction Industry'. *CLR (Construction Labour Research) News*, 3, Brussels.
Cremers, J. (2010). 'In Search of Cheap labour in Europe: Working and Living Conditions of Posted Workers'. *CLR*, Amsterdam. www.efbww.org/pdfs/Part%20 2%20final-november%202010.pdf (accessed August 2015).
——(2011). 'In Search of Cheap Labour in Europe'. *CLR Studies*, 6, Country Report Switzerland. CLR: Brussels. www.clr-news.org/CLR-Studies/Websummary.pdf (accessed August 2015).
Fluder, R., Ruf, H., Schöni, W. and Wicki, M. (1991). *Gewerkschaften und Anges-telltenverbände in der Schweizerischen Privatwirtschaft.Enstehung, Mitgliedschaft, Organisation und Politik seit 1940.* Zürich: Seismo Verlag.
Hobsbawm, E. (1994). *The Age of Extremes: The Short Twentieth Century, 1914–1991.* London: Penguin.
Rieger, A., Ambrosetti, R. and Beck, R. (2008). *Unia: Gewerkschaft im Umbruch.* Zürich: Rüegger Verlag.
Schweizerischer Gewerkschaftsbund (SGB/USS). (2004). 'Migrationspolitik: Welche Antworten?', Dossier No. 26, Bern.
——(2007). 'Organisationen im Umbruch', Dossier No. 51. Bern.
Unia. (2008). *Migration und Integration.* Bern: Unia.
——(2014). *Baracken, Fremdenhass und versteckte Kinder.* Bern: Unia.
Wicker, R., Fibbi, R. and Hang. W. (2003). *Migration und die Schweiz.* Zürich: Seismo Verlag.

Part III

Asia and the Pacific

8

Migrant Unionism in Hong Kong: A Case Study of Experiences of Foreign Domestic Workers in Union Organising

Asia Pacific Mission for Migrants

Labour export as a major economic policy for many countries in the Global South, and as an outsourcing strategy for countries in the Global North, creates an arena of widespread violations of core labour standards. Despite efforts to secure the rights of migrant workers, they remain a largely abused and exploited workforce. The implementation of these core labour standards has not been able to progress with the ever-increasing migrant labour phenomenon under neoliberal globalisation. Without mechanisms to enforce these standards, they cannot promote decent work for migrant workers or address their conditions.

One of these core labour standards – self-organisation through trade unions or multi-functional worker's associations – is deemed to be one of the most effective solutions to the problems faced by workers. Strengthening organised labour tactics can lead to effective advocacy and foster the empowerment of workers. Among the many forms of organising, the Asia Pacific Mission for Migrants (APMM, 2011) contends that trade unionism is an effective approach to migrant organising because of its platform for asserting economic demands through collective bargaining, whether at the firm, industry or sectoral level.

This approach has achieved many successes worldwide, particularly in Hong Kong, where there is a large migrant workforce composed mainly of foreign domestic workers. This chapter discusses migrant Indonesian, Filipino and Nepalese labour organising in Hong Kong, mainly among domestic workers. Ally (2005) speaks of the unionisation of domestic workers specifically in the context of migrant labour. She analyses two modes of organisation, non-union and union. The first of these is the association model which is 'a non-union-based model of representation in which migrant, ethnic, women's, human rights, legal advocacy, and non-governmental organisations mobilise, and on a wider range of issues than just employment' (2005: 192). The second is the union model, which fights for economic rights and focuses on defending workers against class exploitation. Ally argues that these two models complement each other and in turn create a strong movement through partnership.

Hong Kong provides a unique case for migrant labour unions because of the coverage which its labour provisions afford to the migrant community and the response of the workers to these stipulations. Hong Kong law provides some basic rights to the migrant workforce. Article 24 of the Hong Kong Basic Law states that: 'residents of the Hong Kong Special Administrative Region ("Hong Kong residents") shall include permanent residents and non-permanent residents' (Hong Kong Government, No Date: 1). Migrant labourers, and specifically domestic workers, fall under the non-permanent resident status and as such have the right to join trade unions.

The particularities of the migrant labour force in Hong Kong allow for an interesting study on unionism and organising that may be emulated wherever similar conditions exist. The APMM, a Hong Kong-based regional migrant service institution founded in 1984, conducted this case study to show the effectiveness of migrant labour unionism in the specific context of societies where the so-called 'rule of law' allows for a high level of tolerance for trade unionism in general. The migrant unions in this study are the Indonesian Migrant Workers' Union (IMWU), the Filipino Migrant Workers' Union (FMWU) and the Overseas Nepalese Workers Union (ONWU).

This study's methodology consisted of a focus-group discussion with the leaders of each union as well as follow-up interviews with some of the organisers. Between June and October 2012, 21 migrant union organisers took part in the three focus-group discussions (seven in each batch), while five grassroots migrant and local labour leaders were interviewed individually. The goal was to show the background, the emergence of the union, the internal development and the future of each organisation. The purpose was to showcase these successes in order to inspire migrant labour unionism in other parts of the world. IMWU, FMWU and ONWU were chosen because these are organisations that have been created, expanded and sustained by a migrant labour force, something that is quite unique to Hong Kong. These organisations are focused on domestic worker issues, but they also tackle concerns that affect migrant labour in general.

THE INDONESIAN MIGRANT WORKERS' UNION (IMWU)

Systematic labour exportation from Indonesia to Hong Kong began in the 1970s and exploded in the last ten years. According to news reports based on Hong Kong Labour Department statistics (Benitez, 2006; *Hong Kong News*, 2012), in 1993 there were 6,100 women, in 2007 there were 68,880 and in 2012 there were 151,382 registered Indonesian domestic workers (IDWs) in Hong Kong. The explosion in numbers is due to several sociopolitical and economic factors in Indonesia. It is also due to the growing preference of employers for IDWs who are perceived as more docile, less educated and more easily compelled to accept lower wages then their Filipina counterparts.[1]

The Indonesian community grew substantially stronger with the emergence of hundreds of organisations targeting different aspects of the migrant labour phenomenon. Among these are very active organisations like PILAR (United Indonesians Against Overcharging), ATKI (Association of Indonesian Migrant Workers), LIPMI (League of Indonesian Workers) and GAMMI (Indonesian Migrant Muslim Alliance) that fight to protect the rights of the Indonesian community and domestic workers in general. One very notable organisation among these is the IMWU, a formally recognised union established and led by domestic workers.

In Hong Kong, the difference between a union and an association hinges primarily on the provisions that are stipulated for dealing with the Labour Department. Associations are merely registered under the Hong Kong Societies Ordinance and are only accountable to the police, which is tasked with licence distribution. Unions on the other hand are able to represent labour cases after proper registration with the Labour Department. Associations cannot do any kind of legal support and welfare provision. Each union in this chapter provides interesting stories because they are respected and highly effective and have proven their capacity through successful dealings with the Labour Department and other migrant organisations.

Background of Establishment

Prior to its establishment and registration as a union, IMWU was a traditional migrant association called 'Indonesian Group' which began in 1994. The shift to becoming a migrant union in 1999 was done to challenge the problems that domestic workers are exposed to. Some of the general issues faced by domestic workers in Hong Kong are underpayment of salary, premature termination of contracts, refusal of mandatory days off, long working hours and occasionally physical, psychological or sexual abuse. Campaigns also address the right of abode, the abolition of the two-week rule,[2] lax regulation of placement agencies and an increase in the minimum allowable wage.

The exploitation begins in Indonesia where the workers receive pre-departure 'training' that teaches them subservience while omitting any reference to their rights as workers in Hong Kong. Then the workers are made to pay exorbitant fees, which amount to HK$21,000 (US$2700) or seven months' salary. If for any reason the worker is sent back to Indonesia, they are still indebted to the agencies and have to find ways to pay the fees. Also, every time a worker changes employers they must go through the same agency for a contract and are forced to pay the fees once again.

With the abuse and exploitation coming from several different fronts, the Indonesians have established a strong network of informal and formal organisations to provide respite, as well as to actively fight for increased rights. The organisation began as a migrants' association, but with the help of the Filipino community it changed leadership and was able to kick-start a very successful union that had 2,000 members in 1999. This change came from the recognition of its limitations as an association, which led to the decision that the logical move would be to establish a union in order to enter the formal labour sector.

Capacity Building

Membership is an essential part of capacity building for any organisation. Greater numbers give unions greater collective bargaining power. The IMWU began with a membership of 2,000 in 1999, then 600 in 2008 and is currently at 165 members. The fluctuation in membership is due to several restrictions placed on their organisational capacity in Victoria Park,[3] the area where the Indonesian community congregates on Sundays, as well as the weeding out from the membership list those who have returned to Indonesia for good.

Despite these challenges, the IMWU's organisation provides for a unique and effective approach to recruitment and mobilisation. The IMWU has nine executive committees, each tasked with a different occupation ranging from advocacy and education, to dance and 'beauty training'. These committees are separated by region, and the programmes are specific to the needs of the workers. The tactic of recruitment is to create programmes in which the members and potential recruits will willingly participate. The recruits attend rallies coordinated by these committees. Also, on certain Sundays the recruits are encouraged to attend a programme about human rights in Indonesia and Hong Kong.

Once the recruit becomes interested they are assigned to one of eight groups. These groups are meant to diffuse the organisational responsibilities and to facilitate Sunday activities, all coordinated through WhatsApp, the free Internet messaging application, a very important tool for the migrant labour community. Initially the member receives orientation training about the basic rights of domestic workers, the IMWU's mission, what it means to be a labour union in Hong Kong and the history of Indonesian migrant workers and the government. Once they have completed three months and have proven to be contributing members interested in furthering the goals of a union, they are given leadership training.

They are taught skills such as public speaking, English lessons, how to handle members, how to build alliances, and receive a deeper analysis of human rights issues at the advanced level of training. They are able to actively promote the goals of the IMWU in recruitment and advocacy upon completion of the training. The next level of training deals with paralegal skills, which facilitate the work that the IMWU does in the Labour Department. The Hong Kong Confederation of Trade Unions (HKCTU) and the experienced officers of IMWU facilitate this facet of the programme by mobilising likely participants and giving them the necessary workshops in facilities provided by the HKCTU.

The IMWU also engages in advocacy dealing with the social and political aspects of the domestic workers' lives in Hong Kong. For example, the petition for the abolition of the insurance card policy (E-Card) reached 36,000 signatures.[4] They are also urging the Indonesian and Hong Kong governments to sign the ILO Domestic Workers' Convention (C189) that promotes decent work for domestic workers. Much of their strength as an organisation comes from their work in building alliances. The IMWU cites this part of organising as a collective action tool that effectively pressures both the Indonesian and Hong Kong governments. Through alliance building, they are also able to expand their campaigns to address issues pertaining to migrant workers in Hong Kong as a whole rather than focusing solely on Indonesian issues.

Problems and Obstacles

Funding is a major problem for the organisation. Training materials, execution of planned activities and office space rent take up most of their membership dues. They also have to pay for membership to the various unions that they are a part of such as the HKCTU. HKCTU allows them to print materials in their office but that is the extent of their aid. Since the budget is tight, they are unable to offer welfare programmes for their members. Any member who needs financial assistance will receive it from the members themselves, but the IMWU does not have a formal system of welfare.

Other obstacles are the time/space barriers to organising inherent in domestic work in Hong Kong. Domestic workers are supposed to receive one day off per week as specified in the labour contract. But according to the IMWU members, about 60 per cent do not receive their weekly rest day. This is a detriment to organising because, if a member cannot follow IMWU activities every week, coordination for groups or committees become very limited. Even with the facilitation of communication online, sometimes employers do not allow domestic workers to use their cell phones. Since the domestic workers live with their employers, it is sometimes difficult for the IMWU officers to meet with other union members.

The Hong Kong government used to allow the IMWU to apply for work visas for full-time employees sponsored through a parent organisation, but now they are no longer able to do so. Not having full-time staff makes it difficult for them to fulfil the tasks required of trade unions registered with the government. They have to allot time to meticulous record keeping, since they are required to pay a government auditor every year to review their records. They also have to report membership statistics every year to the Hong Kong government, which keeps a comprehensive account of all of the unions and their affiliate members. This type of administration work is difficult without full-time staff, and detracts from the planning of other union activities.

In terms of their power as a collective bargaining unit, their reach is limited due to their position as domestic workers. The IMWU has connections with the Indonesian government through tripartite negotiations, but that avenue is lacking in Hong Kong. The HKCTU is much more effective in collective bargaining, but they deal largely with issues that workers face in Hong Kong without specifically addressing problems faced by domestic workers. Since the nature of domestic work makes it difficult to target the employer, the IMWU focuses a great deal of their collective effort to change policies, which in turn affect the working conditions of the domestic worker.

The IMWU does have some limitations to their power as a union, but they have been able to organise effectively and fight for domestic workers for almost 13 years.

Work as a Migrant Union and Successes

In terms of advocacy work, the IMWU has been successful in mobilising workers to challenge government policies. In 2010, the Indonesian consulate would not allow domestic workers to change agencies before their contract ended and would force them to get new contracts through the same agencies. After the workers protested, the policy was revised. The price of the mandatory insurance[5] has also been reduced because of their collective efforts.

In terms of Labour Department interventions on cases involving IDWs, Sringatin, an IMWU officer and spokesperson, states that nine out of ten cases brought to IMWU are won in the labour tribunal or minor employment claims. Some of the cases may take up to a year to settle but most are settled within a couple of months depending on the severity. The cases that are settled quickly are those which concern underpayment or contract terminations. Cases that deal with physical or sexual abuse or with agency fees take longer to facilitate and can take an average of three months to even begin the process in court.

Forward Thinking

In terms of forward thinking, the IMWU expressed its desire to become a fully functioning migrant union and be recognised as a trade union by the government and labour federations in Indonesia and at the international level. It hopes to achieve this through a substantial increase in membership, something that it cites as a short- and long-term goal of the organisation. Also, it would like to push for an opportunity to keep full-time staff that can facilitate the organisation of people and potential recruits so that the members can focus on other aspects of a strong organisation.

THE FILIPINO MIGRANT WORKERS' UNION (FMWU)

The Philippines is the largest exporter of labour to Hong Kong. An estimated 160,000 Filipino migrant workers live in Hong Kong, the majority of whom are domestic workers. This trend has been fuelled by push and pull factors of the economies of the sending and receiving countries. Hong Kong was in need of foreign labour to fill the positions vacated by women entering the formal workforce, who then needed to hire someone else to fulfil domestic duties. The Philippines also went through several changes in the 1970s that helped to facilitate this phenomenon. Then Philippine President Ferdinand Marcos created incentives for foreign investment into the country but the outflow of money was high, which proved detrimental to the economy. The cost of living went up, real wages decreased, unemployment rose as sectors of the industry closed down, and by the 1980s an estimated two-thirds of the population lived below the poverty line (Constable, 2007).

In order to ease unemployment, the Marcos government promoted a labour export policy, which became the push factor for Filipinos to become migrant workers overseas. This migration policy was affected by several economic global factors that perpetuated the need for migrant work. Remittances flowed into the country, propping up the economy, filling government coffers and provided much-needed foreign currency used to service debt payments (Rodriguez, 2010). Remittances reached an estimated US$21.3 billion in 2010, making the Philippines the fourth largest recipient of remittances worldwide (World Bank, 2011).

With such an influx of foreign labour into Hong Kong, the Filipino community began witnessing abusive and exploitative conditions among their compatriots, which led to the creation of support networks. The mobilisation of the Filipino community has given it a unique ability to tackle issues related to migrant workers in Hong Kong. This then led to the establishment of the FMWU.

Background

The Filipino community has been tremendously successful in building a strong support network for migrant workers in Hong Kong. It has services that cater to the various needs of domestic workers. These social service and advocacy networks do a great deal in protecting the worker community from abuse and exploitation. The FMWU is a strong example of an organisation that not only deals with labour issues, but which is committed to empowerment and advocacy through its extensive network.

FMWU was self-organised and established in October 1998. In the beginning, it was difficult to organise effectively and grow in membership. Some of the problems were attributed to the diverse backgrounds of the migrant community as well as the hesitance of workers to join a union. Some migrants were familiar with the concept of organising and unions because they participated in, or were exposed to them in their home country, while many others had no background knowledge regarding unions and needed persuading. They were able to revive the union with the help of the Mission for Migrant Workers (MFMW) after some initial obstacles. The MFMW is a Hong Kong-based migrant service institution operating under the Anglican Church that provides direct assistance and capacity building to distressed FDWs of all nationalities.

The MFMW taught them several valuable tactics in organising, such as how to take part in alliance work and network with other organisations. The FMWU was established during a time when the migrant community was experiencing many problems. Many dealt with employer abuse, working conditions were poor, and they had to work long hours. Emotional and psychological problems were becoming widespread and workers were unable to protect themselves without collective action. The organisation was able to teach the FDWs how to defend themselves, how to be self-reliant, how to fight for their rights and most importantly, how to organise. This was done mainly through such capacity-building activities as education, advocacy and legal trainings.

Although some organisations were looking to achieve these same values, they ultimately did not reflect the needs of the migrants. In its inception, the FMWU frequently received phone calls and inquiries from migrants who had been working in Hong Kong for several years but were unfamiliar with their rights as workers. One of the biggest problems at that time was the lack of knowledge about how to approach and succeed in the Labour Department when making claims. This then became a prominent feature of the union's work. The goal became to create members who possessed the knowledge and skills to help other migrant workers in order to curtail abuses.

Issues, Campaigns and Work as a Trade Union

Existing programmes attending to the rights and welfare of its members include several advocacy campaigns dealing with wages and working conditions. For example, there is the 'Ratify C189!' campaign[6] that is important for the international welfare of domestic workers, as well as the right of abode campaign that addresses the inability of migrant workers to become citizens, leaving them in a permanent state of being second-class citizens. The push to abolish the two-week rule for domestic workers is also a major campaign for the migrant community.

Another core campaign is the fight against illegal agency fees, which have become a money-making scheme in both the Philippines and Hong Kong. This campaign deals with the current ban on direct hiring in Hong Kong, which forces workers to go to placement agencies with high fees to find them jobs. The fees range from about HK$11,000–13,000. FMWU has then taken up the call to abolish this type of injustice in Hong Kong and the Philippines.

In terms of its work as a labour union, FMWU handles labour cases in the beginning stages. Throughout their years as a union, and through the support of the MFMW, it has been able to establish a strong support network for labour tribunal proceedings. Once a case has been brought to their attention, representatives from the MFMW are the caseworkers who accompany the client to the labour tribunal and act as paralegals. Although FMWU is a member of HKCTU, it relies mostly on the migrant community to further its sociopolitical and economic agenda.

The FMWU highlights the fact that unions exist for collective interests and not for the sole interest of any individual. Open-mindedness is cited as the key to a successful organisation and effective campaigning. There are some problems in terms of the work required to further the goals of the organisation, such as the 'socialisation aspect' of a union occasionally conflicting with a successful campaign or strategy. By socialisation, we mean activities like parties, parlour games, picnics and hiking/outdoor tours designed principally for interpersonal bonding rather than political advocacy.

Although in practice, migrant organisers often mix political content into these.

Capacity Building

The organisational capacity of the FMWU has created a union that has roughly 400 members, 98 of whom are active members. It has also been able to establish a number of chapters under the FMWU umbrella with an organising strategy that involves several aspects of recruitment, mobilisation and organisation.

The following is the step-by-step strategy:

1. Contact-building: the process begins here. Workers share their experiences with the union members, and the members share their knowledge with the worker and give them advice whenever possible.
2. Education: the second step is educating the migrant worker about the issues that affect them in Hong Kong and the Philippines. Through this learning, they become aware of their situation and are more likely to understand that they have options.
3. Recruitment: the FMWU recruits through conversations with domestic workers. As the domestic worker becomes aware of the issues and develops an interest in the organisation, then they can be considered a prospective recruit. The recruitment rate for the FMWU is about two out of every ten 'approached' domestic workers.
4. Organising: workers can be recruited into a particular chapter of 15 members and upwards, or simply as members of the FMWU.

Officer training is another facet of the FMWU's organisational capacity. Through the training, officers are given leadership skills through intensive discussion of manuals, one of which is called 'Know Your Rights'. They also go through paralegal and welfare trainings to better equip them to counsel migrant workers. Furthermore, they train in issues relating to money, such as how to improve the migrant's economic capacity and how to minimise debt. Lastly, they train in advocacy, alliance building, networking and organising.

Goals and Challenges

The short- and long-term goals all involve strengthening the movement through advocacy and recruitment in order to build more chapters. In order to expand, the FMWU acknowledges that there needs to be an increase in capacity training to address the different issues pertaining to migrant labourers. The challenge lies in the FMWU's ability to become a collective bargaining centre for migrant workers' economic demands in Hong Kong, in similar ways to how the local trade unions have played this role for formal sector workers. The FMWU admits that despite the efforts to make that a reality it is unlikely due to the nature of their work. The workers all have different employers and do not work under one company. Their work is individual work instead of collective work, which means that collective agreements can only take a sectoral form.

THE OVERSEAS NEPALESE WORKERS' UNION (ONWU)

Foreign labour migration has also become an essential contributor to the Nepalese economy.[7] Poverty in Nepal remains at around 30–45 per cent, and the government is unable to provide its people with social, political and economic security. According to the United Nations Development Fund for Women (UNIFEM, 2009: 23), 'over two million Nepalese have migrated in search of alternative livelihoods and escape endemic poverty and unemployment'. About 5 per cent of this total migrant population is women. These conditions set in motion the push factors for people to leave the country as migrant workers, facilitated by the labour export policy established in 1985. Yet Nepal's Labour Act has failed to provide a comprehensive policy towards migrant labour and has led to differing avenues for job placements abroad. One of the most notable has been the personal connection that Gurkhas[8] provided in Hong Kong for the Nepalese workers. Due to these connections and because of the need for domestic workers, Hong Kong received an influx of Nepalese workers. There are estimated to be approximately 30,000 Nepalese in Hong Kong, of whom about 700 are women domestic workers.

The Nepalese have a peculiar standing in Hong Kong because many are permanent residents. After the handover in 1997, the Gurkhas and their families were allowed to stay in Hong Kong. On 6 June 2005, the Hong Kong government stopped accepting work or study visas from Nepalese immigrants, and the ban remains in effect (UNIFEM, 2009). This factor, along with many other issues, creates the need for NGOs to provide services to Nepalese workers. Of these groups, the ONWU was established to aid in alleviating the labour problems faced by the Nepalese in Hong Kong.

Background and Organisation

Seven people[9] founded the ONWU on 6 December 2003. This came after years of disparity in the way female and male contract workers were treated. Labour laws protected the men, who were also paid higher wages, while the women faced many problems. The membership then grew to 20 members through community outreach. ONWU membership is restricted to low-income contract workers such as domestic workers, bodyguards, drivers and restaurant workers.

Most of the ONWU's members are female domestic workers, although there are some male members. The Far East Overseas Nepalese Association was the first Nepalese organisation in Hong Kong, and helped the migrant workers in the beginning stages. Yet the Labour Department would not allow them to represent workers. Other nationalities also gave their support and stood as examples for the ONWU. In the beginning, they were part of a Nepalese group, but one which mostly functioned for socialisation purposes. They were in need of an organisation that would address the needs of workers specifically. At the time of ONWU's creation, there were 48 Nepalese organisations. But ONWU remains the only union that represents Nepalese workers in Hong Kong.

The ONWU did not receive much direction in the initial stages of the union's establishment. Kumar Gurung, the leader of ONWU, went to the Labour Department and inquired about the differences between an association and a union. Most of the Nepalese groups did not advocate for their rights through mobilisation tactics, and thus there needed to be an organisation that defended their rights as workers. He was told that the unions could work with both the employee and employer, and they would need to be registered with the Labour Department, rather than just the police. Most of the ONWU's work concerns workers' economic rights. It will only get involved in political aspects if those issues affect the economic rights of the workers.

The ONWU has 165 official members of whom about 100 are active. Some participate voluntarily and others come when they are in need of assistance. There are six officers, namely: chairman, vice-chairman, secretary, vice-secretary, treasurer, vice-treasurer and one auditor. The union has seven committees that all work under the same platform, allowing for a cohesive understanding of the objectives of the organisation. Members are recruited through friends, relatives and personal networks rather than through outright recruitment processes. The union holds monthly training sessions for its membership on Labour Department issues. There are no part-time or full-time organisers since most members cannot attend the union meetings.

Problems and Cases

A major issue in mobilisation is that the Nepalese have been banned from coming to Hong Kong since 2005 and if they leave, they cannot come back. Even in transit, they need to have a special transit visa to pass through Hong Kong. The ban plays a big role in union membership, and contributes to the decline in membership numbers. Participation is also an obstacle. Of those that are involved, most do not want to participate in training. They tried to have an educational programme, but not many members participated and few members go to rallies. Nepalese migrants are difficult to organise because domestic workers are afraid of losing their jobs, especially because they are not able to come back if this happens due to the ban.

Capacity training is also an obstacle. ONWU officers used to attend training at the MFMW, but that proved to be difficult because not all members have Sundays off. Membership services are difficult to maintain because of lack of funds. The HK$50 one-time membership fee is not enough to generate services to provide for the members. When it collects the money initially, the ONWU asks the new members if they are willing to donate more money to the organisation.

Regardless of the obstacles, the ONWU has been quite effective in the Labour Department, utilising their resources to attend to the rights of migrant workers. The cases brought to ONWU reflect the following examples.

Advocacy and Networking

The ONWU focuses on many issues, but its main goal is to repeal the visa ban. It also takes on issues like underpayment, right of abode (many members have been in Hong Kong for more than seven years) and wage increases. The advocacy is mostly related to Hong Kong issues and rarely connects to issues in Nepal, as the ONWU does not think that these are connected. It does not have any alliances with any other Nepalese organisations because the ONWU considers its work different from that of other organisations. It is not yet a member of the HKCTU (unlike the FMWU and the IMWU), but it plans to join in the future and has already begun the long process of doing so.

The ONWU has to figure out how to reach out to migrant workers and show them how effective it can be at protecting migrant rights. The obstacle to achieving this lies in the fact that many of the Nepalese in Hong Kong are already ONWU members and no new migrants are coming because of the ban. It hopes to strengthen the expansion of the organisation by establishing itself as a collective bargaining centre in the future.

CONCLUSION

The most evident benefit of establishing a migrant labour trade union in Hong Kong, especially one consisting of domestic workers, is the Labour Department recognising and conceding to the notion that domestic work is formal labour. Thus, it should be afforded the labour protections that other professions receive. With the recognition of different types of work in the informal sector, the ILO's principles of 'decent work' can guide Hong Kong's core labour standards. Through collective organising via an association, or preferably a union, alliance activities become part of a greater effort to enter formal sector negotiations. This is important for building a bridge between the formal and informal sectors of the Hong Kong economy and political structure.

Migrant labour unions in Hong Kong have achieved this transition from the informal to the formal sector through union dynamics, with members being considered as part of the labour sector at large. As has been shown by the experiences of the FMWU and the IMWU, migrant unions by their very nature possess a relatively advanced awareness of common labour issues that impels them to link up with formal sector unions, thereby narrowing gaps and strengthening solidarity among workers of all types in host countries. In this sense, migrant unionism has served as a bridge between traditional migrant associations and local workers' organisations.

Another aspect of significance in these practices is the affirmation of the validity and viability of migrant unionism as an organising approach, despite the fact that they face problems of expanding their base due to high turnover rates among FDWs in Hong Kong. They can play an indispensable role in elevating migrant sectoral struggles to the point where it can help influence macroeconomic policies affecting the whole labour sector, such as compelling the Hong Kong government to conduct a public consultation that will guide the expected reduction of overly long working hours in the territory. Being tightly connected with formal sector unions is certainly one way of facilitating this process, as the multi-layered fight for higher wages in Hong Kong has shown. Greater integration and coordination among various subsectors within the labour sector can thus result in regular wage increases and some incremental improvements in working conditions, hopefully not only in Hong Kong but also in other migrant-receiving countries.

NOTES

1. For contemporary views (stereotypes) of Filipino, Indonesian and Thai FDWs in Hong Kong, see: http://open388.com/0388-001/388-view.php?Redir=dhfaq#Par01 (accessed August 2014).
2. The two-week rule is a requirement by Hong Kong's Immigration Department, which requires FDWs to exit the territory if no new contract is signed within two weeks after the end of an existing contract. This exposes desperate FDWs to a plethora of abuses by placement agencies.
3. A 1997 amendment to Hong Kong's Public Order Ordinance requires a 'no objection' notification from the police commissioner for any 'public procession' larger than 30 people, which has to be obtained one week prior to the activity. As failure to comply may be punished with five years' imprisonment, the provision had a dampening effect on large gatherings of Indonesian migrants in Victoria Park.
4. The E-Card is required for Indonesian FDWs in Hong Kong to access the Online System, which is a computerised system implemented in March 2011 that connects agencies in Hong Kong and Indonesia. Indonesian FDW organisations oppose the Online System as another scheme to make money from FDWs and bind them to placement agencies.
5. The Indonesian and Philippine governments require their migrant workers to pay a one-time general insurance fee that covers hospitalisation, money-claim compensation and emergency repatriation. As coverage of this insurance policy lasts only up to two years, few migrant workers are able to take advantage of its benefits, and the agencies reap windfall profits from its extraction.
6. 'Ratify C189!' is a grassroots-based FDW campaign initiated by APMM and the Asia Migrants Coordinating Body (of which FMWU is a member) to push for the adoption of the ILO Domestic Workers' Convention in the region, especially in China (for Hong Kong and Macau).
7. The information presented in this section came from the focus-group discussions that the APMM conducted with ONWU leaders, as well as interviews with Kumar Gurung.
8. The Gurkhas are indigenous people mainly from Nepal who enlisted in military units in the British army.
9. Seven is the minimum number of people required to form a union, according to Hong Kong's Employment Ordinance.

REFERENCES

Ally, S. (2005). 'Caring about Care Workers: Organizing in the Female Shadow of Globalization'. *Labour, Capital and Society*, 38 (1/2), 184–207.

APMM (Asia Pacific Mission for Migrants). (2011, January). *APMM Program Concept on Migrant Trade Unionism*. Hong Kong: Asia Pacific Mission for Migrants.

Benitez, M. A. (2006). 'Number of Indonesian Domestic Helpers Tops 100,000'. *South China Morning Post*, 22 July. www.scmp.com/article/557535/number-indonesian-domestic-helpers-tops-100000 (accessed August 2015).

Constable, N. (2007). *Maid to Order in Hong Kong: Stories of Migrant Workers*. Ithaca, NY: Cornell University Press.

Hong Kong Government. (No Date). *The Basic Law*. www.basiclaw.gov.hk/en/basiclawtext/index.html (accessed August 2015).

Hong Kong News. (2012). 'Filipino Workers Surpass Indonesians'. *Hong Kong News*. http://hongkongnews.com.hk/filipino-workers-surpass-indonesians/ (accessed August 2015).

Hong Kong Labour Department. (No Date). *Importation of Labour: Foreign Domestic Helpers*. Public Services. www.labour.gov.hk/eng/plan/iwFDH.htm (accessed August 2015).

www.ilo.org/wcmsp5/groups/public/@dgreports/@dcomm/@webdev/documents/publication/wcms_082607.pdf (accessed August 2015).

Rodriguez, R. M. (2010). *Migrants for Export: How the Philippine State Brokers Labor to the World*. Minneapolis: University of Minnesota Press.

UNIFEM (United Nations Development Fund for Women). (2009). 'An In Depth Study on the Realities and Concerns of Nepalese Domestic Workers in Hong Kong'. East and Southeast Asia Regional Office.

World Bank. (2011). *Migration and Remittances Factbook*. http://siteresources.worldbank.org/INTLAC/Resources/Factbook2011-Ebook.pdf (accessed August 2015).

9

The Possibilities and Limitations of Organising Immigrant Workers in Japan: The Case of the Local Union of the All-Japan Metal and Information Machinery Workers' Union

Hiroshi Ueki

The Lehman Shock of September 2008 had extremely negative effects not only on the global economy many months later, but also on Japanese factories. It resulted in a widespread phenomenon called 'temp cuts', in which both Japanese and foreign nationals lost their jobs and their homes at the conclusion of their employment contracts. By the end of that year – with non-profit organisations, labour unions and other organisations providing food and support to help these temporary employees who had no place to go over the New Year – the 'Village to Get the Temporary Workers Through the New Year' had become well known, offering assistance in finding work and a place to live. Japanese-Brazilian workers (the subject of this chapter), met with the same 'temp cuts', termination of their employment contracts and job loss. However, they joined labour unions and fought back.

There has been little prior research on the organisation of immigrant workers by Japanese labour unions. However, pioneering research on the Kanagawa City Union (KCU), a union for individuals, documents this union's progress in actively organising its activities, beginning in the mid-1990s, and focuses on South Koreans and

Peruvians (Ogawa, 2000; Urano, 2007). Other research has discussed the General Union, which made some progress in Osaka by focusing on the organisation of such workers as English language instructors from the United States and the United Kingdom (Weathers, 2012). Besides the National Capital Region and Kansai region, there is also a concentration of foreign nationals in Japan's Tokai region (Aichi, Shizuoka, Gifu and Mie prefectures). These workers mainly comprise Japanese-Brazilians, and efforts are being made to organise them. The union that is the focus of this chapter, the JMIU Shizuoka-Ken Seibu Chiiki Shibu (hereafter referred to as JMIU-SSCS, the Local Union of JMIU in Western Shizuoka), is one of these.

Existing activity reports (Nakayasu, 2007) prepared by labour union activists, and introductions from researchers (Hyodo, 2013), are based on the organisation's perspective, and lack the perspectives of those being organised. This chapter endeavours to analyse the organisation of immigrant workers by industry labour unions in Japan in detail, by observing JMIU-SSCS activities, and documenting the perspectives of Brazilian nationals, in order to understand why they became activists, and why they continue to be so engaged.

To this end, I provide an overview of the circumstances of immigration including Japanese-Brazilians and describe work environments in Japan. Labour unions have been working since 2000 to organise non-organised and irregular workers, including foreign workers. I then explain how Japanese unions have worked to organise irregular workers since this time, by analysing JMIU-SSCS activities.

IMMIGRATION AND JAPANESE-BRAZILIANS IN JAPAN

According to Japan's Ministry of Justice, as reported in 'Statistics on Foreign National Residents', the number of foreign nationals living in Japan has gradually increased since the second half of the 1980s, exceeding one million for the first time in 1990. There has, however, been a further large increase since 2000. This number passed two million in 2005, and by 2008 a record 2.217 million foreign nationals were living in Japan (1.73 per cent of the total population). This number subsequently fell to 2.066 million as of 2013, due to the Lehman Shock. As of 2012, at 652,000 (32.1 per cent), the largest number of foreign nationals by nationality came from China. There were 530,000 foreign nationals from South and North Korea (26.1 per cent), 203,000 from the Philippines (10.0 per cent) and 190,000 from Brazil (9.4 per cent). Foreign nationals from these four countries represented 87.2 per cent of Japan's total foreign national population.

The proportion of immigrants as a percentage of Japan's total population is very low when compared with the average of 12.4 per cent for the other OECD (Organisation for Economic Co-operation and Development) countries (OECD, 2014). Discussions of immigration in Japan always involve arguments over the pros and cons of introducing foreign national workers. On the other hand, many immigrants reside permanently in specific areas, as for example in Oizumimachi in Gunma prefecture, where they represent 14.5 per cent of the population.

Immigration came into full swing at the end of the 1980s, when Japan experienced its bubble economy. Since young Japanese workers shunned the manufacturing industry at that time, labour shortages became a serious issue. This shortage was filled by Japanese-Brazilians and Japanese-Peruvians arriving from South America. Industrial trainees and technical interns from other Asian countries such as China later added to this number.[1] The former group worked in small- and medium-sized automotive companies and the electronics industry, and the latter group worked in small businesses such as textiles and farming. Compared to that time, even now many immigrants of Japanese descent continue to work in the manufacturing industry. But for the Chinese there is a wide range of employment opportunities, not only in manufacturing but including everything from part-time work for international students to work in the fields of research and education. As a result, by 2013, of the approximately 720,000 foreign nationals working in Japan, 304,000 (42.4 per cent) were Chinese, 95,000 (13.3 per cent) were Brazilian, 80,000 (11.2 per cent) were from the Philippines, 34,000 (4.8 per cent) were from South Korea and 70 per cent of all the ethnic Japanese immigrants came from these four countries (Ministry of Health, Labour and Welfare, 2014).

The descendants of Japanese who immigrated to Brazil between the 1900s and the 1970s are among the immigrants who came from

Brazil and Peru. Japanese emigration was a nationwide phenomenon before the Second World War, when many people emigrated from Okinawa and Hiroshima prefectures to Hawaii, the US and South America. The Japanese who immigrated to Brazil came from a tradition emphasising education, and after two generations a large proportion of these immigrants had high-income occupations in Brazil (Miyao, 2002).

However, in the 1980s economic uncertainty increased in Brazil, as a result of natural disasters such as the destruction of coffee trees from drought, the lowering of real wages and increases in real estate prices caused by 1,700 per cent annual hyperinflation, and deteriorating public safety due to economic stagnation that led to increasing unemployment levels. Hence the number of people moving to Japan to make a living began to increase. Japan was in the midst of a bubble economy at that time, and there were ongoing labour shortages in many companies in the manufacturing sector. Against this backdrop, the Immigration Control and Refugee Recognition Act was revised in 1990 to allow a permanent residency visa for second- and third-generation descendants of Japanese immigrants visiting Japanese relatives. The place of work and residence could be freely established under this visa. As a result, from that year many ethnic Japanese from South America went to Japan for work.

With the Japanese economy stagnating in the mid-1990s, immigrant workers of Japanese origin employed in assembly factories for large automakers lost their jobs. However, they remain permanent residents of Japan, in spite of earning reduced wages and experiencing instability in their lives, including being employed as temporary labour on contracts at companies such as parts makers.

When the ethnic Japanese began living in low-income public housing, they encountered difficulties with their Japanese neighbours, due to having different customs. Further problems arose because their children were not able to perform well in Japanese schools. These problems have occurred in cities such as Hamamatsu where there is a large ethnic Japanese immigrant population. These cities have been dealing with these issues since 2000, by forming the Committee for Localities with a Concentrated Foreigner Population (CLCF) to encourage mutual exchanges (Ueki, 2015).

CHANGES IN JAPAN'S EMPLOYMENT ENVIRONMENT SINCE 1990

The 1990 revision of Japan's Immigration Control and Refugee Recognition Act led to an increase in the number of foreign nationals working in Japan. During this time, ethnic Japanese workers arrived from South America, with countries such as Brazil and Peru representing the largest number of immigrant workers. During the 25 years since Japan began accepting foreign workers there have also been significant changes in how workers in Japan do their jobs. These changes have intensified the need for foreign workers.

For a long time, Japanese male workers were engaged in regular employment that fulfilled the following three principles: direct employment by the employer, open-ended employment contracts (open-ended employment) and regular work hours (full-time). These employment practices were widespread up to the early 1990s. According to Japan's Employment Status Survey (MIC, 1983, 1993), of the nine million additional workers who entered the workforce in the ten-year period from 1982 to 1992, 5.05 million were regular workers and 3.84 million were irregular workers. The proportion of irregular male workers was exceptionally low, at 10 per cent or less.

In the late 1990s, the number of irregular workers increased significantly. By 2002, as a result of bankruptcies in financial institutions and the frequent large-scale restructuring of major corporations, the number of regular employees had fallen by four million workers in the previous five years. In addition, the number of regular male employees had been falling from a 1997 peak of 26.787 million (MIC, 1998, 2003). The number of irregular workers, however, increased by 3.616 million in the five years after 1997, with men constituting 1.422 million of them. Since then, with the easing of regulations, including the removal of a ban on the dispatch of temporary workers in the manufacturing industry due to the 2004 amendment of the Temporary Staffing Services Law, and the extension from one to three years of fixed-term employment contract limits due to revisions of the Labour Standards Act in the same year, the proportion of irregular workers rose from 24.6 per cent in 1997 to 38.2 per cent in 2012. This trend was conspicuous among young, middle aged and older male workers. Moreover, the proportion of women was even higher, at 57.5 per cent (MIC, 2013).

Irregular work comprises three main aspects. First, the principle of equal wages for equal work does not apply in irregular employment, and irregular employees are left with low wages that do not allow them to support themselves. Second, irregular employment is unstable, based on repetitive, short-term, fixed-term employment contracts (from three months to one year). Third, employees are not eligible for social insurance benefits (Goka, 2014). Temporary and contract workers in indirect employment are the ones most likely to have irregular employment. These temporary workers come from regions with low effective job opening-to-application ratios, such as Hokkaido, Tohoku, Kyushu and Okinawa, to jobs in Kanto, Tokai and Kansai (where manufacturing industries are concentrated, and where they are hired by staffing companies that send them to factories there), where they lose their jobs due to the vicissitudes of the industry, and return home to another region, or go to work somewhere else (Kinoshita, 2010). Ethnic Japanese workers from South America have the same type of existence, in that they continue changing jobs around the Tokai region, using Brazilian and employment agency networks.

ORGANISATION OF IRREGULAR WORKERS BY THE LABOUR UNION

Along with a dramatic increase in the number of irregular workers since 2000, Japanese labour unions have begun to organise these workers. This is one observable measure that has been taken in response to the downward trends. According to the *Basic Survey on Labour Unions* (Ministry of Health, Labour and Welfare, 2014), of the 55.71 million people employed in 2013, 9.874 million belonged to labour unions, a unionisation rate of 17.7 per cent. The number of labour union members began to fall from a peak in 1994 of 12.698 million, sank below ten million in 2011, and has continued falling. On the other hand, the unionisation rate peaked at 55.8 per cent in 1949, right after the Second World War, and then began a downward trend, finally falling to around 30 per cent in the high-growth period of the 1960s. The organisation rate of around 30 per cent continued until the oil shock of the mid-1970s. Since then, the rate has been on a long-term, consistent downturn.

This separation between the total number of union members and the percentage of members who are organised indicates an increase in the membership of regular employees in corporate unions, due to a hiring increase in large companies during the high-growth period. They are surrounded by the remaining non-unionised workers, including irregular workers, and at least 60 per cent of the small- to medium-sized companies. This reflects a strengthening of the corporate labour union character, with greater cooperation between labour and management in large private sector companies since the mid-1960s (Hyodo, 2006).

In the 1980s, the right wing Domei, made up of large private sector corporate labour unions mainly in the metal, auto and textile industries, took the initiative of reorganising the national centre. The left wing Toitsu Rouso Kon labour union was formed in opposition.

As part of this process, the three national centres were consolidated in 1989, under Rengo (Japan Trade Union Confederation), Zenroren (National Confederation of Trade Unions) and Zenrokyo (National Trade Union Council), with Rengo continuing the right wing line, and Zenroren and Zenrokyo on the left.

In terms of current union membership, Rengo, which encompasses most of the major corporate labour unions, is the largest, with 6.839 million people, followed by Zenroren, which organises small- and medium-sized companies and non-organised workers in outlying regions, with 827,000 members, and Zenrokyo, with 124,000 members.

According to the *Survey on the Status of Labour Unions* (Ministry of Health, Labour and Welfare, 2013), in unions with irregular office workers, 62.8 per cent were part-time workers and 44.6 per cent were temporary workers. However, for labour unions with actual members, the numbers decreased to 10.9 per cent for part-time workers and 0.8 per cent for temporary workers. Most part-time workers are married women who work during the day, with the greatest number in the retail industry. On the other hand, since it is difficult for temporary employees to remain in the same workplace, and the unions where they are temporarily employed do not organise them, organisation has not progressed at all.

In response to this situation, Rengo, Zenroren and others that make up the National Centre began working in earnest to organise irregular workers in 2000 using unions for individuals. This term describes labour unions which an individual from any industry in the region can join, regardless of employment status, and where individuals can receive labour consultations and help in resolving labour disputes. The origins of such unions lie in the Edogawa Union founded in 1984. Similar types of unions, called 'community unions', were subsequently founded nationwide. This type of labour activity later influenced the organisation of irregular workers of the National Centre (Oh, 2012; Endo, 2012). In Zenroren, organisations that fall under the unions for individuals' descriptor are called 'local unions', but to avoid confusion with the regional chapters of industrial unions they are called unions for individuals.

Rengo set up a union for individuals in 1996. In the Action Plan 21 presented at its seventh General Meeting in 2001, it appropriated one billion yen (equivalent to 20 per cent of its overall budget, about US$8.4 million) and increased the number of organisation expansion managers from four to 20 to expand its organisation. In addition, it established a Centre for Non-Regular Employment (Hiseiki Rodo Senta) in 2007, worked to improve the treatment of workers, and as of 2010 had organised about 15,000 workers (Hayakawa, 2006; Goto, 2013; Oh, 2012).

On the other hand, in 2002 Zenroren hammered out a policy to establish unions for individuals under the aegis of labour unions in each region, and worked even more substantially on efforts such as stationing twelve organisers in eight regional blocs in 2004. In 2008, it launched a Contingent Workers' Action Centre (Hiseiki Koyo Rodosya Zenkoku Senta), and gave it the role of supporting the following four existing liaison groups: the Part-Time and Temporary Workers' Union Liaison Group, Helper Net, the Temporary and Contract Worker Liaison Group, and the Foreign National Worker Issues Liaison Group (Terama, 2010).

As a result, the Zenroren union for individuals, which had only 1,923 members in 2000, increased its membership to 4,678 in 2005, and 11,338 in 2010. The reason for the increase in union members was the progress that had been made towards orderly organisational growth by greatly increasing the number of consultations at the permanent regional labour consultation centres, from 3,300 in 1998, to 29,057 in 2009, and by increasing the number of dedicated labour consultants from 18 in 1998 to 235 in 2009 (Terama, 2012).

As can be seen from the above, even though overall union membership continues to slide downwards, unions for individuals have increased their membership. The industry unions that make up Zenroren are working actively to organise irregular workers. Among these, the JMIU (All-Japan Metal and Information Machinery Workers' Union), formed in February 1989, organised workers in private sector engineering and metalworking industries, as well as in telecommunications. These efforts are based on organising the ethnic and other minority groups found mainly in small and medium enterprises and major companies, and the principle of 'a single organisation of individuals across industries' is featured in the JMIU rules.

Since 2003, JMIU has embarked in earnest on organising non-organised workers. Also during this time, Zenroren worked to strengthen unions for individuals. These activities, along with establishing permanent organisers nationwide, have made progress in adding volunteers at each regional branch by involving retiree activists. Against this backdrop, the decision was made to focus on encouraging union membership among irregular workers such as part-time workers, temporary workers and foreign workers, through advertising and work consultations.

As an industry labour union headquarters, they pursued the policy of signing labour agreements with each company that undertook collective bargaining. This policy is necessary for workers at small- and medium-sized companies and irregular workers who are forced into low wages and non-acquisition of paid vacation in comparison with regular workers of large companies (Hasegawa, 2006).

Nonetheless, JMIU membership is also steadily decreasing. After reaching a peak of 12,369 in 1991, the number dropped to 7,241 in 2013. Furthermore, the majority of activists who had worked to establish JMIU in the 1980s are now in their fifties and sixties. So an increasing number of activists and workers will be retiring, and there are concerns that this will lead to a decrease in union membership. Despite the overall decline, there are examples of success in organising non-organised workers. One of the most successful is the case of Koyo Sealing Techno in Tokushima prefecture. Here, temporary workers in the same company formed a union chapter under which to fight, while cooperating with the regular employees' union that was also part of JMIU. As a result, all employees became regular company employees, and there were other victories as well (Ito, 2013). Further, as discussed in the next section, JMIU-SSCS succeeded in organising many Japanese-Brazilians. On the one hand, this chapter is a regional chapter (Local Union) of an industry labour union, while on the other hand it represents the interests of individuals (Hyodo, 2013).

ORGANISATION OF JAPANESE-BRAZILIAN WORKERS BY JMIU-SSCS

JMIU-SSCS is located in the Hamamatsu City of Shizuoka prefecture. Hamamatsu has long been the central metropolis of a region with a concentration of large and small manufacturing industries, beginning with musical instruments and transport machinery (such as Kawai Musical Instruments, Honda and Suzuki). Beginning in the 1990s, Japanese-Brazilian workers in this region have been employed as essential labour in the manufacturing process. They have mainly been irregular workers hired as contract and temporary labour.

According to Nakayasu (2007), the issues of Japanese-Brazilians seeking labour consultations were grouped as follows: (1) fixed-term employment contracts and 'fake contracts'; (2) the common occurrence of labour accidents due to unsafe working conditions; (3) a lack of paid holidays; (4) the lack of social insurance coverage; and (5) gender discrimination. With regard to fixed-term employment contracts and fake contracts, there were many irregular workers with roughly three-month, short-term employment contracts, and indirect employment.

'Fake contracts' became a prominent social issue in the 2000s, even though dispatching temporary workers to the manufacturing industry was forbidden in Japan until the 2004 revision of the Temporary Staffing Services Law. The term refers to contracts signed by a temporary employment agency and by someone from the place of the temporary assignment giving instructions to the workers for actual temporary work.

The work day was eleven hours long, spread over two shifts, and included three hours of compulsory overtime. Including a one-hour break, workers were confined to the factory for twelve hours a day. As a result, labour accidents were common among foreign workers, with 159 in 2001 and 234 in 2005. Taking paid holidays was not allowed, and if they were taken, the worker's contract would not be renewed. Since the temporary employment agency (the employer) did not participate in providing social insurance benefits, according to a 2007 Hamamatsu City survey, only 7.1 per cent of resident foreign nationals participated in the welfare pension system. Moreover, if women workers became pregnant, they were forced out of the temporary workplace, and a short time later their contracts were terminated or they were forced to retire by the temporary employment agency. In Hamamatsu and the surrounding area, the prevailing wages of Japanese-Brazilians were different between men and women, at 1,300 Japanese yen/hour for men (about US$10.90/hour), and 900 yen/hour for women (about US$7.57/hour).

Moreover, Japanese-Brazilians worked under poor labour conditions compared to those provided to the Japanese. For example, even if both were factory workers with fixed-term employment contracts, there were discriminatory labour management practices such as six-month terms being offered to Japanese workers, but only two-month terms being offered to the ethnic Japanese immigrants, or Japanese workers having access to opportunities for regular employment, while similar opportunities were not made available to ethnic Japanese immigrant workers (Ueki, 2012).

The JMIU-SSCS was formed in 2003 to receive non-organised workers in the region, beginning with the Japanese-Brazilians. There is one dedicated, full-time staff member, but at Kawai Musical Instruments and Honda, former instructors and others have been conducting labour consultations on a day-by-day, volunteer basis. They began with about ten union members, but at the time of the

Zenroren nationwide labour consultation in November 2003, the fact that they had Portuguese-speaking interpreters was reported in the *International Press*, a newspaper for Brazilians in Japan, and consequently workers from the Hamamatsu area came in on a daily basis to request labour consultations. According to the chapter's monthly summary report, the following statement was made in October 2005: 'There is a recent trend of a large number of labour consultations being introduced through Brazilian union members, and there is a growing need for simultaneous translation' (unpublished internal report, 2005[2]). The union's existence has become known among local Japanese-Brazilians through introductions from Brazilian union members. Moreover, in April 2006, a debate appeared in a newspaper for Japanese-Brazilians, in which members of the same union participated, and that was broadcast on television news programmes. As a result, due to activities such as labour consultations and even consultations on forming unions requested by other prefectures, it became clear that the union was widely known outside of western Shizuoka prefecture. Thus, of the 17 labour consultants on staff in June 2006, 15 were foreign nationals, including Japanese-Brazilians.

The organisation of Japanese-Brazilians progressed rapidly through handling a large number of labour consultations and resolving individual issues, and in 2007, out of 380 union members, 320, or 84.2 per cent, were Japanese-Brazilians. Thanks to increasing union membership, Japanese-Brazilians – who had joined the union after the temporary employment agency K Company rescinded their terminations in May 2007 – ended up attending many meetings to learn about such matters as workers' rights, legal protections, union management methods and the status of union organisation in Japan. They then formed a local union branch in October 2007 to improve labour conditions in their own workplaces. Ethnic Japanese-Brazilian union members became key members, because they had acted to protect worker rights.

Mass terminations of irregular employment following the Lehman Shock sped this process along, and increased the number of labour consultations and the growth of organisations from September 2008 to April 2009. By November 2008, the number of labour consultations had increased to over 30, but in the three months from December 2008 to February 2009 there was a rapid jump in the number of consultations from 43 to 65, and then to 79. Looking at the number of people who had joined the union, in the three months from January 2009 to March 2009 the numbers were 75, 85 and 46, which was two to three times the normal growth in membership. The sudden increase in membership is tied to the formation of multiple chapters, and during this time five chapters were formed.

How did this regional chapter succeed in organising Japanese-Brazilians? Nakayasu (2007) offers the following as lessons for organisations. First, they made resolving the consultations a premise for joining the union. Second, they conducted a large number of consultations. At the same time, they held a regular study group once a month, and as they grew, foreign national workers and Japanese staff influenced one another. Of these, their approach to consultations is thought to have led to the sudden expansion in union membership. With the number of Japanese-Brazilians and Japanese staff growing at the same time, regular study groups and learning from each other are reasons for the qualitative leap in labour movements shown in the formation of chapters. In other ways, they formed a base from which both groups influenced one another through daily associations, such as encouraging exchanges between Japanese staff and ethnic Japanese-Brazilians by holding barbecues and issuing a Portuguese version of the chapter newsletter, with the help of the Japanese-Brazilians.

JAPANESE-BRAZILIANS' INVOLVEMENT IN JMIU-SSCS

Finally, I would like to consider how Japanese-Brazilians became involved in unions in Japan, using the case of Mr M, who is the director of a chapter. He came to Japan about 20 years ago, and in the beginning worked in a factory in Hiroshima. In the late 1990s, he moved to the Hamamatsu City area, where he worked at an affiliate of a major Japanese auto parts maker. He liked the workplace atmosphere and the relatively high hourly wage there. In the roughly ten years before his employment was terminated, he was directly employed, but under continually renewable, two-month, fixed-term employment contracts. In the mid-2000s, the company grew rapidly and hired nearly 1,000 Japanese-Brazilian workers. The earlier workplace atmosphere disappeared, and a unit workplace system with Japanese managers and group leaders was created, which included a subservient relationship with the Japanese-Brazilians. Discriminatory behaviour occurred on a daily basis.

Even though some Japanese-Brazilians achieved the same performance levels as the group leaders, the attitude among Japanese regular employees was that the Japanese-Brazilians were all performing 'simple work'. This demoralising attitude was prevalent, but not discussed publicly while contracts were being renewed. It surfaced with the terminations after the Lehman Shock, and at once workers began joining the union and forming chapters. The company's cold-hearted approach during these terminations was Mr M's direct motivation for joining the union.

Earlier, another Japanese-Brazilian worker had been the director of this chapter, but when he returned to Brazil Mr M became the director. After forming the chapter, they continued negotiating with the company for the payment of salaries while they were being laid off, and to have the terminations rescinded. In this dispute, through the efforts of the Shizuoka prefecture Labour Relations Commission, the company agreed to pay 420,000 yen (about US$3,500) in settlement money to 33 people. Since then they have been negotiating with the company for the re-employment of union members.

Mr M had no previous experience with unions before joining the JMIU-SSCS. Although he was an older worker, with his inherently bright disposition, positive attitude towards others and persistence, he has continued to serve as chapter director up to now. In expressing his motivation for continuing his union activities, he shows anger when he says, 'If I stopped, the chapter would fall apart. That would be accepting how the company does things.' However, he also gets satisfaction and excitement from his union activities in a number of ways. As a result of forming the chapter, he no longer cries himself to sleep, and he has been able to raise issues to intermediaries. Members' interpersonal relations had been limited to ethnic Japanese-Brazilian society, but they came to know many Japanese through their involvement in the unions. Another favourable outcome has been that ethnic Japanese-Brazilians who do not understand Japanese, or the Japanese system, have come to rely on him to help them understand social insurance benefits and labour laws. I asked Mr M what worries he had about union membership. He replied with a laugh that '[t]here is no possibility that the temporary staffing services hire me ... because I might protest about working conditions by organising Japanese-Brazilians.' However, this is not a serious problem for him, since he can speak Japanese fluently, and could find a job through Hello Work, a Japanese public employment agency.

CONCLUSION

The JMIU-SSCS is a chapter of an industrial labour union that also has the characteristics of a union for individuals. The former is the side that promotes activities aimed at improving workplace conditions by organising workers in the metalworking and telecommunications industries, and forming chapters in workplaces. The latter is the side that promotes the resolution of the individual disputes of non-organised irregular workers, such as temporary workers, who are joining the union. While accepting a wide range of irregular workers as members, the JMIU-SSCS offers an entry point for workers who include ethnic Japanese-Brazilians, for daily association, including study activities and recreation. It has developed a stratum of members that can assume leadership, and has succeeded in developing leaders from within this group (such as Mr M), who also serve as the executives of regional chapters. On the one hand, as of December 2014 only two chapters remained, and the number of ethnic Japanese-Brazilians had fallen to around 40. This is a problem, in that it is difficult to organise continuously, as is necessary since irregular workers are the group's focus. There was a further limitation, however, in that unions could not fully support ethnic Japanese-Brazilians in adverse circumstances due to personal issues. For example, those temporary workers who were left out in the cold after the Lehman Shock were able to feed themselves every day, thanks to the distribution of food by local Japanese-Brazilian associations such as churches, but the regional chapters were not involved in these types of activities. In the future, Japanese labour unions must establish a system that will allow them to respond more broadly to labour and life issues, by supporting irregular workers – including immigrant workers – and developing networks capable of offering livelihood support.

NOTES

1. Under the Industrial Trainee and Technical Internship Programme, workers are allowed to come to Japan from other Asian countries for a maximum of three years, for the purpose of receiving training in small companies in a regional textile industry that was already in decline in the 1970s, and an industry that Japanese people avoided. However, there is no freedom to switch jobs under this programme, and immigrants incur large debts upon arrival. There are many problems with this system, including the fact that the training allowance of 300 yen (US$2.50/hour) is well below the minimum wage (the national average wage was 749 yen/hour in 2012 = US$6.20/hour) (Gaikokujin Kensyusei Mondai Network, 2006).

2. The union's internal reports are created in order to report to the union's upper body, and are not normally intended to be viewed outside of this context. In this case, I was granted permission to cite this document.

REFERENCES

Endo, K. (2012). 'Atarashii Rodosya Soshiki no Igi (The Meaning of New Workers' Association)'. In Endo, K. (Ed.), *Kojinkamei Union to RodoNPO: Haijyosareta Rodosya no Kenri Yogo* (pp. 1–32). Kyoto: Mineruva shobo.

Gaikokujin Kensyusei Mondai Network. (2006). *Gaikokujin Kensyusei Jikyu 300 yen no Rodosya (Foreign Trainee – Hourly Wage of 300 yen)*. Tokyo: Akashi Syoten.

Goka, K. (2014). *Hiseiki Taikoku Nippon no Koyo to Rodo. (The Employment and Work of Many Irregular Workers in Japan)*. Tokyo: Shinnihon Syupansya.

Gotou, K. (2013). 'Kumiaiin Needs no Hirogari (The Spread of Needs at Union Member)'. *Nihon Rodo Kenkyu Zashi*, 55(7), 77–87.

Hasegawa, Y. (2006). 'Chusho Kigyo no Rodosya wo Taisyo toshita Soshiki Kakudai (The Trial to Enlarge the Organization of the Small and Medium Enterprise Workers)'. In Suzuki, R. and Hayakawa, S. (Eds), *Rodo Kumiai no Soshiki Kakudai Senryaku* (pp. 183–208). Tokyo: Ochanomizu Shobo.

Hayakawa, S. (2006). 'Rengo to Zenroren no Soshiki Kakudai Senryaku (The Labour Union Expansion Strategy of Rengo and Zenroren)'. In Suzuki R. and Hayakawa, S. (Eds), *Rodo Kumiai no Soshiki Kakudai Senryaku* (pp. 69–98). Tokyo: Ochanomizu Shobo.

Hyodo, A. (2006). 'Nihon no Rodokumiai Undo niokeru Soshikika Katsudo no Shiteki Tenkai (The History of Labour Movement in Japan)'. In Suzuki R. and

Just Work?

Hayakawa, S. (Eds), *Rodo Kumiai no Soshiki Kakudai Senryaku* (pp. 3–36). Tokyo: Ochanomizu Shobo.

—— (2013). 'Sangyo Betu Rodo Kumiai Chiiki Shibu ni yoru Gaikoku-Jin Rodosya no Soshikika (The Organization of Foreign Workers by a Regional Chapter of an Industry Labour Union)'. *Sensyu Daigaku Syakai Kagaku Gepou*, 597, 25–36.

Ito, T. (2013) *Hiseiki Koyo to Rodo Undo (The Temporary Workers And Labor Movement)*. Kyoto: Houritsu Jyunpo Sya.

Kinoshita, T. (2010). 'Working Poor no Zodai to Atarashii Union Undo (The Increase of Working Poor and New Labour Union)'. *Syakai Seisaku*, 1(4), 41–61.

MIC (Ministry of Internal Affairs and Communications). (1983). *1982 Employment Status Survey*. Tokyo: MIC.

—— (1993). *1992 Employment Status Survey*. Tokyo: MIC.

—— (1998). *1997 Employment Status Survey*. Tokyo: MIC.

—— (2003). *2002 Employment Status Survey*. Tokyo: MIC.

—— (2013). *2012 Employment Status Survey*. Tokyo: MIC.

Ministry of Health, Labour and Welfare (MHLW). (2003). *Survey on Status of Labour Unions 2003*, Tokyo: MHLW.

—— (2014). *Basic Survey on Labour Unions 2014*. Tokyo: MHLW.

—— (2014). *Foreign National Employment Notification Status Report October 2013*. Tokyo: MHLW.

Miyao, S. (2002). *Borderless ni naru Nikkeijin (The Borderless of Japanese-Brazilians)*. São-Paulo: Centro de Estudos Nipo-Brasileiros .

Nakayasu, T. (2007). 'Nikkei Brazil-jin Rodosya no Genjyo to Soshikika (The Present Situation and Organizing of Ethnic Japanese-Brazilians)'. *Keizai*, 147, 59–67.

OECD (Organisation for Economic Co-operation and Development). (2014). *International Migration Outlook 2014*. Paris: OECD.

Ogawa, K. (2000). 'Nihon ni okeru Gaikoku-jin Rodosya no Soshiki-Ka (The Organizing of Foreign Workers in Japan)'. *Rodo Houritsu Jyunpo*, 1481, 41–9.

Oh, H. (2012). *Roushi Kankei no Frontier (The Frontier of Industry Relations)*. Tokyo: The Japan Institute for Labour Policy and Training.

Terama, S. (2010). 'Local Union to Hiseiki Rodosya no Soshikika (The Local Union and Organizing of Irregular Workers)'. *Keizai Kagaku Tuushin*, 124, 78–86.

—— (2012). 'Zenroren ni okeru Soshiki Kakudai Kyoka no Torikumi (The Trial to Enlarge and Reinforcement of Zenroren)'. *Keizai Kagaku Tuushin*, 129, 37–41.

Ueki, H. (2012). 'Nikkei Brazil-jin heno Roumu Kanri (The Labour Management for Ethnic Japanese-Brazilian)'. *Thingin to Syakaihosyo*, 1570, 48–64.

—— (2015). 'Nihon ni okeru Gaikoku-jin Rodosya: New Comer no 25nen (Foreign Workers in Japan: 25 years of New Comer)'. In Toyofuku, Y. (Ed.), *Shihonsyugi no Genzai* (pp. 180–98). Kyoto: Bunrikaku.

Urano, E. I. (2007). 'Zainichi Latin America-jin Rodosya no Soshikika no Kanousei (The Possibilities of Organizing of Latin American Workers in Japan)'. *Rodo Houritsu Jyunpo*, 1650, 54–64.

Weathers, C. (2012). 'General Union to Osaka no Gaikokujin Hiseikirodosya (The General Union and Contingent Workers in Osaka)'. In Endo K. (Ed.), *Kojinkamei Union to RodoNPO: Haijyosareta Rodosya no Kenri Yogo* (pp. 83–106). Kyoto Mineruva Shobo.

10

Disaster Capitalism and Migrant Worker Organising in Aotearoa/New Zealand

Edward Miller and Dennis Maga

Only a crisis – actual or perceived – produces real change.
When that crisis occurs, the actions that are taken depend on the
ideas that are lying around.
>   Milton Friedman and Rose D. Friedman (1982: ix)

Migrant workers have long occupied an important role in the development of capitalism in Aotearoa/New Zealand. This chapter argues that migrant workers are now indispensable to the reconstruction projects that have followed the Christchurch earthquakes of 2010 and 2011, and that this has brought with it a significant rise in migrant worker exploitation. We begin with a short history of labour migration in Aotearoa/New Zealand, focusing specifically on the impact of neoliberalism in the country and its impact on the labour market and migration policy. Then we address some of the policies passed in the wake of those earthquakes, using the 'disaster capitalism' lens to argue that neoliberalism benefits from moments of collective trauma to justify the implementation of unpopular policies. Next we discuss the development of community-based migrant worker organising through the Union Network of Migrants (UNEMIG, a division of FIRST Union) and its approach to organising migrants. Finally, we look at the evolution of that approach in the response to disaster capitalism, stressing the importance of broader community engagement and ideological preparedness for disasters.

NEOLIBERALISM AND MIGRATION IN AOTEAROA/NEW ZEALAND

Labour migration has played a central role in the development of capitalism in Aotearoa/New Zealand. Labour migration was predominantly shaped by colonial relations, both as a settler state and quasi-colonial power in the South Pacific, until the neoliberal labour migration reforms of the 1980s. Like Australia and Canada, British colonial ties shaped the first century of immigration policy, imposing narrow racial preferences for immigrants from the United Kingdom (UK), and slowly expanding to other parts of Europe (Hiebert et al., 2003). Post-Second World War policy was shaped by Keynesian ideas of state-managed protectionist capitalism, employment-focused trade and monetary policy and an active, interventionist welfare state. This created a high demand for labour, and in 1944 the government passed the Manpower Act to facilitate internal migration of Maori, a key cause of the rapid post-war Maori urbanisation. After a few decades this proved insufficient to feed Aotearoa/New Zealand's fledgling industrial expansion, and by the 1960s and 1970s many semi-skilled and unskilled migrants from the South Pacific were granted short-term working visas.[1] Many of these workers had illegally overstayed their visa conditions, but the government largely ignored this due to the critical role these workers played in keeping wages down.

The entry of the UK into the European Community and spikes in oil prices sent the economy into a downturn. Rising unemployment fuelled populist xenophobia against Pacific migrants (termed 'overstayers'), prompting a re-evaluation of migration policy and a heavy-handed policing response including proof of residency laws, police raids and deportations (Hiebert et al., 2003). Immigration policy reverted back to its European, particularly British, preference. This was intended to address racist concerns within Aotearoa/New Zealand society, but did little to allay the global crisis eating into capitalism's profitability. Finance capital, however, had a new plan to restore profitability, which involved free trade and investment policies, financial and labour market deregulation, privatisation of state assets and cuts to public spending. These ideas, later labelled neoliberalism, had a profound impact on Aotearoa/New Zealand political society, alongside Thatcherism and Reaganomics in the UK and US.

Neoliberalism's implementation in Aotearoa/New Zealand has relied on shock and crisis. Financial and political elites had long worked on an alternative economic vision, and working with former Labour Party MP and finance minister Roger Douglas in the early 1980s led to 'Rogernomics' reforms, where the role of the state in the economy was dramatically reduced. This radical financial and labour market deregulation was described by economist Brian Easton as the 'blitzkrieg' approach, which required 'implement[ing] it as quickly as possible to overwhelm the opposition' (Kelsey, 1995: 33–4). The neoliberal assault on the labour market began with an about-turn on monetary policy. The use of a targeted inflation window pushed up interest rates dramatically, rendering credit unaffordable to many firms. Grinding austerity prevented firms taking on new workers, while many others were laid off during the corporatisation and privatisation of state-run assets and industries. From the late 1980s, Aotearoa/New Zealand has grappled with structural unemployment, which, combined with cuts to state unemployment assistance, has kept labour cheap and well-disciplined. Inequality grew dramatically. From the mid-1980s until 2004, Aotearoa/New Zealand saw the greatest increase in income inequality in any OECD country for which data is available, and between 1981 and 2002 the share of income going to wage and salary earners fell from 60 per cent to 46 per cent. This was aided by draconian anti-union laws like the 1991 Employment Contracts Act, which quickly eroded trade union density, and Aotearoa/New Zealand also quickly slipped down the OECD rankings for employment protection laws. From 1981 to 2011, labour productivity growth outpaced wages by 30 per cent (Rosenberg, 2013). Labour became cheaper and more flexible, buoyed by the threat of financial crises and economic disaster.

Neoliberalism has intensified successive New Zealand governments' focus on the global market, which have been active participants in bilateral, multilateral and global trade and investment liberalisation negotiations. While these agreements have liberalised the movement of goods and capital, the movement of labour has been subject to increased complexity and criminalisation, rendering workers more vulnerable and making labour cheaper and more pliant (Gomberg-Muñoz, 2012). At the same time the global unemployment that has resulted from debt crises in the Global South, and IMF-imposed structural adjustment policies and free trade and investment agreements, have also markedly increased global immigration flows. Aotearoa/New Zealand's embrace of neoliberal immigration reforms in the 1980s facilitated the selection of immigrants on the basis of international competitiveness and labour demand rather than ethnic/racial background, in a move away from the earlier preference for European migrants (Hiebert et al., 2003). By the late 1990s Aotearoa/New Zealand had the highest per capita immigrant intake in the OECD, and waves of Asian immigration (largely from India and China) fuelled racial tensions.

State retreat exacerbated these tensions. The obsessive neoliberal focus on individualism privileged a depiction of immigrants as 'competitive responsibilised and entrepreneurial selves' (Lewis et al., 2009: 167), able to rationally exploit the marketplace for their own benefit. Skills shortages during the Labour government of 1999–2008 saw the moderation of this approach, and community-based migrant resettlement and support services (including adult education and language courses) received greater funding. The election of a National government (the traditionally conservative party) in 2008 and international economic instability resulted in widespread budget cuts from 2009 onwards, hollowing out migrant assistance spending (Spoonley and Cain, 2013). The Immigration Act 2009 underscored the neoliberal focus on individualism; its purpose provisions include explicitly referencing 'access to skills and labour'. The Act contains eight visa categories,[2] with the most common being student visas (limiting hours at certain times but open in terms of employers) and work visas (can be limited by time, skill and employers). Subsequent governments showed little derogation from the model of state retreat and neoliberalism. However, its implementation slowed, and to win the 2008 election the incoming National government appealed to centrist voters. A few years later, the Christchurch earthquakes provided a powerful justification to reaccelerate the process of neo-liberalisation, as well as opening up the most recent chapter of labour migration in Aotearoa/New Zealand.

DISASTER CAPITALISM IN CHRISTCHURCH

Naomi Klein argues that moments of collective trauma – such as *coups d'état* or natural disasters – can be exploited by policymakers 'to engage in radical social and economic engineering' (Klein, 2007: 8). These events suspend and even redefine reality, creating a sense of crisis that temporarily immobilises the everyday routine of a community or country. Taking advantage of these events can facilitate the imposition of unpopular or anti-democratic policies with limited resistance. She details the implementation of neoliberalism under cover of crisis – in *coups d'état* in Argentina, Chile, Brazil and Indonesia, following natural disasters in Sri Lanka and New Orleans, as well as in the wake of wars or terrorist attacks – concluding that the faster this is undertaken, the less chance there is of any countermovement developing. The implementation of neoliberalism, in other words, has relied on the suspension of democracy through shock.

The reconstruction of New Orleans after Hurricane Katrina demonstrates the dynamics of disaster capitalism. As think tanks began isolating the areas of law that needed reform to lubricate the reconstruction (including living wage and migrant protection laws), major contractors were handed bloated no-bid disaster-relief and construction contracts from taxpayers' money (many of which were also war profiteers during the Iraq invasion and reconstruction). The deal was even sweetened with the relaxation of local labour and wage regulations. Bringing in migrant workers helps to keep labour costs down, and complaints soon began to emerge from New Orleans of poorly monitored construction sites with large numbers of poorly paid migrant workers working with toxic substances and living in inadequate housing with poor healthcare facilities (Southern Poverty Law Centre, 2006: 1). Klein argues that the contractors exhibited 'an aversion to hiring local people', citing one study suggesting that almost a quarter of rebuild workers didn't have immigration papers (Klein, 2007: 410). Competition and widespread subcontracting put enormous downward pressure on labour – one journalist described a subcontracting chain where of the NZ$175 (around US$111) a contractor was paid per square foot for installing (government-purchased) tarpaulin, only NZ$2 (around US$1.27) reached the worker's pockets (Davis, 2006).

In Aotearoa/New Zealand, the Christchurch earthquakes of 2010 and 2011 invoked a similar sense of nationwide shock. On 4 September 2010 a magnitude 7.1 earthquake shook the Canterbury region 40 km west of the city of Christchurch. There was minimal loss of life but the scale of property damage, both to private residences and public infrastructure, was already forecast to be enormous. The worst was yet to come. At 12:51 pm on 22 February 2011 a second powerful earthquake shook Christchurch violently. The cumulative effect of the earthquakes on an already damaged city literally tore buildings apart. A total of 181 people died, including 115 in one building alone. Most New Zealanders were affected in some way, thinking of family members, friends and workmates in Christchurch. For a moment, the country stood still.

The government's immediate response to the crisis consisted of an executive power-grab. During a weeklong regional state of emergency[3] (NZPA, 2010a), the government introduced, read, passed and assented to the Canterbury Earthquake Response and Recovery Act 2010. Until April 2012, the law gave the newly appointed minister for Canterbury Earthquake recovery the power to 'grant an exemption from, or modify, or extend any provision of any enactment', or create 'Orders of Council' with full legislative force. This was described by 27 legal scholars as 'an extraordinarily broad transfer of lawmaking power away from Parliament and to the executive branch, with minimal constraints on how that power may be used' (Legal Scholars, 2010). Similar legislation followed the second quake, extending these powers until 2016. Christchurch remained in shock, but political elites, business columnists and right wing think tanks soon spoke up. It was two weeks before suggestions began to surface, like cutting spending on unemployment benefits and student loans (O'Sullivan, 2011) or the sell-down of local government's shareholding in 'commercial businesses' like transport and electricity infrastructure (NZPA, 2011a). Government departments were instructed to consider private finance initiatives to bridge funding gaps (Rosenberg, 2012), and the prime minister suggested that Christchurch would have to consider partial asset sales to cover rebuild costs (APNZ, 2012). A raft of unpopular corporate-friendly policies were passed, including replacing Canterbury's statutory environmental decision maker (facilitating the expansion of irrigation consents in Canterbury's agricultural frontier), the implementation of for-profit charter schools (Gordon, 2012; Post Primary Teachers Association, 2014) and myriad planning decisions to the benefit of property developers (opening space to facilitate migrant worker exploitation).

In the Christchurch earthquakes, neoliberal policymakers found a powerful justification to impose a dramatic geographical and ethnic transformation, thus feeding an emerging frontier for profit accumulation and associated exploitation. As the rebuild began, the scope for capital accumulation increased the demand for labour. The scramble to keep labour costs low meant that rather than training Aotearoa/New Zealand's unemployed workforce or stemming the export of skilled and semi-skilled labour (particularly to Australia), private firms began a lucrative trade of cross-border labour migration, primarily from the Philippines. Throughout 2013, trade unions in the Christchurch area began to receive complaints from workers dealing with serious employment irregularities, prompting FIRST Union to get involved.

THE BIRTH OF THE UNEMIG ORGANISING MODEL

Migrant worker organising has not always been seen as a priority of unions in Aotearoa/New Zealand; however, cross-border labour flows have now become a consistent factor shaping the global economy. The changing nature of the workforce and the demographics of the sectors covered by the National Distribution Union (NDU),[4] with the assistance of other trade unions, forced the union movement to confront the issue and consider what kind of organising approach this demanded.

The NDU (FIRST Union's predecessor) actively opposed the racist nature of the dawn raids against Pacific Island workers during the 1970s. It was the first private sector trade union in the country to develop an internal structure – the Fono – within the union to advocate for the interests of Pacific workers, in the mid-1990s. While the Fono network plays an important role in advocating the interests of Pacific workers within the union, workers are not actively recruited on the basis of ethnicity or status as a Pacific migrant worker. Indeed, many Pacific workers are second- or even third-generation New Zealanders. In 2009, the NDU formed its initial migrant workers network, a structural step within the union towards recognising the prevalence of migrant worker exploitation. The NDU recognised that labour migration can be a positive experience for both workers and the receiving countries, but that regulation and enforcement are critical. It understood that exploited migrant workers can be used to drive down wages and conditions across the labour market, and can engender deep social divisions. Without embedding migrant workers' interests within the interests of the broader labour movement, trade unions risk alienating their base altogether.

Initially, the NDU's migrant worker organising approach was distinct from traditional union organising models, but still relatively unsophisticated. Where migrant workers were engaged, organisers would be encouraged to identify the relevant ethnicities they could work with, develop a network of contacts and, where possible, make some of them union delegates. At the time, migrant worker organising was largely focused in Auckland, and mainly with workers of Filipino and Indian origin. As cases came forward from different industries, the union used a combination of legal advocacy with media campaigns to alert workers of their rights and encourage others to come forward, alerting employers that these cases were being taken seriously.

The NDU's migrant worker network began addressing the concerns of migrant workers in different industries, often engaging with different unions. One of the earliest cases involved the use of migrant workers (particularly Fijian Indians) replacing drivers who had quit the company NZ Bus over low wages. The workers' work visas were being consistently renewed, but only for a one-year period, leaving them with vulnerable immigration status. Negotiations and high-level dialogue took place between the NDU, the New Zealand Council of Trade Unions (NZCTU), NZ Bus and Immigration New Zealand. Visa extensions were achieved, but the workers were denied permanent residency. These cases highlighted the importance of unions having a well thought out strategy for dealing with migrant worker issues.

A 2009 case involved the government telecommunications firm Chorus, which contracted work out to a company called Transfield that employed Filipino line maintenance engineers. When Transfield lost the contract to another contractor, VisionStream, the workers were informed that work would henceforth be transferred to a subcontracting model, meaning the workers were not guaranteed a job and thus no work visa. Working with both the relevant union (the Engineers, Printers and Manufacturers Union (EPMU)) and MIGRANTE,[5] the migrant workers formed the backbone of strike action against the company, the first time migrant workers had engaged in strike action since the 1980s. Industrial action failed to prevent the introduction of the subcontracting model, but saved the workers' jobs and forced the company to negotiate a pathway to residency.

These cases encouraged the NDU to refine their migrant worker organising approach, and a cross-union workshop was facilitated by the NZCTU to formalise this. The end result was a five-step approach for organising migrant workers, which organisers and delegates were encouraged to adopt:

1. An organiser or workplace activist needs to ascertain the nationalities of workers on the site. This helps identify the dynamics of power in the workplace by highlighting the potential allies available to work with, and recognising potential obstacles so the organiser can start thinking about how to deal with them. Mapping is an ongoing process and will always help the organisers or activists in organising work as well as identify possible obstacles.

2. Organisers/activists are encouraged to engage migrant workers in discussions about their day-to-day problems and help them address them. Some common problems include discrimination, dealing with substandard contracts or intimidation from their

employers. Addressing these problems helps to build confidence in the union.

3. Organisers need to be prepared to overcome common objections such as knowledge gaps around migrants' rights to join a union (many fear losing their visa), negative views about unions (often from past experiences in their country of origin) and membership costs. Addressing these objections helps explain the role and importance of trade unions to workers regardless of immigration status. While many migrants know they are paid less than local workers, few know how collective agreements can alter this imbalance, or that unions can assist them in negotiating work visa renewals. Inviting migrant workers from a unionised workplace can also be useful in overcoming fears and objections.

4. As with all union members, migrant workers' commitment will vary, and organisers need to identify the key migrant contacts and potential activists. Those who are staunch supporters should be encouraged to become union leaders or delegates, while those with less confidence can play other roles.

5. In workplaces where there are workers of different nationalities, organisers are encouraged to develop a Workplace Migrants Network. The network helped the union to overcome language and cultural barriers. Communicating in workers' mother tongues became an effective tool to collectivise and unionise the new and recent migrants. These networks assist union delegates and union officials in organising different nationalities in tasks like translation and organising events outside their workplaces.

By 2012, the growing prevalence and visibility of migrant worker exploitation meant that the NDU's successor, FIRST Union, was approached on average once a week with migrant worker cases to address. In the majority of cases the mere fact of union intervention was sufficient to resolve the issue without the need to pursue legal action. However, between 2012 and 2013 a legal case would have to be taken approximately every two months.

One case involved a live-in domestic worker on a student visa[6] who had been seriously underpaid, was working over 65 hours a week, was not receiving other minimum legal entitlements, and was under a high degree of surveillance and control from her employer. After being contacted by a friend, the union staged a direct intervention at the house where the worker lived with news media present. The worker was immediately taken to a doctor where she was put on a drip to treat severe dehydration, and soon after returned to the Philippines. The case was highly publicised (One News, 2012), and the union secured a mediated settlement of almost NZ$40,000. Another domestic worker was also working 65 hours a week, which, given her monthly pay of NZ$400 a month, worked out to NZ$1.50 an hour, with the hourly minimum wage being NZ$13.50 at the time. This worker's passport was held by her employer as a mechanism of control. A similar intervention was staged and legal case won; the worker has remained in Aotearoa/New Zealand and is still a union member.

By this stage it was becoming clear that migrant workers were spread across too many industries – including domestic work, hospitality, construction, IT services, dairy farming, horticulture and many more – for FIRST Union alone to deal with within its existing structures. In response to this, UNEMIG was formed on 19 August 2012 as a cross-sector cross-union organisation to deal with migrant worker abuse. UNEMIG works on the basis of community union membership rather than an industry or worksite basis. It is open to all new and recent migrants regardless of their employment or immigration status. Members can avail themselves of employment advice and representation, immigration assistance, settlement support, and rights at work seminars for migrants and community linking which are not usually provided by local unions. UNEMIG will organise members on sites that have no collective employment agreement or union. However, membership is intended to be transitional. Once a site has been organised, membership is transferred to the relevant union for bargaining purposes while they remain members of UNEMIG. UNEMIG itself is not a bargaining union; its members are associate members of FIRST Union. This means that they do not pay full fees or union dues and they are not automatically entitled to full benefits of a regular member of FIRST Union due to the absence of a collective agreement.

This community approach combining advocacy and direct action made UNEMIG the leading voice on the issue of migrant worker exploitation. The aftermath of the Canterbury earthquakes appeared to provide some of its most significant challenges to date. As Christchurch became gripped by disaster capitalism in the wake of its earthquakes, the attenuation of democracy and social movements opened a space in which exploitation could flourish. This took the form of a search for cheap and pliable labour to satisfy the profit-making demands of construction companies that won contracts to rebuild the shattered city.

MIGRANT WORKER ORGANISING IN THE CANTERBURY REBUILD

At the beginning of 2014, HSBC bank economist Paul Bloxham predicted Aotearoa/New Zealand would be the 'rock star' economy of that year (Fairfax Media, 2014). Economists now regularly refer to the Canterbury Rebuild as one of the key growth engines behind that success (Wakefield, 2014), and the National government (2008 onwards) has highlighted it as one of its four major economic priorities (Bridges, 2014). Yet the rebuild has been built on a foundation of exploitation. In Christchurch, the reliance of construction firms on migrant workers from the Philippines, whose employment and visa status rendered them vulnerable and difficult to organise, served as the basis for enormous accumulation of profits.

The Christchurch Rebuild is the largest building project in the country's history, including an estimated 10,000 demolished homes and over 100,000 damaged homes. Rebuild costs were initially estimated at NZ$15–20 billion, but by April 2013 were scaled up to around NZ$40 billion – almost a fifth of the country's gross domestic product (GDP), including a total government contribution of $15.2 billion (One News, 2013). The economic stimulus effect of rebuild activity to the national economy has steadily grown, and is expected to peak in 2017 at 2 per cent of GDP (Bagrie and Zöllner, 2014). After the October 2010 earthquake, Fletchers Construction won a billion-dollar contract to run the state earthquake insurer the Earthquake Commission's (EQC) project management office overseeing the rebuild (NZPA, 2010b). The second major earthquake doubled the scope of Fletchers' contract, to 100,000 homes. Fletchers, the largest listed company in Aotearoa/New Zealand, established a 'Fletchers Earthquake Recovery' business unit responsible for coordinating repairs on homes with damage assessed between NZ$15,000 and NZ$100,000. As repairs initially began in November 2010, Fletchers and the EQC addressed a meeting of 700 builders at the Christchurch AMI Stadium, telling them they would be paid NZ$45 an hour when subcontracted for quake-recovery work (Heather, 2010). Subsequent thoroughgoing assessment work showed the full extent of damage: by August 2011, 312,000 insurance claims had been received by the EQC (Boiser et al., 2011: 2).

It soon became clear that the local skilled labour force would be extremely insufficient to cope with the pace of construction required. By September 2012, the industry's labour demand model forecast that the rebuild would require 10,000–17,000 additional construction workers and as many as 15,000 additional workers in supporting roles, peaking in the fourth quarter of 2014 (Construction Sector Leaders Group, 2013). Christchurch's unemployment rate began dropping rapidly in 2012, and by 2013 the intention to use migrant workers had grown strongly among firms engaged in the rebuild. Migrants initially came from the UK, Ireland and the United States, but firms soon looked further afield (Chang-Richards et al., 2013: 4). By July 2013, Christchurch was bringing in migrants at a rate of 22 per day, with the Philippines now joining the UK as the greatest source countries (Stewart, 2013). Between 2006 and 2013 the Filipino-speaking population of Christchurch and Canterbury almost trebled (Canterbury Development Corporation, 2013).[7] The formalisation of this labour importing supply chain appears to have begun in September 2012, when staff from Leighs Construction, a Christchurch-headquartered company, travelled to Manila and worked with a local recruitment agency to find 25 Filipino carpenters, arriving in Christchurch on two-year single-employer work visas (this information has now been removed from the firm's website).[8] The Aotearoa/New Zealand construction sector is largely deunionised, which meant the large arrival of foreign migrant workers into the region was met with little organised opposition. At the time of writing it is estimated that there are 2,500–3,000 Filipino migrant workers in

Christchurch, and many more have already stayed in Christchurch for the duration of their visas.

Around the end of 2013, UNEMIG started receiving communications from Filipino migrant workers working in construction on the Canterbury Rebuild. Their complaints included unpaid wages, breaches of the minimum wage, issues regarding settlement support such as poor housing conditions and overpriced rent, and significant recruitment and record-keeping anomalies. One case that UNEMIG dealt with involved a subcontractor that had forced a group of 40 Filipino workers to labour for free on Saturdays. Another well-publicised case involved a group of 15 workers who had not been paid for periods of between six and eleven weeks (NZN/Radiolive, 2014). Other cases involved arbitrary job losses, working without pay, crowded, overpriced accommodation, and oppressive contracts that require a penalty payment of NZ$10,000 if an employee does not complete their contract. One worker described the condition as 'a chain in our neck. That contract is a chain for us. It's squeezing us. We don't have freedom' (Morrah, 2014).

Due to the limited migrant workers' assistance channels available in Christchurch, UNEMIG began working with the EPMU – the union with traditional coverage of construction workers. Long deunionised, the sector is characterised by complex chains of subcontracting, preventing the EPMU from organising them easily. Multinational labour supply chains make these issues more complex. The migrant workers are engaged in the Philippines by a recruitment agency, where they sign a Filipino employment contract that is lodged with the Philippine Overseas Employment Administration Office, a Philippine government body. The Filipino employment agency then coordinates with an Aotearoa/New Zealand-based employment agency that substitutes their employment contract, deals with their New Zealand visa status with Immigration New Zealand (the government agency) and places them with a Christchurch-based firm. In many situations the employment relationship is triangular – while the work they do is for the benefit of the construction firm, it is the recruitment agency that hires them. This makes the process of organising migrant workers much more difficult.

UNEMIG's organising has relied very heavily on working with ethnic communities, and in Christchurch this work has intensified. UNEMIG employed a part-time Filipina organiser in Christchurch who was already active on these issues, and her work involves educating workers about their rights. Working with MIGRANTE Aotearoa, a short informative video named 'Juan in TraNZit' has been produced in Tagalog, with English subtitles. It depicts Filipino everyman 'Juan' going through the process of applying for a visa and migrating, and provides information on Aotearoa/New Zealand and Maori culture, politics, history and other valuable information. Juan then meets with workers in the dairy sector, learns how to get a tax number, gets a job in the construction sector and joins FIRST Union to learn his employment rights.

The increased social tension that accompanied the significant influx of Filipino workers has created another line of work. Rather than being seen as the victims of exploitation amid multinational labour supply chains, migrant workers are often seen as taking the jobs and occupying the houses that 'rightfully' belong to New Zealanders. The trade union movement is not immune to these attitudes, and care must be taken to ensure that unions are not providing a home to these views. Actively involving migrants in a broad range of community decision-making exercises is critical to ensuring that these divisions do not deepen. UNEMIG has been active in working with other unions in Christchurch to organise community events – to ensure the wider community has an understanding of the issues that migrant workers face and the importance of creating a social environment that supports new migrants.

UNEMIG has also found that more established migrants of the same nationality can play antagonistic roles. They are often involved in the establishment of exploitative labour supply chains, and some Christchurch-based Filipinos now act as labour brokers that headhunt migrant workers for their own profit. Community leaders have magnified this influence: when addressing a meeting of the Canterbury Philippine Assistance Group, the Philippines Ambassador to Aotearoa/New Zealand told migrant workers not to approach unions, 'especially those who post stories in the New Zealand Herald [newspaper]' if they are having employment problems (referring to

UNEMIG). UNEMIG responded immediately by alerting media to this attempt to meddle in Aotearoa/New Zealand's internal affairs, as well as writing to the ambassador and other officials in the Philippines. Another issue for migrant worker organising in this context is housing. The combined impact of the earthquakes on the housing stock and migration on regional demand meant that house prices and rents have risen precipitously, while wages remain low. The average weekly rent in Christchurch increased by 31 per cent between August 2010 and February 2013, from NZ$293 to NZ$384 (Ministry of Business, Innovation and Employment, 2013). Labour shortfalls pushed prices up for a range of commodities, and inflation has consistently been higher than the national average. Christchurch's power prices have been rising at twice the national average (Stylianou, 2013), and rates have increased faster than anywhere in the country as the council tried to patch a NZ$900 million budgetary shortfall (Christchurch City Council, 2014). For migrant workers, these concerns are significantly amplified – as a low cost alternative to the local labour force they are generally housed as cheaply as possible, creating concerns around the safety and quality of housing. UNEMIG has used its public profile to advocate for better housing conditions for migrant workers, but exercises only limited agency in this regard.

CONCLUSION

Migrant workers have long played a role in the development of capitalism in Aotearoa/New Zealand, but for too long they have been forgotten about and their rights ignored. The same is true of the Christchurch Rebuild, although on a scale and intensity that has not been seen in Christchurch before. Given the ongoing housing crisis – particularly in Auckland – it is likely that the demand for migrant workers in the construction sector will continue. UNEMIG is determined to ensure that those workers' rights are recognised.

The fact that in mid-2014 the government committed NZ$7 million over four years to targeting migrant worker exploitation (six new labour inspectors and seven immigration officers) shows that some progress has perhaps been made in pushing this issue on to the government's agenda. However, reliance on the government is not an option. It has a vested interest in getting the rebuild on track as quickly and cheaply as possible, which means keeping a steady flow of migrant workers heading to Christchurch. The Philippines government wants this migration to continue: 13.5 per cent of the Philippines' GDP comes from remittances, and thus the export of cheap labour has attained structural significance for the Philippine economy.

The experience of organising migrant workers in the Christchurch Rebuild has highlighted the importance of instilling UNEMIG members and the broader community with a sense of ideological preparedness to address such a crisis. Union and community organisers both benefit from an understanding of the psychological effects of shocks, crises or disasters, and as Milton Friedman (Friedman and Friedman, 1982) suggests in the opening quote, it is the 'ideas that are lying around' that determine the 'actions taken'. UNEMIG is determined to ensure that in the future, the ideas that lie around reinforce the rights of migrant workers and highlight their role in the historical and future development of the New Zealand economy.

NOTES

1. Both from countries within Aotearoa/New Zealand's quasi-colonial sphere (Cook Islands, Niue and Tokelau) and those with other connections (Samoa and Tonga).
2. Student visa, work visa, open work visa, working for holiday visa, recognised seasonal employer visa, work to residence visa, silver fern visa and interim visa.
3. A state of emergency is an acknowledgment that the situation 'threatens the life of the nation' and may require limitation of Aotearoa/New Zealand's international human rights obligations. For example certain obligations under the International Covenant on Civil and Political Rights are – the right to life, freedom from torture, freedom from slavery, freedom from retrospective punishments and the right to freedom of thought and religion – excluded from application.
4. In 2011, the NDU merged with Finsec to form FIRST Union, which now represents members in a number of sectors: Finance, Industrial (Textile, Clothing, Baking and Wood), Retail, Storage and Transport.
5. MIGRANTE is an international alliance of progressive organisations made up of Filipino migrants that works to secure the rights of the Filipino diaspora across the world.
6. The student visa had been extended for a number of years and, while the worker was ostensibly in the country to study English, it is believed that it was being used as a means of ensuring she could lawfully remain in the country.

7. There are no more accurate figures than this because the 2011 Census was cancelled after the second major earthquake. However, it is believed that the bulk of this change took place in the year or so leading up to the 2013 Census.
8. A 2013 article in *The Press* noted how Leighs had greatly profited hugely as a result of the rebuild; in 2013 annual turnover had hit NZ$70 million (and rising), allowing owner Anthony Leighs to purchase a NZ$3.7 million designer mansion in the Christchurch suburb of Riccarton (McCrone 2013).

REFERENCES

APNZ (Associated Press New Zealand). (2012). 'Christchurch Should Consider Partial Asset Sales – PM'. *The NZ Herald*, 21 May. www.nzherald.co.nz/nz/news/article.cfm?c_id=1&objectid=10807419 (accessed August 2015).

Bagrie, C. and Zöllner, S. (2014). 'Debunking the Post-Rebuild Hole Myth'. *ANZ Economic Comment*, 2 September. www.anz.co.nz/resources/f/9/f9532440-0b61-40bb-9002-f158086142a8/ANZ-Debunking-the-Chch-Myth.pdf?MOD=AJPERES (accessed August 2015).

Boiser, A., Wilkinson, S. and Yan Chang, A. (2011). *Skills Availability for Housing Repair and Reconstruction in Christchurch*. Resilient Organizations Research Programme/University of Auckland. www.recres.org.nz/docs/reports/preliminary_skills_report.pdf (accessed August 2015).

Bridges, Hon S. (2014). *Budget 2014: Tackling Migrant Exploitation in Canterbury*. https://www.national.org.nz/news/news/media-releases/detail/2014/05/20/budget-2014-tackling-migrant-exploitation-in-canterbury (accessed August 2015).

Canterbury Development Corporation. (2013). *Christchurch Increasingly Multicultural, Multilingual – Census 2013*. www.cdc.org.nz/news/christchurch-increasingly-multicultural-multilingual-census-2013/ (accessed August 2015).

Chang-Richards, A., Wilkinson, S., Seville, E. and Brunsdon, D. (2013). 'Resourcing of the Canterbury Rebuild: Case Studies of Construction Organisations'. The University of Auckland. www.resorgs.org.nz/images/stories/pdfs/Reconstruction followingdisaster/case_study_report_resourcing.pdf (accessed August 2015).

Christchurch City Council (2014). *Annual Plan and Rates Rise FAQ*. http://resources.ccc.govt.nz/files/TheCouncil/newsmedia/mediareleases/2014/FAQsAnnualPlanJune2014.pdf (accessed August 2015).

Construction Sector Leaders Group. (2013). *Construction Sector Workforce Plan For Greater Christchurch*. www.constructionstrategygroup.org.nz/downloads/Construction_Sector_Plan_-_FINAL.pdf (accessed August 2015).

Fairfax Media (2014). 'New Zealand 2014's "Rock Star" Economy'. *Business Day*, 7 January. www.stuff.co.nz/business/industries/9583473/New-Zealand-2014s-rock-star-economy (accessed August 2015).

Friedman, M. and Friedman, R. D. (1982). *Capitalism and Freedom*. Chicago: University of Chicago Press.

Gordon, L. (2012). 'The Politics of Charter Schools'. *Foreign Control Watchdog*, 129, April. www.converge.org.nz/watchdog/29/04.htm (accessed August 2015).

Gomberg-Muñoz, R. (2012). 'Inequality in a "Postracial" Era: Race, Immigration, and Criminalization of Low Wage Labor'. *Du Bois Review*, 9(2), 339–53.

Heather, B. (2010). 'Fletcher Hits Back'. *The Press*, 18 November. www.stuff.co.nz/the-press/news/4356780/Fletcher-hits-back (accessed August 2015).

Hiebert, D., Collins, J. and Spoonley, P. (2003). *Uneven Globalization: Neoliberal Regimes, Immigration, and Multiculturalism in Australia, Canada and New Zealand*. Vancouver Centre of Excellence Working Paper Series No. 3–5. http://mbc.metropolis.net/assets/uploads/files/wp/2003/WP03–05.pdf (accessed August 2015).

Kelsey, J. (1995). *The New Zealand Experiment: A World Model for Structural Adjustment?* Auckland: Auckland University Press.

Klein, N. (2007). *The Shock Doctrine: The Rise of Disaster Capitalism*. New York: Metropolitan Books.

Legal Scholars. (2010). *Deep Canterbury Quake Law Concerns*. Media release, 28 September. http://auckland.scoop.co.nz/2010/09/legal-scholars-deep-canterbury-quake-law-concerns/#more-5862 (accessed August 2015).

Lewis, N., Lewis, O. and Underhill-Sem, Y. (2009) 'Filling Hollowed Out Spaces with Localised Meanings, Practices and Hope: Progressive Neoliberal Spaces in Te Rarawa'. *Asia Pacific Viewpoint*, 50(2), 166–84.

McCrone, J. (2013). 'Players at the Helm of a Boom'. *The Press*. www.stuff.co.nz/the-press/business/the-rebuild/8660409/Players-at-the-helm-of-a-boom (accessed August 2015).

Ministry of Business, Innovation and Employment (2013). *Housing Pressures in Christchurch: A Summary of the Evidence*. Wellington: Ministry of Business, Innovation and Employment. www.dbh.govt.nz/UserFiles/File/Publications/Sector/pdf/christchurch-housing-report.pdf (accessed August 2015).

Morrah, M. (2014). 'Christchurch Rebuild Migrants Face Debts, Cramped Accommodation'. *3rd Degree*, 16 July. www.3news.co.nz/tvshows/3rd-degree/christchurch-rebuild-migrants-face-debts-cramped-accommodation-2014071618 (accessed August 2015).

NZN/Radiolive (2014). 'Migrant Rebuild Workers being Exploited, Says Union'. *3 News*, 6 January. www.3news.co.nz/business/migrant-rebuild-workers-being-exploited-says-union-2014010608#axzz3kBZYtVBT (accessed August 2015).

NZPA (New Zealand Press Association). (2010a). 'Canterbury States of Emergency Lifted'. *Otago Daily Times*, 16 September). www.odt.co.nz/news/national/126747/canterbury-states-emergency-lifted (accessed August 2015).

—— (2010b). 'Fletchers gets $1bn Quake Contract'. *The New Zealand Herald*, 15 October. www.nzherald.co.nz/nz/news/article.cfm?c_id=1&objectid=10680864 (accessed August 2015).

—— (2011a). 'Christchurch Earthquake: Roundtable Calls for Sell-Off'. *The New Zealand Herald*, 14 March. www.nzherald.co.nz/business/news/article.cfm?c_id=3andobjectid=10712213 (accessed August 2015).

One News. (2012). 'Migrant Taking Legal Action against Auckland Family'. *Television New Zealand*, 12 October. http://tvnz.co.nz/national-news/migrant-taking-legal-action-against-auckland-family-5128207 (accessed August 2015).

—— 'Cost of Christchurch Rebuild Balloons by $10b'. *Television New Zealand*. http://tvnz.co.nz/national-news/cost-christchurch-rebuild-balloons-10b-5419980?autoStart=true (accessed August 2015).

O'Sullivan, F. (2011). 'Fran O'Sullivan: Key Should Not Hesitate to Seek Nation's Help to Finance Rebuild'. *The New Zealand Herald*, 26 February. www.nzherald.co.nz/politics/news/article.cfm?c_id=280andobjectid=10708760 (accessed August 2015).

Post Primary Teachers' Assocation. (2014). *Charter School, Free School, Models and the New Zealand Education Environment*. Post Primary Teachers' Assocation, 18 March. www.ppta.org.nz/index.php/-issues-in-education/charter-schools/2119-no-charter-schools-nz (accessed August 2015).

Press, The. (2012,). 'Black Day for Democracy in Canterbury and the Nation'. *The Press*, 8 September. www.stuff.co.nz/the-press/opinion/editorials/7636520/Black-day-for-democracy-in-Canterbury-and-the-nation (accessed August 2015).

Robson, S. (2014). 'Battle for Christchurch Seats Intensifies'. *3 News*. www.3news.co.nz/politics/battle-for-christchurch-seats-intensifies-2014091205 (accessed August 2015).

Rosenberg, W. (2012). *The Risks of Private Public Partnerships to the Health System*. www.converge.org.nz/watchdog/30/03.html (accessed August 2015).

—— (2013). *Economics of the Living Wage*. CTU Monthly Economic Bulletin, June. http://union.org.nz/sites/union.org.nz/files/CTU-Monthly-Economic-Bulletin-147-June-2013.pdf (accessed August 2015).

Southern Poverty Law Centre (2006). *Rebuilding after Katrina: A Population-Based Study of Labor and Human Rights in New Orleans*. www.law.berkeley.edu/files/rebuilding_after_katrina.pdf (accessed August 2015).

Spoonley, P. and Cain, T. (2013). *Making it Work: The Mixed Embeddedness of Immigrant Entrepreneurs in New Zealand*. IZA DP No. 7332, April. www.massey.ac.nz/massey/fms/Colleges/College%20of%20Business/ntom/Cain%20and%20Spoonley%202013.pdf (accessed August 2015).

Stewart, A. (2013). 'Christchurch Gains 22 Migrants a Day'. *The Press*. www.stuff.co.nz/the-press/news/8959963/Christchurch-gains-22-migrants-a-day (accessed August 2015).

Stylianou, G. (2013). 'Christchurch Cops Highest Power Price Hikes'. *The Press*, 5 October. www.stuff.co.nz/the-press/news/canterbury/9247139/Christchurch-cops-highest-power-price-hikes (accessed August 2015).

Wakefield, S. (2014). *Budget 2014. Rock Star Economy: Is the Government Hitting the Right Notes?* www.deloitte.com/assets/Dcom-NewZealand/Local%20Assets/Documents/nz_en_Deloitte_Budget_Commentary_2014.pdf (accessed August 2015).

Part IV

North America

11

Migrante, Abante: Building Filipino Migrant Worker Leadership through Participatory Action Research

Valerie Francisco

This chapter discusses the potential of using participatory action research (PAR) methodology in the political organising and mobilising of migrant workers. I argue that democratising research and scientific methods through research training, political education and participation of migrant workers can be a process in which critical consciousness and collective action is pursued. By using the case of Filipino migrant workers in the United States, specifically in the San Francisco/Bay Area, California, this chapter details the strengths and challenges in using PAR for migrant worker organising.

As the baby boom generation continues to age in the US, eldercare has become a crisis of immediate concern. The need for affordable caregivers to look after the elderly has created a demand for migrants seeking employment in different capacities: through assisted living facilities, one-on-one care and part-time care. A steady stream of Filipino migrants to California has become a reliable source of labour for this occupation. In the 2010 census, 460,000 Filipinos were estimated to live in the Bay Area – the largest Asian American population in the whole state of California. Filipino migrants in California can be found in a spectrum of industries. They include contractualised workers in nursing and teaching, temporary migrant workers on contracts and tourist visa holders who overstay to find work. In the San Francisco/Bay Area, the caregiving industry is an attractive economic niche for Filipino migrants seeking work as the need for eldercare workers has not waned. Thus, Filipinos are a sizeable population working in a range of different types of caregiving jobs: as one-on-one care providers, live-in care providers in private homes, workers in home care facilities, in-home support service providers, etc. Many of the opportunities afforded to recent immigrants or visa overstayers are made available through immigrant networks, family and friends, who are also working as caregivers to the elderly. Caregivers also vary in their work capacity depending on their physical limitations and individual motivation. Many are often employed in more than one job, working part-time alongside their full-time jobs. Because various employers allow for differing immigration statuses when it comes to employing Filipino migrants, there is a range of possibility for Filipino migrants with different legal statuses to work as caregivers.

With this context in mind, this chapter will discuss an organising strategy explored by a collaboration between an existing Filipino migrant workers' programme in San Francisco's Filipino Community Center (FCC), Filipino American youth and professionals and academics in the San Francisco/Bay Area to reach this substantial group of migrant workers. I argue that participatory action methodology can develop organising capacity through methods such as talk-story, or what I call *kuwentohan* elsewhere (Francisco, 2013). Coupling participatory research and popular education models to develop migrant workers' critical thinking skills and analysis on the situations emerging from findings of the research project activates what Paolo Freire calls 'conscientisation' (2000) for migrant workers. In examining the CARE (Caregiver Research) Project's approach to migrant worker organising and leadership development, the chapter asks: what strategies, outside of conventional labour and worker centre approaches, can mobilise Filipino migrant workers to find a common basis for uniting across varying work and migratory experiences? What is the role of collective inquiry through participatory research methods and processes in establishing solidarity between Filipino migrants to inspire engagement and commitment to political organising and activity?

The CARE Project began in 2011 when organisers and community members began to observe an increase in the traffic of Filipino caregivers needing services to assist with various workplace issues in the San Francisco/Bay Area. The FCC, a community-based organisation located in the Excelsior district of San Francisco, had been a long-established institution in the Filipino community. It had thus attracted Filipino immigrants and tended to rising needs for advocacy on issues that ranged from wage theft, safe workplace conditions, employment opportunities and immigration. Through the FCC workers' rights programme, community organisers understood the problems of Filipino caregivers as urgent and in need of an organised response. Still there was a need to understand the baseline conditions of caregivers to assist in jumpstarting a long-term solution to the problems facing the community. Therefore, a partnership between the FCC, Filipino American scholars and their students began to explore an alternative avenue in studying and organising around Filipino migrant caregivers' issues.

The project was a scholarly inquiry into a community-based need. At its outset, the parties involved accepted that a hybrid of community-based research, service provision and political organising components must be included in answering the call of Filipino caregivers in the San Francisco/Bay Area. The conceptualisation of research methods resulted from a core group of Filipino community organisers, caregivers, youth and academics which came to an agreement that a research project could be one step in understanding the lives and issues of Filipino caregivers in the Bay Area. Yet research alone would not suffice as a response to the growing numbers of Filipino caregivers approaching the FCC for services, so the project had to maintain an orientation towards action and organising. Therefore, with the help of academic partners, a core committee developed the CARE Project as a participatory action research project putting migrant workers at the centre of the collective inquiry, which would answer the need for research on the conditions of Filipino caregivers but also attend to the need for organising and leadership among the ranks of migrant workers.

Thus the project's ultimate objective was to use community-based research to develop a core of caregiver-organisers and migrant leaders. The project's projected outcomes were two-fold. First, it sought to collect the stories of caregivers in the Filipino community and analyse the work conditions of immigrants in the caregiving industry. Second, the research process aimed to integrate leadership development and popular education focused on topics such as US immigration policies, globalisation and forced migration. The aim was that the interplay between the two objectives would assist migrants in identifying relevant key issues and potential organising strategies for them.

During the project's inception, the type of organisation or programme that was to address the needs of Filipino caregivers was unclear. The collaborators agreed to let the research process and leadership development of participating migrant workers inform the end goal. In what follows, I outline the context and lessons learned conducting participatory action research methods through the CARE Project and the subsequent establishment of Migrante Northern California, a grassroots Filipino migrant worker organisation, which is also a chapter of Migrante International, a global alliance of Filipino migrant workers in over 22 countries. The experience of collective inquiry as the basis for launching a migrant worker organisation and sustaining migrant worker campaigns is a major lesson learned from the CARE Project. Further, informed by the project's research findings about migrants' issues stretching from the Bay Area to the Philippines, Filipino migrants' choice to form an organisation that is a chapter of an international alliance working on local and transnational issues emerges from the very process that brought migrant workers and community members together. The organising strategy of coupling research and political education supplied the formation of Migrante Northern California with a complex mission and vision for its political organising.

IMMIGRANT WORKER ORGANISING
AND PARTICIPATORY ACTION RESEARCH

In the context of major global economic restructuring under neoliberal globalisation, labour migration has grown exponentially, essentially reconfiguring the labour force in countries like the United

States. In the US, immigrant workers occupy jobs in low-wage service industries that are insecure, precarious and unstable. At times, these conditions give way to breakthrough organising in sectors wherein immigrants and migrants realise a collective identity to protest and advocate for basic worker standards such as a living wage, decent working conditions and dignified work, to name a few (Ness, 2005). Scholars have studied different forms of immigrant organising (Schrover and Vermeulen, 2005) under traditional labour organising through collective bargaining agreements and unionism (Delgado, 1993) and alternative approaches to labour organising through worker centres (Fine, 2011). The burgeoning literature and research on immigrant worker organising shows the depth and significance of various forms of political organising and participation within immigrant communities that extend beyond conventional labour strategies (Jayaraman and Ness, 2005).

Scholars have engaged in PAR or community-based participatory research (CBPR) in a range of capacities to inform collaborations with immigrant worker organisations (Calderon et al., 2005; Chang et al., 2013). Often these projects' aims are to systematically investigate and develop deeper understandings of the needs of immigrant workers while supporting emergent forms of organising. The methodological values of democratising research and the production of knowledge towards social justice and collective action make PAR and some CBPR projects a suitable endeavour for many collaborations across academic and activist circles (Billies et al., 2010; Torre et al., 2012). Politically and ethically, a participatory research process calls into question who are considered experts and who are 'studied' as objects of interest, thus challenging the purposes and accountability of research practitioners and their products (Cammarota and Fine, 2008; Fals-Borda and Rahman, 1991). The critical approach to power relations in knowledge production and research as the foundation of PAR lends itself to be a viable springboard for grassroots organisations that are organising and developing critical consciousness in the communities in which they are working.

To this end, studies have shown that the research processes can draw in the voices and participation of immigrant workers, thus leading participants to engage in critical dialogue about the sociopolitical conditions under which they live and work (Calderon et al., 2005; Chang et al., 2013). The integration of political education and capacity-building components in the research process has increased immigrant workers' interest and involvement in political organising thereafter (Chang et al., 2013). Given that immigrant worker organising has seen continued success when workers can articulate their many intersecting subjectivities through their activism and organising (Chun et al., 2013), the conscientising approach to alternative learning and collective inquiry of PAR gave them opportunities to realise these political subjectivities. Scholars have found that hybrid approaches to immigrant organising which include providing services and engaging immigrant workers in education and organising also keeps participants engaged in their activism (Cordero-Guzmán, 2005; Gates, 2014). Through PAR methods, immigrant workers were engaged in shaping the direction of research on their own lives and work conditions. They were considered to be experts in their field as they participated in conducting data gathering, analysis and production of research. Collaborations between immigrant workers, scholars and community organisers also see the benefit of alternative forms of education and pedagogy, as they often foster opportunities to develop important organising skills such as public speaking, systematic inquiry and consensus building. With this in mind, CARE Project collaborators shared a hope in beginning a PAR project in the Filipino community.

THE CARE PROJECT

The CARE Project commenced in August 2011 during many meetings and consultations defining the objectives, timeline and logistics for a PAR project. The collaborators on the CARE Project were Filipino caregivers, Filipino immigrants and second-generation immigrants who had been affiliated with the FCC for various services, organisers of the workers' rights programme at the FCC, other grassroots Filipino American organisations such as Gabriela San Francisco, the League of Filipino Students at San Francisco State University and the Samahan Filipino Student Association at the University of San Francisco, and two sociologists, Dr Robyn Rodriguez from the

University of California, Davis, and myself. Individuals from these groups made up the CARE Project's core committee. (In this chapter, 'we' or 'our' refers to this core committee.)

Early on in the process, the core committee, alongside the first cohort of CARE Project community researchers, decided to adopt a research method called *kuwentohan*, or 'talk-story', as a method of data collection. I introduced my experience with a past research project in New York City with domestic workers and our use of *kuwentohan* (Francisco, 2013) and Filipinos' attraction to sharing their experiences through talk-story, a method that relies on cultural values of sharing experiences with as many as two or more people guiding the direction of the interview. As a group, we decided to continue training in *kuwentohan* method to power the engine of our data collection, as many of the participants felt quite comfortable with the term and had a common cultural understanding of exchanging experiences rather than using a question and answer guide found in traditional qualitative interview methods. Instead of learning an interview process, community researchers were relieved that they could enact something they felt they do in their daily lives already. Through this group interview style of data collection, many community researchers found that they were able to share their own stories of exploitation and abuse to clear the air and allow other caregivers to then share their own stories about difficulties in their work experiences. Scholars have established that methods that rely on cultural values of storytelling have been useful to tap into the wealth of knowledge that marginalised communities maintain in their oral traditions (Francisco, 2013; Jocson, 2009; Kahakalau, 2004; Madriz, 1998).

In October 2011, the core committee convened the first of the CARE Project training sessions with the members of the core committee and 15 Filipino migrants working as caregivers. From October 2011 to April 2012, the CARE Project convened twice a month to hold two and a half hour long training sessions, which consisted of popular education activities, 'theatre of the oppressed' games and research training. These often began with opening activities that centred on theatre of the oppressed games to 'break the ice' between participants who were new to one another. These games' objectives were to break an often long day of work and commuting into laughter and play. This was a key part of these training sessions as many of the participants came from work, which meant they were often in isolation for more than eight hours in a private home or facility where their daily conversations were task-oriented. Play and theatre games enlivened participants to return to a lighter state where they could engage with one another through jokes, stories and laughter. But also, theatre of the oppressed games engage particular skills that participants would need in preparing to think about research. For example, an activity I developed called *ating boses* or 'our voice', inspired by an Augusto Boal game (2000), required all the participants to stand on one side of the room in a line, shoulder to shoulder. One volunteer would stand on the other side of the room facing the rest of the participants and would control the volume and direction of their voices based on how close or how far the volunteer was to the line. If the volunteer was very close or face-to-face with the line of people, voices on the line would be loud. If the volunteer was far from them, the line would be quiet. If the volunteer was on the right or left side of the line, the corresponding side of the line made more noise. The game was supposed to highlight how an interview or *kuwentohan* needs the participation of two or more people. The line represented person(s) or interviewees who were being asked questions. The person controlling the volume of the line would represent the person asking questions. The control the interviewer had in coming close or far from the line represents an affect of *malapit ang loob* or 'warmth and closeness'. The interviewer would show an interest and warmth to their interviewee through asking many open questions, sharing their own stories and listening attentively. This could then result in an interviewee telling their story openly and without restraint, or as we saw in the activity, the line of people getting louder. But if the interview is *malayo ang loob* or 'distant', then the person answering will be less likely to engage in *kuwentohan* as represented by the line's quietness, when the volunteer would be far from the participants. The theatre games accomplished two goals in the training: providing a space of lightness and play, while providing didactic analogies to the research process.

After the opening activities, the training would begin to debrief games through concepts of scientific and sociological research methods such as defining a research topic and question, or surveying data collection methods and data analysis approaches. Through problem-posing pedagogy, facilitators would challenge the assumptions of elitist knowledge production institutions and processes, by centring the CARE Project participants as experts in their own lives and conditions. These discussions affirmed that communities outside of universities, research institutions, government agencies and market research firms had as much right to research (Appadurai, 2006) as other institutions had. During this time, facilitators would alternately introduce topics of interest to the migrant workers in terms of current hot-button issues such as immigration reform, human trafficking cases and wage theft. Lastly, the meetings would end with developing practical research skills for participants. Week by week the participants tackled research skills such as narrowing down a research topic and question, designing a method, crafting an interview instrument, creating a flow chart of topics and specific wording in two languages, Filipino and English, considering best practices in interview or *kuwentohan* methods, analysing transcriptions, sharpening themes within a collected data set, or distilling and delivering the key findings from the data collection. This list of research skills required repetition and overlapping discussion, as meetings only lasted two and a half hours and were held twice a month. At times, review of these skills was necessary before we could continue to learn another component of the research process.

In April 2012, after six months of training and one practice round of data collection and analysis, the CARE Project graduated 15 migrant workers and seven Filipino student leaders and women organisers while also acknowledging the core committee members who went through the training. The graduation served as a launch of the CARE Project data-gathering phase. This community-wide event drew an audience of 150 people, including migrant worker allies from the Progressive Worker Alliance in San Francisco such as the Mujeres Unidas y Activas and Chinese Progressive Association, and San Francisco district supervisors such as David Campos for the Mission district and John Avalos for the Excelsior district. This community-building moment in the CARE Project's history demonstrated the support from multiracial, multicultural communities around the need and initiative of migrant workers to study and investigate their own lives. More importantly, it showed that migrant worker research initiatives could also transform into points of unity and action across communities.

For the following six months, the CARE Project researchers held four sessions of *kapihan at kuwentohan* or 'coffee and talk-story', community events where interviews and focus groups would be held to collect the experiences of Filipino caregivers. These alternating sessions were held in the districts of San Francisco that had high concentrations of Filipinos, in the South of Market (SoMa) district at the SoMa Collective Action Network space, and in the Excelsior district at the FCC. The CARE Project researchers, especially the caregivers, were responsible for inviting and reaching out to their Filipino caregivers' networks in recruiting for the study. Each event would begin with Filipino migrant workers giving a warm welcome and a speech about the project's objectives. They informed the interviewees that any identifying information would be excised from any recording that took place as long as interviewees agreed their stories could be used for research purposes. In teams of two, *kuwentohan* or group interviews would begin with one community researcher following the interview instrument designed by the group and the other community researcher setting up the recording equipment, following up with probing questions and taking notes on the conversation at hand. After about an hour and a half, each *kuwentohan* session would end with a debrief discussion where interviewees had a chance to discuss their experience of being part of the research project and what they learned from the process. The final discussions would include the 30–50 people in attendance in a large group circle, and often concluded with comments of affirmation and gratitude for the space and ability to share such burdensome experiences. To finish the session, the CARE Project researchers led the attendees with a *isang bagsak* – meaning 'one down', one event, one story collected – bringing the group closer to their goal of unity.

After four *kuwentohan* sessions, the CARE Project collected over 50 stories in Filipino and English through group interviews. These comprised roughly 16 Filipino men and 34 Filipina women, 46 of whom worked as caregivers to the elderly and developmentally disabled patients. Four of the migrant workers worked in retail, maintenance and non-profit organisations when participating, but had experience in caregiving. The participants in the study hailed from various provinces in all three major regions of the Philippines: Luzon, Visayas and Mindanao, with the majority coming from Luzon. They had arrived in the US between 1992 and 2012.

Filipino students and women organisers were essential in the transcription phase of the project, as many of the caregiver researchers worked 50–60 hours per week. Funding for transcriptions came through academic collaborators. However, the time and technological dexterity of Filipino American youth and women organisers were key in completing this task. After a majority of interviews were transcribed, researchers came together for data analysis workshops, where each researcher was assigned two to three transcribed interviews to read in search of recurring themes *within* each interview. In these open coding (Charmaz, 2006) sessions, we relied on the data we collected to point us to the most urgent issues in the lives of Filipino caregivers. After two open coding sessions, we conducted a 'theme museum' wherein all researchers wrote the themes they found in their interviews on butcher paper along the FCC wall. As we gleaned from the museum, we identified the recurrent themes *across* all interviews. Through this activity and discussion, we found that issues such as wage theft, health and safety in the workplace, lack of rest and meal breaks, and the lack of formal contracts or the breach of verbal contracts were keeping Filipino caregivers' work insecure and precarious.

From these findings, the researchers began to revisit the dissemination strategies we created earlier in our research process. Filipino caregivers were key in planning a weekend retreat to study the findings more thoroughly and decide on a plan of action. During the July 2012 weekend retreat, community researchers connected the patterns across interviews to their own stories of exploitation and isolation. The discussions generated from the research and subsequent retreat were convincing enough for the researchers to see that a solitary event to share these findings would be an inadequate response to the prevalence of injustice that Filipino caregivers were experiencing. Thus, participants decided that they would hold a community forum to discuss the state of Filipino caregivers and celebrate the establishment of Migrante Northern California – a grassroots migrant worker organisation that would advocate and organise Filipino migrant workers.

Paolo Freire's concept of *conscientizaçao* describes a process in which participants of popular education come to sharpen their analysis about larger social forces as they produce problems and issues of marginalisation and oppression for various groups of people. In the CARE Project, our PAR process not only achieved the objectives to investigate and research the conditions, but also linked Filipino migrant workers' individual circumstances to structural inequalities. During our trainings, we could not avoid engaging in lengthy discussions about which political and economic systems produced issues such as mass emigration from the Philippines or high demand of low-wage care workers in the US. Especially when the findings of the research laid bare the patterns of inequality and exploitation that Filipino migrant workers experienced, CARE Project researchers were invested in deeply understanding *why* their community members were suffering in this manner and *how* it came to be this way. In short, the collective inquiry embedded in the research process provided researchers with fodder to ask critical questions about their work conditions and lives. Since many of the researchers had a stake in conducting research, they were not only interested in its outcomes, but it became important to them to provide analysis and explanation for the project's findings. Rowena, a CARE Project community researcher said:

> Hearing the same stories over and over again, you can't stop and think about 'why?' Why is this happening to all of us? And we all thought we were the only ones experiencing this one at a time. When you hear one story like yours, it's one thing. But when you hear a story like yours, five times, ten times, you ask, why?

For Rowena, a 59-year-old caregiver who worked as a street vendor without formal education besides a high school diploma, and migrated to the US after her children reached adulthood through a tourist visa, the CARE Project was a demanding process which required her to be patient with the experience of being a student again. But as the project progressed through a combination of leadership development training – such as public speaking skills, research skills and substantive worker education (that is, Filipino labour history, the political economy of Filipino migration, know-your-rights workshop) – and data collection, migrant workers such as Rowena were politicised as they gained a new perspective on their shared struggles with other caregivers. Rowena's experience was much like that of many other migrant workers as they shared and met their goals collectively. More importantly, they were moved to ask critical questions about the systematic disadvantages they had as undocumented migrants and low-wage workers.

Because of shared values such as *tiis* (translated in English as 'resolve' or 'determination') or resolve through their experiences of migration, migrant workers related to the reasons why their fellow Filipinos continued to work in exploitative situations or took up more than one job. Angelito, a 63-year-old, comments on the shared experience of caregivers:

> You cannot be choosy after getting here, *tiniis mo na* [just endure it], you already gritted your teeth through it. Please don't be choosy because we know people say that, 'Oh, you're a caregiver, you just clean up people's poop.' And so what, I'm wearing gloves. We work with dignity, my wage is what I work hard for. I don't steal. It's respectful-respectable work. But other people's view is I don't care. But it's the hardest job. You can only know this if you work this job.

Angelito references his migration and transition story in this excerpt as the basis of his understanding of other caregivers. He speaks to an anonymous multitude of current and future caregivers when he gives the advice of 'don't be choosy' because he understands that the work of caregiving is hard labour and lacks social prestige. In his own words, continuing his advice-giving thread, he also asserts that the job, albeit difficult, is dignified and respectable work. Angelito, alongside other caregivers, repeatedly referenced the circumstances of hard labour, both physical and emotional, in caregiving as a point of solidarity between migrant workers. When they had articulated their own experience, it often gave way to them providing a logic of collective action and solidarity. When asked if there is a need for Filipino migrant workers to come together, he stated:

> To help with, what is called, abuse. Because we know what it's like without papers. When they [employers] make use of you. Exploit. Take advantage. I hate it. During my time I am that one. And I'm happy that when others are experiencing it there are people like this CARE Project to help. We can see each other in the stories.

The development of a core of migrant worker leaders through the CARE Project research process rested on the collective inquiry they led together. Based on the findings, migrant worker leaders were able to identify recurring and urgent issues among their fellow caregivers. But more importantly, the process of analysis produced cohesion on the basis of solidarity between researchers. This cohesion was the foundation that led CARE Project researchers to work together to eventually establish an organisation that could provide ongoing programmes and services to migrant workers in similar conditions.

BAKIT PA-R? WHY PAR? CHALLENGES AND LESSONS FOR PARTICIPATORY ACTION RESEARCH WITH MIGRANT WORKERS

Migrant workers who often exchange humorous banter in Filipino slang often use the phrase *bakit pa?* to ridicule one another. It is a question of exasperation that is colloquially and jokingly asked by Tagalog-speaking Filipinos who are asked to do something above and beyond a simple task. Literally translated, it means, 'Why do all of that?' or 'Do we *have* to do all of that?' Although this question taken out of its jocular slang context becomes an overly serious query, this was one of my fears in undertaking such a PAR project with the different collaborators. After all, many scholars have written about the challenges of the methodology (time-consuming processes, privilege and position of academics, etc.) undermining PAR's participatory, ethical and political values (Gianotten and de Wit, 1991; Maguire, 1993; Nygreen, 2009). PAR and immigrant worker organising models have been far from perfect. In the intersection of these two fields of work, the CARE Project was burdened with two major challenges. Logistically, the length of time required for research training, collection and analysis spanned a year and a half. During this time, some researchers dropped off in attendance or moved on to a new job or location. The shifting group of researchers involved in the project would require us to double back on research training or political education that other CARE Project researchers had already taken up. Second, participants questioned how research skills could translate into the betterment of work and life conditions as caregivers. Although they understood the possibilities of hearing people's stories and finding connections between caregivers, many of them were worried that devoting two or three hours twice a month could be better spent either working or taking care of personal matters. For some community researchers this led to a tapering off of their interest or commitment to the project, thus also affecting the morale of others who chose to continue. Given the lengthy amount of time necessary for community researchers to see the gains of the CARE Project, many Filipino migrant workers weren't able to see the fruits of their labours after early contributions to the research. Time became an ethical issue for the core committee, who struggled with a research process that extended training, collection and analysis to over a year.

When these obstacles emerged, I discovered that what kept people committed to PAR methods was that participants were uncovering the impetus for action and change in the lives of Filipino migrant workers. For the immigrant workers and community organisers, the research process was hopeful because the collective action component at the end of the research process served to keep some migrant workers (albeit a vacillating number) interested in the long-term project of organising. The swell and drain in our group was part of the dynamic of recruiting and organising migrant workers. The research provided an opportunity for migrant workers to acquire skills as co-researchers through collecting interviews, examining and analysing data, making provisional conclusions and reporting the findings to our larger community meetings. Additionally, the actions at the end of the PAR process were shared goals for migrant workers/CARE Project researchers to tell their stories to a broader audience which included community meetings, academic conference presentations and publications, mass protests, photo exhibits, or performances. Although time and workload were definite concerns for community partners, the engagement in a learning and research process from start to finish was a promising glue that could hold migrant workers together for some time to help build community, foster trust and plan collective actions. For Filipino migrants and organisers, PAR became a platform to begin to learn ways to resist the oppressive situations even in the face of the inability to overthrow the entire structure.

Lastly, a challenge but a significant lesson in the CARE Project was the context of migrant workers supporting their families in the Philippines. Many participants often needed to detach and reattach during different contact points because of emergencies in the Philippines or during the holidays, as they needed to work overtime or take on extra jobs to send money back to their loved ones. This context was deeply understood by CARE Project participants as it recurred in all of the interviews collected in the research. Thus, the social reality of transnationalism in the lives of migrant workers became the basis for why Filipino migrant workers chose to establish an organisation that is inherently linked to a global alliance of Filipino migrant workers' organisations in Hong Kong, Ontario, Riyadh, London and Manila. Because many participants of the CARE Project who became leaders in Migrante Northern California understood the need to activate transnational networks for their local issues, they also accepted the need to carry out activities that push Filipino migrants out of the Philippines. Migrante Northern California's membership to Migrante International, headquartered in the Philippines, with transnational reach across the world was informed by their *kuwentohan* that spanned the globe as well.

CONCLUSION

The use of PAR is not just a method; it is also an intentional epistemological inquiry that reflects marginalised communities' experiences, both in its gains and challenges. I argue that research and education can become key tools in introducing Filipino migrant workers to collective inquiry, critical learning processes and collective action towards building migrant worker power. But it also presents challenges, as its form of long-term commitment and, at times, intellectual skill building becomes cumbersome for migrant workers who are working physically taxing jobs over long hours.

Still, the Filipino migrant workers in the CARE Project demonstrated that their work as community researchers gave them a basis to invest in a long-term organising project that is now Migrante Northern California. An orientation towards organising and action based on data gave participants a way to use their PAR findings and analysis to organise around wage theft cases that often kept participants from attending to the work of the research project. For example, Migrante Northern California has recently won a campaign for over US$800,000 in back wages for caregivers who suffered from wage theft. With or without legal documentation, caregivers were able to collect the wages that were due to them from the continuous research done by the organisation. The CARE Project, where many of the caregivers began to learn how to conduct research and analyse data, contributed to the strategy of building a campaign using sound information. PAR becomes a way to bring together individual voices and experiences of migrants to amplify them through grassroots organising and collective action.

Many of the challenges of the CARE Project, such as retention and recruitment, remain in Migrante Northern California. But a key lesson to be learned is that social transformation is a process, unable to be constrained in a single project or event (Maguire, 1993). As Migrante Northern California assesses whether it should launch another CARE Project to deepen or widen the reach of the research, organisers now have a sober perspective through which to interpret the use and purpose of research and education in migrant worker organising.

REFERENCES

Appadurai, A. (2006). 'The Right to Research'. *Globalisation, Societies and Education*, 4(2), 167–77.

Billies, M., Francisco, V., Krueger, P. and Linville, D. (2010). 'Participatory Action Research: Our Methodological Roots'. *International Review of Qualitative Research*, 3(3), 277–86.

Boal, A. (2000). *Theater of the Oppressed*. London: Pluto.

Calderon, J., Foster, S. and Rodriguez, S. (2005). 'Organizing Immigrant Workers: Action Research and Strategies in the Pomona Day Labor Center'. In Ochoa, E. and Ochoa, G. L. (Eds), *Latino Los Angeles: Transformations, Communities, and Activism* (pp. 279–97). Tucson: University of Arizona Press.

Cammarota, J. and Fine, M. (2008). *Revolutionizing Education: Youth Participatory Action Research in Motion*. New York: Routledge.

Chang, C., Salvatore, A., Lee, P., Liu, S., Tom, A., Morales, A. and Minkler, M. (2013). 'Adapting to Context in Community-Based Participatory Research: "Participatory Starting Points" in a Chinese Immigrant Worker Community'. *American Journal of Community Psychology*, 51(3/4), 480–91.

Charmaz, K. (2006). *Constructing Grounded Theory: A Practical Guide through Qualitative Analysis*. New York: SAGE.

Chun, J. J., Lipsitz, G. and Shin, Y. (2013). 'Intersectionality as a Social Movement Strategy: Asian Immigrant Women Advocates'. *Signs: Journal of Women in Culture and Society*, 38(4), 917–40.

Cordero-Guzmán, H. R. (2005). 'Community-Based Organizations and Migration in New York City'. *Journal of Ethnic and Migration Studies*, 31(5), 889–909.

Delgado, H. L. (1993). *New Immigrants, Old Unions: Organizing Undocumented Workers in Los Angeles*. Philadelphia, PA: Temple University Press.

Fals-Borda, O. and Rahman, M. A. (1991). *Action and Knowledge: Breaking the Monopoly with Participatory Action Research*. Lanham, MA: Rowman and Littlefield.

Fine, J. R. (2011). 'New Forms to Settle Old Scores: Updating the Worker Centre Story in the United States'. *Industrial Relations*, 66(4), 604–30.

Francisco, V. (2013). '"Ang ating iisang kuwento" Our Collective Story: Migrant Filipino Workers and Participatory Action Research'. *Action Research*, 12(1), 78–93.

Freire, P. (2000). *Pedagogy of the Oppressed*. New York: Continuum.

Gates, A. B. (2014). 'Integrating Social Services and Social Change: Lessons from an Immigrant Worker Center'. *Journal of Community Practice*, 22(1/2), 102–29.

Gianotten, V. and de Wit, T. (1991). 'Action and Participatory Research: A Case of Peasant Organization'. In Fals-Borda, O. and Rahman, M. A. (Eds), *Action and Knowledge: Breaking the Monopoly with Participatory Action-Research* (pp. 64–84). Lanham, MA: Apex Press.

Jayaraman, S. and Ness, I. (2005). *New Urban Immigrant Workforce: Innovative Models for Labor Organizing*. Armonk, NY: M. E. Sharpe.

Jocson, K. M. (2009). 'Whose Story is it Anyway? Teaching Social Studies and Making Use of Kuwento'. *Multicultural Perspectives*, 11(1), 31–6.

Kahakalau, K. (2004). 'Indigenous Heuristic Action Research: Bridging Western and Indigenous Research Methodologies'. *Hulil*, 1(1), 19–33.

Madriz, E. I. (1998). 'Using Focus Groups with Lower Socioeconomic Status Latina Women'. *Qualitative Inquiry*, 4(1), 114–28.

Maguire, P. (1993). 'Challenges, Contradictions, and Celebrations: Attempting Participatory Research as a Doctoral Student'. In Park, P., Brydon-Miller, M., Hall, B. and Jackson, P. (Eds), *Voices of Change: Participatory Research in the United States and Canada* (pp. 157–76). Westport, CT: Bergen and Garvey.

Ness, I. (2005). *Immigrants Unions and the New US Labor Market*. Philadelphia, PA: Temple University Press.

Nygreen, K. (2009). 'Critical Dilemmas in PAR: Toward a New Theory of Engaged Research for Social Change'. *Social Justice*, 36(4), 14–35.

Schrover, M. and Vermeulen, F. (2005). 'Immigrant Organizations'. *Journal of Ethnic and Migration Studies*, 31(5), 823–32.

Torre, M., Fine, M., Stoudt, B. and Fox, M. (2012). 'Critical Participatory Action Research as Public Science'. In Cooper, H. and Camic, P. (Eds), *APA Handbook of Research Methods in Psychology* (pp. 171–84). Washington, DC: American Psychological Association.

12

Temporary Employment Agency Workers in Montreal: Immigrant and Migrant Workers' Struggles in Canada

Aziz Choudry and Mostafa Henaway

There is growing international scholarly interest in the expansion of temporary employment agencies ('temp agencies') in the context of labour deregulation, flexibilisation and economic restructuring. Van Arsdale (2013) suggests that outsourcing labour by the US temp agency industry produces poverty for millions and stagnating wages for all workers. He contends that '[t]emporary help is becoming the great stabilizer of modern capitalism. It will consistently grow as the economy expands over time, encountering occasional downturns as recessions are encountered. Each recession will lead to greater dependency on staffing, as companies transition to hiring temporary workers to sustain economic downturns and labor expenses' (2013: 107). Some authors focus on connections between immigration status, race and agency work in North America (Fuller and Vosko, 2008; Gonos and Martino, 2011; Vosko, 2000). Agencies range from global corporations like Manpower, Randstad and Adecco to small, local (often unregistered) labour agents.

This chapter discusses organising against exploitative practices of Québec's agency industry, in relation to migrant and racialised immigrant workers, and especially the work of Montreal's Immigrant Workers Centre (IWC) and the Temporary Agency Workers

Association (TAWA). The IWC, like many workers' centres, stands at a juncture between traditions of labour unions and community organising. One author (Choudry) is an academic and IWC board member; the other (Henaway) has been an IWC organiser for several years. We build upon the organising experiences and insights of IWC organisers. Knowledge produced by workers is also a vital resource for analysis, education and action for documenting and resisting abusive practices of agencies and businesses which use them.

Fudge (2012: 96) notes that 'different migration statuses, some of which are highly precarious, ... produce a differentiated supply of labour that [in turn] produces precarious workers and precarious employment norms'. This chapter deals with workers with a range of immigration status. Racialised new immigrants are often discriminated against in the labour market and frequently pushed into temporary work upon arrival in Canada (Galabuzi, 2006; Henaway, 2012; Vosko, 2000; Zaman, 2006, 2012). Agencies often justify paying low wages and providing no benefits, by arguing that recent immigrants receive valuable 'Canadian experience' (Cranford and Ladd, 2003; Vosko, 2000). For Vosko (2000: 190), '[j]ust as officials argued that the industry represented an ideal labour force re-entry vehicle for women absent from the labour force while raising children in the late 1960s and early 1970s, they now claim that temporary help work is a suitable means for immigrants to gain experience and exposure in the Canadian market'. New arrivals must often find a way to earn quickly, but claims that temping can help someone gain a foothold in the labour market and stable permanent work are questionable. Hatton (2011) notes that permanent workers are replaced with 'permanent temporaries', shifting workers to agency payrolls, with attendant employer savings and the avoidance of obligations towards workers, and broader, deeper impacts on labour and the nature of work itself. Workers are on permanent probation, and can be dismissed at any time, for any reason, without benefits. Thus, for many, the prevailing trend is not movement from temporary to permanent jobs, but the opposite. Vosko (2000: 193) notes that many recent immigrant workers felt trapped in precarious agency work where the racialised division of labour 'is a product of two overtly racist practices that reveal the ideological nature of the industry's promise of "Canadian experience": namely, placing workers of the same background together intentionally, and thereby perpetuating segmentation, and refusing to provide references to recent immigrants.'

CONDITIONS OF AGENCY WORKERS

Freeman and Gonos (2005: 305) suggest that besides producing subservience and abuse of workers, agencies' negotiating activities 'impede workers' ability to engage in concerted activity to effectuate meaningful bargaining over the terms and conditions of their employment'. For them, agencies' 'substantive bargaining relationship with the user employer is one of collusion with that employer to minimize workers' wages and benefits and to maximize profits' (2005: 307). Vosko (2000, 2008) dubs dominant approaches to theorising the labour market as 'SER-centric' (SER = standard employment relationship). She argues that the SER (a bilateral employment relationship between employee and employer, standardised working time, continuous employment) is not the norm for many workers. There is no direct employment relationship with and supervision by a single employer, but rather a triangular one between worker, agency and client company.

By 2008, over 1,200 agencies operated in Québec, in virtually all sectors of the economy, including office work, cleaning, construction, healthcare, manufacturing and agriculture. In Montreal, Canada's second largest city, there are two major types of agencies – firstly, larger, registered agencies, second, unregulated 'fly-by-nights' which mainly operate outside of the official labour market. Fly-by-night agencies often recruit desperate workers without legal status or those unable to find stable work. They operate mainly in the agricultural/ food processing sector, paying cash, often below minimum wage, with neither health and safety coverage nor basic respect for minimum labour standards. These agencies rely mainly on networks within specific communities. IWC also encountered a case where a popular cafe chain purchased sandwiches through a subcontractor, which hired agency workers. Six Mexican refugee claimants – sandwich-makers paid below the minimum wage – were owed almost three months in unpaid wages. The subcontractor blamed the agency, which blamed the subcontractor. Workers felt unable to complain lest it impact their refugee claims because they were not allowed to work legally.

A critical moment in creating public awareness and leadership building around agency work came in October 2010 with the IWC's collaboration with an investigative documentary. Journalists posing as new immigrants documented the practices of fly-by-nights, working for cash through agencies in chicken-processing plants (*Radio Canada*, 2010). One journalist wore a hidden camera when applying to agencies specialising in placing immigrants who speak no English or French. Assigned to Montreal chicken factories, they worked alongside regular staff, and were never asked for any identity documents. 'If I'd had a workplace accident, what would have happened then? Who would have been responsible for my care?' asked undercover journalist, Martin Movilla, originally from Colombia. They were expected to work long shifts, up to nine hours at a time, sometimes with only one 15-minute break, for between CDN$6.50 and CDN$8.00 per hour (approximately US$4.94–US$6.08). Agencies understand how to leverage workers' immigration status to provide cheap labour. The documentary led to more media focus on agency work and precarity, which served as a critical education tool for a broader audience while giving voice to the first group of agency workers with whom the centre had built relationships.

Broadly, the IWC sees three categories of workers whose precarity and vulnerability is exploited in particular, though overlapping ways. First, the most exploitable comprises those without status. Unable to work legally, they are forced to find any form of work, often through small fly-by-night agencies, because they have no access to social assistance. The second category comprises refugee claimants on social assistance. They cannot work legally, but for people with families, social assistance is insufficient to live on. Many refugee claimants work for fly-by-night agencies in food production for cash. Employers and agencies know that they will probably not make formal complaints because they are particularly vulnerable.

The third category of agency workers that the IWC works with comprises permanent residents and citizens who suffer institutional racism and discrimination. Meaningful employment is difficult for them because their education and qualifications are not recognised, or they may have been laid off from more stable manufacturing or service sector jobs. Many – especially those with limited language skills or without newer skills needed for the labour force – are forced into agency work. Systemic racism tends to push racialised workers into lower-paid, lower-status jobs with lower rates of unionisation and greater precarity than white workers in Canada (Galabuzi, 2006). In a Commission des normes du travail (CNT) survey (CNT, 2012), (Québec's labour standards board), 90 per cent of 1,000 agency workers interviewed reported one or more labour standards violation.

ORGANISATIONS

Agency workers' jobs in and around Montreal are diverse, but reflect growing precarity. One IWC ally, the collective Dignidad Migrante, works with Latino migrants on local migration and work issues, including agency exploitation. Another ally, PINAY, has dealt with agencies around issues faced by migrant Filipina domestic workers under Canada's Live-in Caregiver Program (LCP). LCP workers frequently pay large recruitment fees to agencies to find employers. Many migrant workers have already been exploited by recruiting agencies in their countries of origin in order to get work overseas and are under great pressure to repay debts incurred. In 2009, the IWC began outreach to agency workers, particularly Spanish speakers, working for fly-by-night agencies. One group comprised new immigrants from Mexico working for cash under the table, below minimum wage, in a food processing plant. The agency disappeared, leaving them without wages or access to employment insurance. Yet under existing labour laws the company sourcing workers through the agency was not responsible for the workers' problems, yet created and managed the work environment. The IWC challenged these conditions, first through a public campaign to address the systemic issues of placement agencies. The second method focused on mobilising workers themselves to build their capacity to lead such a campaign and challenge workplace conditions. The IWC has attempted to build a campaign not just based in an immediate fight around one workplace, but rather one that could result in a long-term campaign relevant to the working class as a whole. It wanted to challenge conditions common to different workplaces and communities, and change the conditions of all workers impacted, those with immigration status and without, and including unionised workers. A major goal has been strategically to collectivise isolated and transient agency workers. One means to do this has been the effort to create collective strategies among particular communities, organising among Spanish-speaking workers who share many similar work experiences in slaughter houses, food processing, cleaning and day labour. For many, the primary issue is immigration and working with fly-by-night agencies. Organising strives to create a common narrative among workers to break the isolation and fear of the consequences of complaining about working conditions, and build collective capacity and solidarity.

Given the spectrum of agency workers' situations, what was needed was an umbrella organisation flexible enough to address the particular issues faced by a wide range of agency workers and to build a larger movement that could change policy and act like an independent union run for and by agency workers. Thus TAWA was founded in 2011. Ultimately, a broad organising vision would benefit diverse types of workers, and would weaken the tools that employers and companies can use against workers. A goal was to build more workplace fight-backs locally, while building real leadership among migrant and immigrant workers. Concretely, this meant understanding workers' situations and helping forge relationships among them. This has led to a deeper understanding of how most work has been changing drastically, governed by capitalist restructuring which has been effectively able to undermine gains made by workers in earlier years, advanced on other fronts by free trade and investment policies.

TAWA demands the respect of basic labour rights and better standards of decent work for all agency workers, regardless of immigration status, and aims to support workers on an individual and collective level. TAWA works to bring these non-unionised workers together to challenge individual workplace problems and working conditions for agency workers through solidarity. Agency workers are uniting, building their organisation to defend their rights, providing services and building a community union to meet the real needs of immigrant workers with low wages. The group also seeks to raise awareness on this issue, to pressure the government to take concrete steps to protect the rights of all workers. TAWA also supports justice movements for the regularisation of migrants without status.

One example of agency worker exploitation, which the IWC and TAWA have confronted, concerns Dollarama, Canada's fastest-growing chain of dollar stores. Dollarama has several distribution centres in Montreal that employ many workers from West and North Africa, often through a registered Montreal-based labour agency. Some are permanent residents or citizens, others are refugee claimants. Even workers who have been there for three years were unable to be hired directly by Dollarama. When the IWC attempted to have a white McGill University graduate volunteer 'salt' (that is, attempt to be hired), the agency offered him office work because he looked 'too good' to work in the factory. Conversely, a Haitian worker, a fluently bilingual accountant, who had practised accountancy in Montreal, had repeatedly asked for office work commensurate to his training, yet continued only to be offered warehouse work. Outreach and consistency are pillars of IWC's work in reaching new layers of people. After leafleting for over a month outside the warehouse, the IWC began to make contact with workers, and gain an understanding of a host of issues related to agency work. One group of African workers related their work experience to slavery, and became curious about their rights. One said: 'Certainly one could compare it to slavery, and I've been able to understand in my time here that just by an individual's skin colour, when I go to the placement agency, there's work for those that are black, and there's work for those that are white', adding that he lost jobs to white Quebecois people despite advanced qualifications (Immigrant Workers Centre, 2012). This has been the IWC's starting point in building a longer-term campaign and implementing lessons from previous struggles.

TAWA focuses on outreach in locations where day labourers are picked up and dropped off, and works with other community groups in the Latin American community where many workers are recruited to work for fly-by-night agencies. It also does outreach near distribution centres, where workers are contracted through more established agencies. This includes handing out informational flyers near agencies in key neighbourhoods at periods when workers are getting paid. The work includes holding actions for theft of wages (in the case of some fly-by-night agencies), and, for workers in larger agencies, organising workshops around health and safety rights. Workers also criticised agencies' discriminatory practices in hiring workers mainly from Africa and Haiti regardless of professional experience and desire to be placed in skilled positions in offices, given that the agencies place them in low-wage factory work in different companies. TAWA ran a workshop series in Spanish in collaboration with Dignidad Migrante, which strengthened relationships with Spanish-speaking agency workers. Monthly workshops with lawyers, CNT representatives and labour organisers have addressed issues such as CSST (*Commission de la santé et de la sécurité du travail* – workplace health and safety) and CNT coverage for agency workers, employment insurance and welfare regulations. Further outreach to agency workers happens through multilingual community radio. One Mexican migrant worker recounted his experiences of fly-by-night agencies. After working for agencies since February 2008, he discussed different jobs, such as cleaning trays in a bakery and clearing ice and snow. He said:

> The degree of safety I have had is nil. Let's say the job I had clearing snow on roofs with ice, no cleats, no boots, no helmets and harnesses. The workers from the company had all of these things. Obviously we don't have any rights: we are basically pawns in the system until we can no longer work the machines. ... I was paid CDN$9.00 an hour when I saw a contract that stipulated the person should be paid CDN$17.00 an hour. Also they will pay a person CDN$9.00 an hour for one position that should be done by 2 workers [the Québec minimum wage was $10.15 at that time]. (Immigrant Workers Centre, 2012).

In 2011, Au bas de l'échelle, a Montreal organisation which advocates on issues related to working in precarious situations, published research documenting how agencies undermine labour standards and working conditions and contribute to the growth of precarious labour (Au bas de l'échelle, 2011). The findings are typical of research on working conditions for agency workers in other contexts. They include the general poor working conditions, unequal treatment of workers in the same workplace (that is, regular employees and agency workers), systematic labour code infractions by some agencies, abusive clauses in contracts that some agencies require workers to sign, the lack of responsibility of employers, and the higher level of accidents among agency workers. Some employers have also established their own agencies, which hire specifically for them. One strategy for agencies is to operate through more than one registered company and move workers from one agency to the other to avoid paying overtime.

All of these practices are highly problematic. But the question of the employer not being responsible for violations of workers' rights has major implications for recourse for workers. Vosko (2000: 154) suggests that the temp industry is selling 'a new type of employment relationship to its customers, one that allows both the agency and the customer to adopt a range of distancing strategies'. As Bartkiw (2009) notes, the triangular relationship creates a structural tendency towards underenforcement of existing standards, given the potential for confusion, conflict or outright obfuscation concerning the division of employment law responsibilities between the client and agency. Policymakers and labour law generally assumes the employer to be a unitary entity, which is not the case for agency workers' employment relations. Regardless of whether or not they work for an agency, in Québec workers supposedly have recourse to the CNT if their rights are violated. However, for the CNT, in such cases it is unclear who is responsible, and each situation is determined according to many different variables. This uncertain and legally complex situation acts to deter complaints: employers are protected from complaints against them and have no responsibility for workplace conditions. Besides the personal risk of job loss that workers face when grieving against their boss, the uncertainty of who is responsible further deters action. Without these protections, agency workers are often exposed to high-risk jobs without proper equipment and training. The Institut de recherché Robert-Sauvé en santé et sécurité du travail (2011) found that accident rates for agency workers were ten to eleven times higher than for other workers. One agency worker said: 'I work at a company that hires 90 per cent of its workers from temporary placement agencies. They are fired without cause, work without basic workplace safety requirements, are not given holiday pay and overtime, are not able to make complaints about highly dangerous workplace situations, and are still considered "temporary" workers after years of continuous employment' (Immigrant Workers Centre, 2012).

Workers' knowledge is key to building the organising, strategy and broader campaign work on temporary labour agencies. Besides workers' experiences of exploitation, they are often positioned to be able to shed light on agency identities and (mal)practices. Such knowledge arises in the course of outreach to agency workers, and at meetings where they can pool their experiences and discuss the conditions and possibilities for action. This is key to mapping the sector, especially given the fly-by-night nature of some agencies, and informing the direction of campaigns. The ability to figure out the geography of the agencies could only happen through contacts in different immigrant communities, and with agency workers, especially through assemblies and organising meetings. One worker shared how many of the agencies operate through financial services offices in certain neighbourhoods with sizeable immigrant communities. Some agencies did not pay workers directly – instead they received their pay from these businesses that service working immigrants. Similarly, in the course of outreach, through building a wider contact base, agency workers noted that one way to learn which employers use agencies is to go to various metro (subway) stations at 6:00 am where workers are picked up. This insight has helped locate more companies, especially in the agricultural sector that use agency workers. The IWC and TAWA have tried to collaborate with some local unions or share resources on broader issues of precarious work which the unions are currently engaged in, to put forth a series of demands around temp agencies in Québec and map the agency industry. Work is also being done with engaged academics to try to facilitate research combining the real experiences and knowledge of workers/organisers with the tools and resources available in academia to develop research that is relevant to organising and campaigns.

CHALLENGES OF BUILDING WORKER LEADERSHIP

The IWC and TAWA have focused on building worker leadership. Agency workers who organise risk being moved to another worksite. The agency moved one worker who organised a CSST workshop with the IWC in a Dollarama warehouse to a fish warehouse outside of the city, giving him increasingly difficult work until he finally quit. Yet he felt he achieved his goal, raising awareness about immigrant workers' labour rights, especially health and safety issues. Employers use the fear of being moved from site to site as a key tool of labour discipline. This helps reduce the likelihood that a worker might file a complaint at the CNT for unjust dismissal. The agency may merely say there was no need for that worker to be at a certain enterprise and that they were needed elsewhere. This tactic creates fear among agency workers who hope that the longer they stay at one workplace the better their chances of being hired as a permanent worker are.

Given the many barriers to organising agency workers, creative strategies are needed. Bringing agency workers together within TAWA can build a sense of solidarity, but at the same time different workers face different problems. For one set of workers, mainly in fly-by night agencies, fundamental issues, such as non-payment, lack of overtime and immigration-related concerns, are often priorities. Many agency workers from Latin America face the threat of deportation, making it extremely challenging to organise around workplace issues. The primary focus then is to support their fight for status. This can be difficult because of limited resources and capacity in community labour organisations like the IWC and TAWA. When someone's immigration status becomes precarious and/or they are waiting for another work permit, they lose access to essential social rights like employment insurance and CSST coverage. Workers supported by the IWC and TAWA have had some success in fighting for unemployment insurance for those with expired work permits, but for the workers these battles can become too emotionally draining.

CAMPAIGNS

The IWC and Au bas de l'échelle have campaigned for greater government regulation of agencies, advancing two key demands.

First, agencies must have an operating licence to try to ensure that only credible and responsible agencies can be registered, and that permits should be revoked if an agency does not adhere to established regulations and work standards. Agency registration is one means of forcing them to be accountable, and to ending fly-by-night operations. The second demand was co-responsibility – both agency and employer should be jointly responsible for workplace conditions. This pertains to many issues that IWC came across regarding non-payment of wages and health and safety concerns. A major challenge for organising with agency workers is the lack of a mass collective workforce. Several hundred workers may work for an agency but they are scattered across workplaces, making it hard to forge a common identity or a socialised workforce that can build collective action. Mobilisation can also be difficult because one day a worker can work for one agency or on one worksite, and the next day another. The structure of temp work problematises the idea that the workplace is the main locus for labour organising. Yet trying to build from a community organising perspective is also challenging.

How can campaigns reflect agency workers generally, but understand that within the temp agency industry there are different scales and forms of exploitation, and differences in working conditions? In Québec, many workers who work through major agencies receive payslips indicating deductions and receive vacation pay, and are paid regularly and with some degree of transparency that conforms to labour standards and which provides short-term labour to major corporations. Yet such agencies arguably serve a similar function in the economy as fly-by-night agencies, where working conditions may be terrible because a worker (who may be non-status or on social assistance) is shackled to a phone waiting to see if, where and when they will work, are not properly trained and/or briefed on health and safety issues, and are in a position of never being able to find steady work. These agencies build and maintain a large precarious workforce to be used by corporations and other employers. For workers in larger agencies, priorities may be concerns about discrimination and health and safety, while the other group often focuses on basic demands, such as pay or the struggle for immigration rights and regularisation. In October 2011, on the International Day for Decent

Work, the IWC and Au bas de l'échelle, supported by several unions, organised a rally demanding that agencies be regulated and forced to gain permits allowing them to operate from Québec's Ministry of Labour, so that workers can take them to the CNT to file complaints for non-payment or force them to pay the minimum wage. The IWC also organised a 'bad agency tour', which targeted and highlighted some of the agencies operating in Montreal. This allowed worker-leaders who had worked for these agencies to share their stories in a more powerful way. The tour passed a Dollarama warehouse where agency workers had complained of discrimination, health and safety, and job security problems. The tour and rally helped build alliances with unions and other groups, yet illustrated challenges in building real leadership among agency workers. Those still employed by their respective agency did not want to be seen in public. Thus the strategy was for former agency workers to speak about workplace rights violations and forms of exploitation. The IWC has also worked with those workers who were more vulnerable, helping them to overcome their fear and be more public about the general issues.

Freeman and Gonos (2005) assert that nobody has yet created an effective legal framework that can advance the unionisation and fair treatment of temp workers deployed in the workplace by exploitative temp agencies. The Toronto-based Workers Action Centre led a campaign to defend agency workers, and won some gains through Ontario provincial policy amendments relating to the scope and enforcement of the Employment Standards Act (Vosko, 2010; Workers Action Centre, 2007). Some gains, such as the right of agency workers to be treated like other employees under labour standards, theoretically exist in Québec, but without addressing employer responsibility between agency and employer, and its enforcement, it is unlikely that workers will benefit. Vosko (2010) critiques the Ontario law changes as inadequate. Gellatly et al. (2011) criticise Ontario's individualisation and privatisation of the employment standards enforcement process. They argue that this shifts responsibility for enforcement from government and employers on to individual workers. This approach 'belie[s] an understanding of the complex weaving of gender, race and immigration status that characterises the uneven social relations that shape the experience of employment for many of Ontario's workers' (2011: 99).

Bartkiw (2009: 183) holds that it generates yet more precarious (non-union) employment

> that carries with it the threat of further erosion of union power and growth through labor market undercutting and the increased inability of unions to 'take wages out of competition'. Thus, precarious employment outcomes and restricted access to unionisation become *self-reinforcing*. It follows that labour policy reforms to regulate temporary help agency employment that do not directly address the issue of frustrated access to unionisation under current Canadian regimes will not likely reduce, and indeed are not even *aimed* at reducing, this structural tendency generating labor market precarity.

Similarly, Vosko (2010: 646) argues that there is a 'need for creating new types of bargaining units to enable unionization, benefits beyond job tenure, precarity pay, and parity of treatment for workers regardless of the forms of employment in which they engage'.

Recently, in cooperation with other organisations working on precarious work and migration, the IWC and TAWA began a campaign for a new Québec law on precarious work, including demands around domestic work and access to health and safety coverage. These called for easier access to permanent residence and equal access to government programmes for temporary foreign workers. They also called for a raise in the minimum wage to CDN$12.00 an hour and access to government services for all workers regardless of status. In 2013, in an open letter to Québec's minister of labour, many Dollarama workers demanded the right to be made permanent after three months of work at the same workplace, arguing that merely making agencies co-responsible was not enough. This was critical because agency workers themselves are directly articulating proposals about creating a healthy labour market and workplace conditions.

The agency worker campaign gained some momentum with the creation of the Precarious Worker Coalition that began in response to the belief that Québec's former minister of labour would produce a bill to protect precarious workers. TAWA initiated this coalition with the IWC, Mexicans United for Regularization, Dignidad Migrante and a public campaign with a set of demands around 'precarious work'. The coalition organised press conferences in April and May 2013, resulting in an official consultation involving the leadership of the precarious workers' coalition and TAWA with the Ministry of Labour. In this campaign, the IWC and TAWA were able to build worker leadership and a broader understanding of the centrality precarious migrant workers play in the economy. However, whatever traction there may have been with officials at that point has not yet achieved concrete results.

WORKING WITH UNIONS ON AGENCY EXPLOITATION OF WORKERS AND PRECARITY

As elsewhere, these organising strategies have come at a time when the historical focus and priority of unions, to organise and maintain their traditional industrial base, face sustained challenges from the transformation of work in the context of global capitalist restructuring and anti-labour legislation, and as some strive to think through these challenges and acknowledge the importance of fighting for the rights of non-standard workers as part of a broader strategy to defend the rights of working people. This has included the Québec unions, Centrale des syndicats démocratiques (CSD), Confédération des syndicats nationaux (CSN), Centrale des syndicats du Québec (CSQ), and Fédération des travailleurs et travailleuses du Québec (FTQ), (see CSD/CSN/CSQ/FTQ, 2011). A 2011 joint union report on agency workers was produced in the context of a larger Québec Ministry of Labour consultation on regulating agencies, and a campaign focused around a proposed law to protect precarious workers. This campaign in turn had arisen from earlier pressure from community organisations and unions collaborating in the Front Des Non Syndicats (FDNS), as well as the joint IWC and Au bas de l'échelle campaign which worked with several labour councils during 2011 to support the campaign for agency workers. These actions predated the formation of the current Precarious Workers Coalition, and form part of a broader strategy. The IWC's aim was for the coalition to be a process in which workers could directly address their concerns about agencies to the minister as opposed to a strategy of wider coalition of civil society organisations, to complement the existing strategy of the FDNS.

The campaign demanded that: (a) agencies provide a security deposit in order to reimburse all the necessary fees deducted from the agency workers; (b) agencies promptly report any changes of address or administration; (c) companies using agencies without a proper permit be fined; (d) a principle of co-responsibility be established under Québec's Labour Standards Act between the agencies and their client companies, to guarantee that workers' rights and entitlements are respected; (e) agencies and their client companies be held accountable to the workers they hire where pecuniary obligations (salaries, paid vacations, etc.) are concerned; (f) to hold either the agency, the client company or both liable and responsible in the event that worker rights are violated (in instances of unjust dismissal, psychological or physical harassment, etc.); (g) to enforce labour standards, particularly relating to vacation pay, statutory holiday pay and years of service in general; (h) to ensure joint responsibility between agencies and client-employers for CSST compensation.

The IWC and the TAWA have formed a partnership with the CSN to work with agency workers to create activist-based research from workers, labour rights campaigns and concrete support for TAWA. A coalition of Québec unions believe that the responsibility to pay for CSST coverage should rest on the client-employers rather than co-responsibility with the agencies. It is a challenge to advance these demands because to address them substantively entails placing them within the existing tripartite structure that governs the CNT between the Québec minister of labour, union centrals and representation by employers' associations, which has made it more difficult for the unions to navigate and push for progressive changes to Québec's labour standards. Yet, among a growing number of Québec unions there is a realisation of the broader threats posed to the future of work and workers' rights through the increasing use of agencies.

CONCLUSION

Global capitalism fragments labour and the lives of working people everywhere. Struggles for immigration status, dignity and justice for temporary migrant and immigrant workers are raising some of the most important challenges to capital and state in recent years. The examples in this chapter of struggles to change the economic and social conditions of low-wage agency workers in Montreal highlight the importance of engaging workers in collective self-organisation. Such strategies break from orthodox post-war union organising traditions and create community responses to labour issues. IWC support for a worker-led campaign and organisation to transform agency work has meant the creation of TAWA. It grapples with challenges faced mainly by newer immigrants and migrant workers in more exploitative conditions, contending with both labour problems and the regularisation of status. This organising approach allows the IWC to build a more comprehensive organising strategy, and a sense of solidarity across communities, immigration status and other experiences. Leadership development of workers and education are central to the organising model. It is a hybrid model: first, building a committee or association that can have a broad membership; second, dealing with policy issues at the provincial level; and third, working to resolve individual grievances with agencies and employers around wage theft, health and safety, and other violations. Currently TAWA has a core group of former and current agency workers with a monthly assembly giving a real voice, and leadership from workers themselves. TAWA could act like a union by formalising the membership. The campaign has also seen workers build relationships with different community organisations and unions in order to highlight that agencies and temp work impact all workers, and that for unions to be able to defend the rights of their membership means to end to precarious work as a way of outsourcing decent paying work. Alongside this is an understanding that the nature of work has drastically changed, and thus that the need to support such initiatives and campaigns is vital for a rebirth of the labour movement.

The IWC and TAWA seek to create longer-term alliances and a coherent strategy. Québec unions have emphasised that the employer should be solely responsible for work conditions to clearly identify that the use of agency workers is a way to undermine unions, which allows employers to deny responsibility. They have remained important allies for IWC's campaign through presentations at labour council meetings. In 2011, the Coalition of Labour Councils in Montreal issued a press release calling for the Québec Ministry of Labour to address the demands put forth by the IWC and Au bas de l'échelle. In 2013, the CSN began a formal partnership with the IWC to organise agency workers. These have been critical steps towards creating a real alliance between unions and community groups working towards regulating agency work, and key to understanding the importance of finding ways to fight back. The challenge remains how to organise workplaces staffed by agency workers and workplaces employing both agency workers and unionised workers.

The significance of the work of activists in workers' centres and new organisations like TAWA with temp agency workers lies not simply in organising a smaller, vulnerable workforce. These are testing grounds for alternative approaches or models of collective organisation, and are grounded attempts to work through some of the issues, debates and tensions around the shifting centres and margins of labour market regulation and workers' struggles in Canada today. As the expansion of agency work enhances employers' ability to create a sense of fear, austerity and denial of decent work with job security in order to generate profits, such organising among a changing working class contesting their daily problems arising from precarious work is a key way to highlight local impacts of globalisation. There are challenges for political coordination for organising precarious workers across cities in Canada. This kind of precarious worker organising is a relatively new phenomenon in Canada, by comparison to more established networks in the US. The need for coordination will be crucial between the mainstream labour movement/unions, community-based labour organisations like the IWC, TAWA and other community organisations, to build a broader movement against the agencies and workplaces that exist transnationally and within Canada.

Just Work?

REFERENCES

Au bas de l'échelle. (2011). *Présentation au comité de travail du CCTM Sur la question des agences de placement temporaire*. Au bas de l'échelle, 14 January. www.aubasdelechelle.ca/assets/files/nos%20publications/memoires-avis/CCTM%20FINAL. pdf (accessed August 2015).

Bartkiw, T. J. (2009). 'Baby Steps? Towards the Regulation of Temporary Help Agency Employment in Canada'. *Comparative Labor Law and Policy Journal*, 31(1), 163–206.

CNT (Commission des normes du travail). (2012). 'Sondage visant à évaluer les conditions de travail des salariés temporaires d'agences de placement de personnel et les pratiques de celles-ci. Rapport d'analyse final'. CNT, 2 November. www.cnt. gouv.qc.ca/fileadmin/pdf/enquetes-et-recherches/Rapport-CNT79083-024_nov_2012_VF.pdf (accessed August 2015).

Cranford, C. J. and Ladd, D. (2003). 'Community Unionism: Organising for Fair Employment in Canada'. *Just Labour*, 3, 46–59.

CSD/CSN/CSQ/FTQ. (2011). *Rapport des membres syndicaux du Comité sur les agences de placement temporaire*. CSD/CSN/CSQ/FTQ, 15 September.

Freeman, H. and Gonos, G. (2005). 'Regulating the Employment Sharks: Reconceptualizing the Legal Status of the Commercial Temp Agency'. *WorkingUSA: The Journal of Labor and Society*, 8, 293–314.

Fuller, S. and Vosko, L. F. (2008). 'Temporary Employment and Social Inequality in Canada: Exploring Intersections of Gender, Race and Immigration Status'. *Social Indicators Research*, 88, 31–50.

Fudge, J. (2012). 'The Precarious Migrant Status and Precarious Employment: The Paradox of International Rights for Migrant Workers'. *Comparative Labor Law and Policy Journal*, 34(1), 95–132.

Galabuzi, G. (2006). *Canada's Economic Apartheid: The Social Exclusion of Racialized Groups in the New Century*. Toronto: Canadian Scholars' Press.

Gellatly, M., Grundy, J., Mirchandani, K., Perry, J. A., Thomas, M. and Vosko, L. (2011). 'Modernizing Employment Standards? Efficiency, Market Regulation, and the Production of the Illegal Claimant in Ontario'. *The Economic and Labour Relations Review*, 22(2), 81–106.

Gonos, G. and Martino, M. (2011). 'Temp Agency Workers in New Jersey's Logistics Hub: The Case for a Union Hiring Hall'. *WorkingUSA: The Journal of Labor and Society*, 14(4), 499–525.

Hatton, E. (2011). *The Temp Economy: From Kelly Girls to Permatemps in Postwar America*. Philadelphia: Temple University Press.

Henaway, M. (2012). 'Immigrant Worker Organizing in a Time of Crisis: Adapting to the New Realities of Class and Resistance'. In Choudry, A., Hanley, J. and Shragge, E. (Eds) *Organize! Building from the Local for Global Justice* (pp. 144–55). Oakland, CA: PM Press.

Immigrant Workers Centre. (2012). 'Migrant Voices. Temporary Agency Workers Testimony', 2 July. http://iwc-cti.org/migrant-voices-iwc-radio/2012 (accessed August 2015).

Institut de recherché Robert-Sauvé en santé et sécurité du travail. (2011). *Enquête québécoise sur des conditions de travail, d'emploi et de santé et de sécurité du travail.* September. www.travail.gouv.qc.ca/fileadmin/fichiers/Documents/conditions_de_travail/EQCOTESST_R-691_RAPPORT.pdf (accessed August 2015).

Radio Canada. (2010). 'La jungle des agences de placement'. *Radio Canada,* 21 October. www.youtube.com/watch?v=yVOLMYzdZmE (accessed August 2015).

Van Arsdale, D. G. (2013). 'The Temporary Work Revolution: The Shift from Jobs that Solve Poverty to Jobs that Make Poverty'. *WorkingUSA: The Journal of Labor and Society,* 16, 87–112.

Vosko, L. F. (2000). *Temporary Work: The Gendered Rise of a Precarious Employment Relationship.* Toronto: University of Toronto Press.

—— (2008). 'Temporary Work in Transnational Labor Regulation: SER-Centrism and the Risk of Exacerbating Gendered Precariousness'. *Social Indicators Research,* 88, 131–45.

—— (2010). 'A New Approach to Regulating Temporary Agency Work in Ontario or Back to the Future?'. *Industrial Relations,* 65(4), 632–53.

Workers Action Centre. (2007). *Working on the Edge.* Toronto: WAC.

Zaman, H. (2006). *Breaking the Iron Wall: Decommodification and Immigrant Women's Labor in Canada.* Lanham, MD: Rowman and Littlefield.

—— (2012). *Asian Immigrants in 'Two Canadas': Racialization, Marginalization and Deregulated Work:* Halifax and Winnipeg: Fernwood.

Contributor Biographies

Asia Pacific Mission for Migrants (APMM) is a regional migrant service institution based in Hong Kong. Founded in 1984 as a regional research, advocacy and movement-building organisation, APMM is currently the secretariat of the International Migrants Alliance. https://ima2008.wordpress.com
www.apmigrants.org

Baba Ayelabola is Deputy Secretary General and Head of the Education and Research department of the Medical and Health Workers' Union of Nigeria. He is also a leading social movement activist, and is currently National Convener of United Action for Democracy, the pan-Nigerian coalition of political rights-based civil society organisations He studied industrial relations and personnel management, human resource management, and labour policies and globalisation at the universities of Lagos, Nigeria and Kassel respectively. A writer and poet, he is the author of *Era of Crises and Revolts* as well as several articles in journals, newspapers and magazines. A guest columnist of the *African Herald Express* and *Amandla!*, Baba Aye' currently serves on the Editorial Working Group of the *Review of African Political Economy*. He is presently Chair of the Socialist Workers League Editorial Board.

Marek Čaněk is Director of the Migration Program in the Multicultural Centre, Prague. He specialises in political and social regulation of labour migration and the approach of the trade unions towards immigrants in the Czech Republic. He obtained his PhD from the Department of Political Science of Charles University in Prague. From 2008 to 2009 he was a Fulbright Scholar at Rutgers, the State University of New Jersey. From 2011 to 2012 he was a fellow of Erste Foundation Fellowship for Social Research. Until recently he was an advocacy officer of the Consortium of Migrants' Assisting NGOs in the Czech Republic.

Aziz Choudry is Associate Professor in the Department of Integrated Studies in Education at McGill University, Montreal, and visiting professor at the Centre for Education Rights and Transformation at the University of Johannesburg. He is author of *Learning Activism: The Intellectual Life of Contemporary Social Movements* (University of Toronto Press, 2015), co-author of *Fight Back: Workplace Justice for Immigrants* (Fernwood, 2009), and co-editor of *Learning from the Ground Up: Global Perspectives on Social Movements and Knowledge Production* (Palgrave Macmillan, 2010), *Organize! Building from the local for Global Justice,* (PM Press/Between the Lines, 2012), and *NGOization: Complicity, Contradictions and Prospects* (Zed Books, 2013). With a long history as a social and political activist, educator and researcher, he serves on the boards of the Immigrant Workers Centre, Montreal and the Global Justice Ecology Project.

Valerie Francisco is an Assistant Professor in the Department of Sociology at the University of Portland in Oregon. Francisco received her PhD from the Department of Sociology at City University of New York, The Graduate Center. Francisco's dissertation examined the strategies of maintaining a transnational family from the perspectives of Filipino migrant women working as domestic workers in New York City all the way to their families in the Philippines. In journals like *The Philippine Sociological Review* and *Critical Sociology*, Francisco writes about how families are changing under neoliberal immigration policies, and what types of political subjectivities emerge from those conditions. Francisco's research is informed by her participation in transnational activism with GABRIELA, an alliance of progressive Filipino women's organisations in the Philippines and MIGRANTE International, an international alliance of Filipino migrant workers.

Adam Hanieh is a Senior Lecturer in Development Studies at the School of Oriental and African Studies (SOAS), University of London. Prior to joining SOAS, Adam taught at Zayed University, United Arab Emirates. From 1997–2003, he lived and worked in

Ramallah, Palestine, where he completed an MA in Regional Studies at Al Quds University. He holds a PhD in Political Science from York University, Canada. Adam is an editorial board member of the journal *Historical Materialism: Research in Critical Marxist Theory*, a founding member of the SOAS Centre for Palestine Studies, and a member of the committee of management for the Council for British Research in the Levant. His most recent book is *Lineages of Revolt: Issues of Contemporary Capitalism in the Middle East* (Haymarket Press, 2013). He is also author of *Capitalism and Class in the Gulf Arab States* (Palgrave Macmillan, 2011).

Mostafa Henaway is a writer and community organiser, and worked at the Immigrant Workers Centre, Montreal, from 2007 to 2014. He has recently completed the masters programme of the Global Labour University, and has been active in campaigns on temporary agency workers, temporary foreign workers and laid-off textile workers. Prior to this, in Toronto he organised with the Ontario Coalition Against Poverty and the Toronto Coalition of Concerned Taxi drivers. He has a book chapter in *Organize! Building from the Local for Global Justice* (2012) on immigrant and migrant worker organising, as well as co-authoring articles in *Canadian Dimension, Global Labour Journal*, and *Labour, Capital and Society*.

Mondli Hlatshwayo is a senior lecturer in the Centre for Education Rights and Transformation at the University of Johannesburg. Previously he worked for Khanya College, a Johannesburg-based NGO, as an educator and researcher. His areas of research include post-schooling, adult and youth education, workers' education, xenophobia, trade unions and social movements. Hlatshwayo has published a number of peer-reviewed journal articles and book chapters on the following topics: xenophobia and trade unions, football world cup and stadia, education and immigrant learners, and trade unions and technology.

Jake Lagnado was a Latin American Workers Association (LAWAS) committee member from 2004–6 and 2008–10, being secretary for three of these years. Based in the UK, he was also an active member of Unite and Industrial Workers of the World (IWW) during these periods, and previously lived for six years in Peru and Colombia. He has worked most recently as a translator and trade union tutor.

Dennis Maga is a union organiser for FIRST Union in Aotearoa/New Zealand and is well known and respected for his advocacy work on migrant employment matters. In 2007, he worked as a Migrant Worker Project Coordinator for the New Zealand Council of Trade Unions. In 2009, Maga established the Migrant Workers Network within the National Distribution Union (NDU). The NDU amalgamated with the Finance Sector Union (FINSEC) in 2012 and formed FIRST Union, one of the biggest private sector unions in Aotearoa/New Zealand. The Migrant Workers Network was relaunched in August 2012 as the Union Network of Migrants (UNEMIG), an integrated structure within FIRST Union. Maga acts as UNEMIG secretary, engaging with community groups and institutions for the promotion and protection of migrants' rights and welfare. He is also the National Coordinator of Migrante Aotearoa, a Filipino migrants' organisation with four chapters in Aotearoa/New Zealand.

Edward Miller is a strategic adviser for FIRST Union, Aotearoa New Zealand.

Vasco Pedrina began his active commitment to migrant workers' rights in the 1970s. He became central secretary of the building and wood workers' union (FOBB) in 1988, responsible for migrant workers' affairs. In 1991, he assumed the union's presidency. Following the merger with the chemical, textile and paper workers' union, two years later he became the president of the building and industry union (SIB). After the merger with the metal workers' union and two services unions, he became co-president of the inter-industrial union Unia (www.unia.ch) in 2004 and stayed in that position until 2006 (200,000 members, 50 per cent migrants). During the 1990s, he served for four years as co-president of the Swiss Federation of Trade Unions (USS, www.uss.ch). From 2006 to 2013, he was also vice-president of the BWI (Building and Wood Workers' International Federation). Today, he is a board member of the Global Labour Institute (GLI).

Hiroshi Ueki is an Assistant Professor at the Department of Living, Tottori College, Tottori, Japan. His major research interests include problems of migrant workers, non-regular workers and union activities in Japan. He has investigated industrial relations (e.g. labour management, labour process) of immigrant workers at the subcontractor of an automobile company in Japan.

Index